T0247612

OUR PORTION OF HELL

OUR
PORTION
OF
HELL

FAYETTE COUNTY, TENNESSEE:
An Oral History of the
Struggle for Civil Rights

ROBERT HAMBURGER

University Press of Mississippi / Jackson

The University Press of Mississippi is the scholarly publishing agency of
the Mississippi Institutions of Higher Learning: Alcorn State University,
Delta State University, Jackson State University, Mississippi State University,
Mississippi University for Women, Mississippi Valley State University,
University of Mississippi, and University of Southern Mississippi.

www.upress.state.ms.us

The University Press of Mississippi is a member
of the Association of University Presses.

Any discriminatory or derogatory language or hate speech regarding
race, ethnicity, religion, sex, gender, class, national origin, age, or
disability that has been retained or appears in elided form is in no way
an endorsement of the use of such language outside a scholarly context.

First printing 2022

∞

Library of Congress Cataloging-in-Publication Data

Names: Hamburger, Robert, 1943– author.
Title: Our portion of Hell : Fayette County, Tennessee: an oral history of
the struggle for Civil Rights / Robert Hamburger.
Description: [New edition]. | Jackson : University Press of Mississippi,
[2022] | Includes bibliographical references.
Identifiers: LCCN 2022030309 (print) | LCCN 2022030310 (ebook)
| ISBN 9781496842343 (hardback) | ISBN 9781496842350 (trade
paperback) | ISBN 9781496842367 (epub) | ISBN 9781496842374 (epub) |
ISBN 9781496842381 (pdf) | ISBN 9781496842398 (pdf)
Subjects: LCSH: Civil rights—Tennessee—Fayette County. | Civil rights
movements—Tennessee. | African Americans—Tennessee—Fayette
County—Interviews. | African Americans—Suffrage. | Community
organization—Tennessee—Fayette County. | Sharecropping—
Tennessee—Fayette County—History—20th century. | Fayette County
(Tenn.)—Race relations.
Classification: LCC F443.F3 H35 2022 (print) | LCC F443.F3 (ebook) |
DDC 305.896/073076821—dc23/eng/20220712
LC record available at https://lccn.loc.gov/2022030309
LC ebook record available at https://lccn.loc.gov/2022030310

British Library Cataloging-in-Publication Data available

CONTENTS

PREFACE TO THE NEW EDITION

In 1973, *Our Portion of Hell* was published by Links Books in New York. This reissued edition includes the entire text of the original version, unchanged in any essential way. Michael Abramson's suite of photographs for the original edition is even more compelling now, some fifty years later, in the photos' depiction of an environment and a way of life that has been transformed in so many ways. However, Michael did not visit Fayette County until 1971, a good ten years after the tumultuous voter registration drives and the events surrounding Tent City. In preparing this reissued edition, I've had access to the archives of Ernest Withers, Art Shay, Archie Allen, Nick Lawrence, and the *Commercial Appeal*—allowing me to gather images that bear witness to the important events of the early 1960s. By availing myself of their work, *Our Portion of Hell* now offers on-the-spot images that document events recounted by the book's speakers. In addition, I've included a brief afterword in which I share personal reflections about the making of this book, as well as thoughts about what has changed and what has not changed in the fifty years that have passed since I conducted my interviews.

OUR PORTION OF HELL

INTRODUCTION

Fayette County is in the southwest corner of Tennessee, a forty-minute drive from Memphis. The Mississippi border is just fifteen minutes from Somerville, the county seat. Fayette County is the third-poorest county in America. About 60 percent of the population is Black, and most of these Blacks are sharecroppers working on land owned by whites. In statistical terms Fayette County is typical of severe poverty in the rural South. What makes this county unique and significant is the way Blacks have changed their attitude toward themselves and America as a result of the civil rights movement.

Fayette County Blacks did not wait for the movement in the South to stimulate this new consciousness. They did not wait for the organized activism of SNCC or SCLC or any of the other groups that did so much to shake up the structure of life in the Deep South. Leadership and momentum came from the people, born and raised in Fayette County.

Community action began fourteen years ago. The struggle still continues. The power structure continues to use all the economic, legal, and physical means at its disposal to obstruct progress and destroy the movement. People have died. Others have been shot and beaten. Still more have been thrown in jail, dismissed from jobs, and persecuted by the legal system that is supposed to protect them. There have been some positive changes—schools and public facilities have been integrated; various federal assistance programs are operating—but none of these changes came about without bitter, painful struggle, and all of these changes are continually subverted by the cynical operation of economic and legal power. And what makes the situation even more difficult, more desperate, is that the movement has been all but abandoned by those outside the South who once cared or were forced to care.

3

Under President Nixon's southern strategy the federal government is no longer an aggressive ally of the movement. During the Kennedy and Johnson administrations, leaders in the Fayette County struggle could pick up the phone and speak directly to the attorney general's office. Today the attorney general does not appear to like tying up his lines with such callers. And the national media has also abandoned the movement.

Of course, there has been lots of other news in the past fourteen years. Many issues besides the civil rights movement demand our attention and commitment. But old issues do not disappear just because our nation's leaders choose to ignore them. New issues do not eradicate old ones. The struggle for civil rights in the South continues. It is still a cruel and difficult journey. And the lives of those who have embarked on this journey have a moral significance that we must not ignore.

I first went to Fayette County in the spring of 1965 to help build a community center. Over the years I returned when I could to visit friends I'd made, people I loved. When I visited my friends in 1970, I felt torn apart with love and anger. John McFerren had been beaten almost to death, school integration was being obstructed by astonishing abuse of Black children, a seventy-year-old woman, her two daughters, and her grandchild were clubbed and beaten by two rednecks. People were getting messed over as viciously as they ever were years ago when such events flashed across the media as "national news."

During the summer and autumn of 1971 and the spring of 1972 I lived in Fayette County and tape-recorded the interviews that make up this book. A book exists as something real and tangible. Perhaps the lives of these ignored people will regain a kind of reality to outsiders if a book, their book, exists.

I'm already in hell. This is it. This is hell here. This is all I expect to go to.
Well, we've had our portion of it. . . . I don't think I'll wait around for all this peace
and happiness to come. I'm gonna raise all the hell I can to move some of this away.

—MAGGIE MAE HORTON

We knew from the beginnin that we didn't have no education—we didn't have that speakin
part that dress things up so we just were tellin the story just like it was. We had had experience
of these things and we just only told it like it was. We didn't dress it up, we didn't undress it—
we just told the straight truth and that was the problems we was dealin with every day.

—HARPMAN JAMESON

Cotton Pickers

"I was paid fifty cents a day. In the mornin we'd wake up round at four o'clock in the mornin. We'd go to the fields by five o'clock, stay in the field till twelve o'clock, then come out, and at one o'clock go back in the field, then we'd stay in the field until sundown. That's twelve or sometimes fourteen hours. That's fifty cents a day, four cents an hour."
—Square Mormon

Gertrude Beasley and her family

"When I was quite small, I remember we couldn't have any shoes to wear
in wintertime. When the weather got bad I had to stay in the house. . . .
There was eight of us. Fourteen in all, but some died real young."
—Porter Shields

PART I

"THINKIN FOR MYSELF"

The Beginning: 1959–1960

The trial of Burton Dodson in 1959 is what started things changing in Fayette County, Tennessee. Back in 1941, Dodson, a Black farmer, was accused of murder. The circumstances surrounding his alleged crime were not unusual for that time in the South. Dodson had argued with a white man. They came to blows. The indignant white man gathered a mob, they were deputized, and then they descended upon Dodson's isolated farmhouse. Harpman Jameson can tell you the rest:

A mob went out to his house. This was in the early hours in the mornin—around three o'clock in the mornin. I understand there was a warrant had been gotten out for Burton Dodson. They went to his house—I understood it from one of his boys talkin at the trial—they went out to his house to hang him. They went up there to get him outa the house and they couldn't get him out. One of Dodson's boys testified in court. And this particular boy was shot by the mob—a glance in the head with a bullet. And he said they were shootin everywhere around there. And the state attorney asked him what did he mean about shootin from everywhere. He said, "They were shootin from the smokehouse and outa the top of trees and all out from around the house." I don't know how Dodson come out, but the deputy sheriff said Dodson come outa the house runnin west, shootin back, and that the mob chased him into the woods. What I never could figure out—I was in the court there, see—the house was up there on the hill and he was runnin down the hill west from the house shootin back. And this man got killed over on the east side of the house, down the hill behind a tree. Now how could this bullet come back up the hill and go down the hill and kill a man behind a tree? And you know it was at night—a man shootin back, he couldn't see nothin. So I never did believe that Dodson killed a man. The way I saw it, the way this deputy sheriff told it there in court, he had cleared Dodson.

In all likelihood the deputy was slain by the confused and excited crossfire of the mob he came with. They had stormed Dodson's farm to kill. They succeeded, but the man they came for was alive and free. Dodson was now sought as a murderer.

Eighteen years later, in 1959, at a time when the Dodson episode had seemingly taken its place as just another event in the county's terrible ledger of violence. Burton Dodson, now well into his seventies, was discovered in East St. Louis, Illinois, and brought back to Fayette County to face charges of homicide. The issues embodied in the Dodson case were not unusual—the reckless, lawless white mob, the sudden ruin of a Black family, the looming threat of southern justice—these were ugly but familiar facts of life to the Black men and women of Fayette County. What gave the trial its special significance was not the case itself but rather the appearance of a Black lawyer, J. F. Estes, who drove out from Memphis to defend Dodson. People in Fayette County knew that the only way a Black man got into the courthouse was either as a doomed defendant or as a janitor. A Black lawyer appearing to defend a Black man was unheard of. People put aside their farm work and flocked to the courthouse to see it for themselves. Because they were not registered voters they were unable to qualify as prospective jurors, but they watched with pride and astonishment as Estes coolly questioned prospective jurors on their racial attitudes. "Do you believe Negroes should have the right to vote?" Estes would ask. Caught by surprise and anxious to win a place on the jury, some whites answered yes. At the time of the trial there were 16,927 Blacks in Fayette County—they made up 68.9 percent of the county's population—but only one Black out of every thousand, seventeen people in all, voted between 1952 and 1959. And now in the prelude to the Burton Dodson trial, Estes had drawn from Fayette County whites verbal support of the idea that Blacks deserved to vote. It was an extraordinary moment. Needless to say, these prospective jurors had been caught off guard. Neither they, nor Estes, nor the men and women who attended hearings had any idea where all this would lead.

Among the Black farmers who came in from the fields to watch the proceedings were two men in their early thirties—John McFerren and Harpman Jameson. When Estes appealed for money to hire a recording secretary for the hearings, John and Harpman went among their friends and acquaintances to raise the necessary sum. This was the first indication that the Black community in Fayette County was prepared to join together. John and Harpman were hardly aware of it at the time, but this was the beginning of the civil rights movement in Fayette County. Southern justice prevailed over Estes's defense and Burton Dodson was given a twenty-year sentence that was later reduced to ten years. Nevertheless, the trial had set lives in motion. Fayette County would never be the same.

With Estes providing the necessary legal advice, John McFerren, Harpman Jameson, Scott Franklin, Floyd Franklin, John Lewis, and nine others filed a charter for the Fayette County Civic and Welfare League in the spring of 1959. Its stated purpose—"To promote civil and political and economic welfare for the community progress"—sounds moderate and wholly reasonable, but in Fayette County even general goals such as political equality and economic welfare seemed militant and dangerous to the white power structure. The political and economic system of the rural South depends upon the powerlessness of Blacks. It is a system that abhors change. "Political progress" could only mean Black voting power. "Economic welfare" could only mean fair wages, fair distribution of money from state and federal assistance programs, and fair hiring practice in local stores and local light industry. In short, the simple justice of the league's goals represented a powerful threat to a system built upon the accumulated injustice of a hundred years.

The first concerted action of the league was to encourage voter registration. There was no precedent for this in the rural South. The civil rights movement had scarcely begun. Two years earlier, in 1957, Congress passed its first Civil Rights Act in seventy-five years, an act that seemed to give the Justice Department power to sue in support of any American citizen deprived of his civil rights. But the Justice Department had not yet used its new powers. In June and July of 1959 a few hundred Blacks managed to register at the Fayette County courthouse in Somerville, but when the Democratic primary was held in August Black voters were turned away. There was no possible legal justification for this. Twenty-five years earlier the Supreme Court had examined the segregated Texas Democratic primary and ruled that the state could not permit racial discrimination in such a significant part of the election process. The league filed a federal suit against the local Democratic party and in April 1960 the court ruling gave Fayette County Blacks their first victory.

There was no time for rejoicing though. The white community began using its economic power to punish Blacks who registered. Blacks who registered lost insurance policies and credit in local stores. Many Blacks found that local banks would no longer supply the annual loan that made their spring farm work possible. Still others lost their jobs with white employers.

An economic squeeze was on. In spite of this, voter registration continued. Before 1960 ended, fourteen hundred people had registered. By the end of 1960 the white community expanded its economic squeeze. White landlords began evicting Black tenant farmers who had registered to vote. Scores of families, 257 people in all, were thrown off their farms. The blow came suddenly, unexpectedly, but the league and its supporters improvised quickly and imaginatively. Tents were pitched on the land of Shepard Towles, an independent Black landowner, and the evicted families moved in and prepared to face the damp, chilly winter months as best they could. Tent City, as it was called, was the scene of severe hardship, but it became a symbol of defiance and fierce pride.

In February Estes, John McFerren, Harpman Jameson, and two others drove to Washington to demand federal action as authorized by the Civil Rights Act of 1957. Ten months later, on December 14, 1960, the Justice Department invoked its unused powers and filed a suit against forty-five landowners, twenty-four merchants, and a bank—all seventy parties were accused of violating the civil rights of Black citizens of Fayette County. The league had won another important victory. But while the Justice Department prepared its case the white community tightened the economic screws. A blacklist was compiled with a complete listing of those Blacks who had managed to register. Any Black whose name appeared on the list soon discovered he was unable to buy anything anywhere within the county. It was not easy to adjust to this strategy. For farmers working twelve hours a day in the fields a fifty-mile trip into Memphis to buy groceries was an exhausting, time-consuming chore.

And for families living way below the national standards of poverty the extra money spent on gas mileage was a cruel expense. Day-to-day existence was a continuous strain. People were pushed to their limits, but they refused to suffer any longer as victims of history. They were determined to shape their own lives.

John McFerren

My name is John McFerren. I'm forty-six years old. I'm a Negro was born and raised in West Tennessee, the county of Fayette, District 1. My foreparents was brought here from North Carolina five years before the Civil War and since then we have a very good history of stayin in Fayette County. My people was brought here in covered wagons because the rumor got out among the slaveholders that West Tennessee was still goin to be a slaveholder state. And my people was brought over here and sold. And after the Civil War my people settled in West Tennessee. That's why Fayette and Haywood counties have a great number of Negroes.

Back in 1957 and '58 there was a Negro man accused of killin a deputy sheriff. This was Burton Dodson. He was brought back after he'd been gone twenty years. J. F. Estes was the lawyer defendin him. Myself and him both was in the army together. And the stimulation from the trial got me interested in the way justice was bein used. The only way to bring justice would be through the ballot box.

In 1959 we got out a charter called the Fayette County Civic and Welfare League. Fourteen of us started out in that charter. We tried to support a white liberal candidate that was named L. T. Redfearn in the sheriff election and the local Democrat party refused to let Negroes vote.

We brought a suit against the Democrat party and I went to Washington for a civil rights hearing. Myself and Estes and Harpman Jameson made the trip. It took us twenty-two hours steady drivin. We met John Doar who took us over to the Justice Department canteen where you eat. While we were walkin down the street and goin over there to eat, I was lookin all up—lotsa big, tall buildins. I had never seen old, tall buildins like that before. After talkin to him we come on back to the Justice Department building and we sat out in the hall while he had a meetin inside the attorney general's office. And when they come out they told us they was gonna indict the landowners who kept us from voting. That night we were so poor with finance that three of us slept in one bed and four of us slept on the floor at a friend of ours house up there cause we wasn't able to go to a hotel. And when we came back we drove a Chrysler nonstop twenty-one hours back to Memphis—only stopped for gas and oil check.

Just after that, in 1960, in January, we organized a thousand Negroes to line up at the courthouse to register to vote. We started pourin in with big numbers—in this county it was 72 percent Negroes—when we started to register to vote to change the situation. In the followin September an article came out in the editorial of the Fayette *Falcon* that they would evict a thousand Negroes offa the land. So in October and November they started puttin our people offa the land. Once you registered you had to move. Once you registered they took your job. Then after they done that, in November, we had three hundred people forced to live in tents on Shepard Towles's land. And when we started puttin em in tents, then that's when the White Citizens Council and the Ku Klux Klan started shootin in the tents to run us out.

Tent City was parta an economic squeeze. The local merchants run me outa the stores and said I went to Washington and caused this mess to start. The first store I went in after I come back from Washington in 1959—I had been tradin there many years—was Farmer's Hardware. And I went in that day and went on back and done my buyin. The colored fellow who's been there for years waited on me—and when I started out the door the store owner called me and said, "John, come here." I went on back to the cash register. He says, "That mess you went to Washington on, that Democratic primary. You started somethin. I can't sell you nothin. I can't. I can't. I don't want you to come in my store anymore." So I come on out. They had a blacklist—once you registered and your name appeared on the registration books, your name would appear on the blacklist. And they had the list sent around to all merchants. Once you registered you couldn't buy for credit or cash. But the best thing in the world was when they run me outa them stores. It started me thinkin for myself.

After they put the economic screws on us my brother just got tired of pressure. He was in business and he left in the first of 1960. And an old fella by the name of John Lewis, he was eighty-three years old at the time—he was very good support for myself and the other coordinators with me—he told me, he said, "John, whyn't you go in that store and put somethin in there for us to buy cause they're puttin the screws on us?" And I attempted, I went into business the first of 1960, to supply the Negroes who could not buy for cash or for credit. It was very hard. I had to haul everything I bought from other towns. When they run me outa all the nearby towns I had to go fifty miles every other night to pick up bread and milk and groceries for my store. I used to have to go into the city of Memphis bout every other night and the White Citizens Council in our district chased me just about every time. I had a '55 Ford with a Thunderbird motor in it and two four-barreled carburetors on it. And it would run about 135. The sheriff told me one day, he says, "Every time we get after you, I just sees two balls of fire goin over the hill. That's all I see."

One night I went out to Mr. L. T. Redfearn's house. He was a friend of ours. He was in the suit with us against the Democratic Committee. The Ku Klux Klan was waitin out there in the intersection of the road when I came out there from his house. They wasn't sure who I was till I slowed up at the stop sign at the highway; then all those car lights flashed on to get after me. They chased me through the town runnin ninety miles an hour. They were lookin for me to come straight home, but I made a right turn and went a back way and come home behind my house. And the deputy was in his car runnin up and down the road lookin for me with no license on his car. Reason I know it was the dep's was that this car had a taillight broke out on the left side. I went in town the day after they chased me and looked at the dep's car—his taillight was broke out on the left side.

After six or eight months I found some friends in New Orleans to lend me the money to build a bigger grocery store. And when I got my buildin about 90 percent finished, their office was raided and they were called Communist, and I had three lawsuits against me in about three weeks' time. And one of the men that was in the Small Business Administration told me that the Small Business Administration let my record out for the local authorities to frame lawsuits. The Justice Department has this on record and yet the Justice Department has done nothin. In many other instances they hadn't did nothin. They brought suit against the big landowners, but yet and still they did not break the boycott against me. They did somethin and then left and did nothin no more.

And at the same time the inspectin engineer of the Small Business Administration, he got the word indirectly not to the buildin that I had built and constructed. But when he went down here for a final inspection he passed the buildin. They didn't fire him, they eliminated him. That's the way I see it. They cut back to cut him out because he passed the loans to me. Back then I didn't know that when a Negro in the South goes into business and tries to make substantial gains he is violatin the white man's civil rights. I didn't know that at the time. The engineer said I had one of the best-constructed buildins that he know'd of. Durin one of the trumped-up lawsuits that they had me in court on, the lawyer for the other side told the judge that I don't need a buildin that good. Out in open court. I'm convinced that the Negro or any other minority group has to be economically strong. That's the only way the Negro can have his civil rights.

Durin the time that the squeeze was put on me the Coca-Cola Bottling Company, they didn't sell to me until the Tennessee Council of Human Relations threatened to file a suit against them. The worst part was the big oil companies. They put the national screws on us. I tried to buy from major oil companies all over America. They would not sell to me. The first shipment of gas I bought, the deputy sheriff put a gun on the driver and made him carry the shipment back to Memphis. It was six months again before we had gasoline in our tanks.

Both Tad Davis, the deputy sheriff who blocked delivery of the gas shipment, and the town mayor held personal interests in the distribution of petroleum products within Fayette County. When John turned to national distributors, Gulf, Texaco, Amoco, and Esso all turned their backs on his urgent pleas. National executives of these firms insisted that they had no influence over local distribution procedures. Only after the NAACP urged a nationwide boycott of these companies did they manage to fill John's orders. In those difficult months before the squeeze was broken John and his wife Viola faced a severe and dangerous challenge. Here is Viola's account of those days.

We were trying to make contact with oil companies and we were being—we were just really given the runaround. Nobody wanted to be bothered with us and I suppose the blacklist had had its effect. And as a matter of fact, one oil company told us that a committee of people had been there from Fayette County and had threatened them that if they sold gasoline to John McFerren they would inform many of their other customers. They guaranteed them that they would be boycotted. They were simply afraid to sell us gasoline products.

It had been in the press all over the country. Quite a few people had come to Fayette County to see what kind of place was there and if the stories they was hearing was true. I remember quite well, one day, about noon, when a beautiful automobile drove into the yard, driven by a white fellow who didn't look like a Fayette Countyan at all. And I went to the door. And he looked so friendly; he had a smile on his face and this is what I had not seen from white people in Fayette County for months. And I knew, "You must be a friend to us if you can smile like this." I allowed him to come into the house cause I was just glad to see a smile on a white person's face one more time. He came in and he asked me if I was Mrs. John McFerren.

I said, "Yes."

I asked him who he was and he said, "I'm sorry, but I can't tell you who I am. But I'm your friend and I came to help you. Is Mr. McFerren around?"

I told him no he wasn't and I didn't expect him till about was six at night.

And he said, "Well I'll be back. Would you say about seven o'clock?"

And I said, "Probably."

He said, "Well I'll be back. I can't tell you who I am, but I am your friend and I came to help." And he left.

John came home that night before the man returned and he was in bed asleep, but I wasn't. It was warm weather and the window was raised by the side of the bed. This car drove in and headed right down by the side of the window. This frightened me a little bit. I couldn't figure out why the person drove there. Then, when the car door was being opened and the light was on, I saw the white person that had been earlier. And I waked John up and I told him that this man was back. John asked him in and he said, "I came to help you. I can't tell you who I am, but I want to help you to get gasoline in your tanks and I can have this gasoline in here tonight, about two o'clock in the morning, if you have your tanks ready."

In preparing the tanks we had just a little bit of money that we had saved the eight years we had been married. With all the community work John had done all the money was gone. He was using money every day—he had to stay out there where the people were. He had to do what he could to help them. But he did manage to get two tanks outa what we had. He brought these tanks on his own log truck from the place he had purchased them far outside of Fayette County. And he left them here at the grocery. And at night the whites would drive out and shoot these tanks while they were on top of the ground. And John said, "Well they're trying to puncture my tanks and I've spent all of my money. I don't want this to happen." So then he would go up each night with a shotgun to guard his tanks. After they found out he was up there this ceased. But he had to stay there. The only relief was to get those tanks underground where they belonged. He had been trying to get the kind of equipment he had to have to dig the pits out for these tanks. They had to be six feet under the ground. The two tanks he had at the time were 6000-gallon capacity which meant a good bit of digging. A machine would have been the thing to have. He couldn't get any white person who had this kind of equipment to dig the thing out cause they were bitter or they were afraid of pressure. Then he found this Black man in another county that had this equipment. The man came. He broke something on his machine, and when he went back into Memphis to replace his piece that was broken he said he was stopped by some white people and told if he didn't get that machine back from digging that pit out for John McFerren what they would do for him. And it scared him. So he came back and carried his equipment away and never did return. The tanks were yet on top of the ground.

Then finally, during the mass meetings, it was suggested that men would come with their picks and shovels and mules and scoops and tractors and help to dig the pit out so he could get his tanks underground before something happened to them and so John could come home at night instead of staying up there. They did. If I'm remembering properly, it took about six weeks for the men and scoops and mules and all that to get the pit dug. But they did it. It was sometime after the tanks were under and John had filled these tanks with water because he said he had to fill them with something to keep them under there, and he had pumped all this water into the storage tanks, and then finally this man arrived and said, "I can get you gasoline by two o'clock in the morning if your tanks are ready."

John told him, "My tanks are filled with water and I'll have to pump the water out first. I can't have that water out by two o'clock in the morning."

Then this guy told John, he said, "Well, we'll get the gasoline next night if you can start working on getting the water out now."

Then John said, "I don't even have the kind of pump that is necessary to pump the water out with. I know a Negro who's in the well-drilling business who has that kind of pump, but I'm a little bit afraid that if I go to borrow that pump to get that water out that he will get suspicious and he might mention it to someone else and then the secret is gone because people would normally know that if you're getting the water out of the tanks you'd expect to put gasoline in them."

Then this man said, "Well don't contact him. I will go back and I will bring a pump that you can use and no one will know."

He went back into Memphis and brought this new pump out and he and John set this pump up. And John suggested that we pump this water out to the back of the store and not let it flow to the front cause when the passersby see all this water coming out of the tank it will tell them that the water's coming out and gasoline's going in and this will only put the whites on guard. So they pumped this water out of the tanks on the backs.

After they got all of this water out John told this man that he had to get his money together for the gasoline. Then John decided that he would check with his people and I jumped in the car and away I went to Mississippi and Memphis to check with my people to see if we could borrow enough money from all of them together to get the gasoline shipment. As I said, the little bit we could find was so small that we still didn't have enough, but we felt we were fairly safe to go on with the gasoline coming. And on the night the gasoline was coming this gentleman returned and when he returned he parked again by the side of our window and I was in the kitchen wrapping corn for the store. And he asked John if I was wrapping this for money to help buy the gasoline shipment. And John told him, "Yes." And he said, "John, why didn't you tell me your wife is up this time of night trying to get the money together? I could've arranged that you could have paid later. You didn't have to stay up and go through this kind of punishment. The main thing is to have gasoline in your tanks to shut your mouth up."

So we managed to have it together then. We had borrowed from everybody that we could and with that little we put together by ourselves, we had enough to buy the gasoline shipment. That night the gasoline came in about two o'clock. It came in the back way. It didn't come in through town. The two huge gasoline trucks—it was simply something that would bring tears to your eyes to see. A thirsty county of Black folks that couldn't get gasoline, that had to park their automobiles and couldn't even begin their farm programs because of not having line. It was just something that would make you cry—to see the two trucks bringing gasoline to a place that had been in the news for months and no relief all that time.

After that gasoline had been used we were told how to make contact when we needed more. We made our contact for the second shipment. The second shipment came. But when the second shipment came there were whites patrolling the roads at the time and they saw the trucks at the place. Then after this the owner of this truck line told us he received all kinds of calls from up here in Fayette County calling him everything and saying what they would do to him and that they would refuse to allow any products that they used to be hauled by this company if he were going to haul to that nigger John McFerren. He recorded these conversations over the telephone and then he invited us down to his house and played them back for us to hear what these people were saying. And these were people that we knew. We really got a firsthand report on how they felt about us.

The third time we made our contact they didn't respond. We were out again. And it was approaching farm season for that year. We went down to the refinery here. John asked to go with him. I didn't want to go because he had had it so rough and I was afraid that someone was going to hurt him—they had been so bitter against us—and I didn't want to be on the scene when it happened. I tried to get out of it, but I thought, I said, "Well, if something happens to him, I don't think any other person deserves to know what happens and how it happened more than I do." I went along. When we got to this refinery the manager finally asked us into his office. And John told him he wanted to buy a shipment of gasoline.

And this man stood up and shook his finger in John's face and asked him, "What are you trying to do out there, nigger? Are you trying to run over those white people? And if you think I'm going to sell you gasoline, and you're trying to run over those people out there, you're just wrong. I'll never sell you a drop of gasoline." And he told him to get up and get out of there. This frightened me a little bit because he looked like he was angry enough to do anything. I stood up. I felt that if I stood John would come on out. John wouldn't leave. He stood there and told this man how he felt about him and what he had said.

After he finally did decide to leave, he said, "I'm leaving, but you will read about this." I was so nervous and upset. So when we finally got to the car, I told him I was afraid this man was going to shoot him. He said, "Yes, I thought that too and that's why I didn't try to leave at that time, because if I had turned to leave it might have been a better opportunity for him to shoot. So I stood up, cause if he had pulled his gun I was going to take it from him. I could've helped protect myself from his shooting me by catching his hand."

When we left there we called a news conference and we told what had happened and after a short while this story was circulated. This man that had delivered gasoline to us had been under terrific pressure. He was really upset about things people were trying to do to him. He worked along with us and he made affidavits along with us to the United States Department of Justice. Attorney Harold Flannery came by the store and he wanted to know had we gotten gasoline from the time had made the affidavits. Apparently the Justice Department was moving in on that faster than we realized. Anyway we had not, and he left hurriedly. But he wouldn't tell us where he was going. At this time, you see, we were not able to deal with the refineries at all. We were set up legally to do our own transactions with them, but they would not recognize us at all.

We had also sent a letter to the president of the refinery in regards to this treatment in his office. I don't know how long after, but it wasn't a long time afterward—one morning about nine o'clock the telephone rang. I answered.

And this was a white voice. It said, "Is Mr. McFerren home?"

And I said, "To whom am I speaking?" I was very reluctant to give out information and didn't know who I was talking with cause things were pretty bad.

He said, "I am a salesman from the refinery that you visited not long ago and I want to quote him some gasoline prices."

And I said, "Where are you?"

He said, "I'm in Somerville."

And I asked him if he could come on out to our house.

He came in and he had the gasoline prices. He asked us if we would like to buy gasoline from his refinery. So we arrived at the amount that we could afford to purchase at the time. We didn't want them to have an excuse. We went into the bank in Memphis, Tri-State Bank, a Black bank, and bought a cashier's check made out to this refinery in the exact amount tended to buy. So if we offered a personal check they wouldn't have to say, "Well we don't know if we can honor this." Then we proceeded to go back to this refinery. We got back there and they were so nice. We went into the office and they talked to us as if we were human, whereas just a few weeks ago it was completely different. We paid for this amount of gasoline and we asked that it be delivered at this given time. It was delivered on time and it came in the bright daylight. And it was so relieving to know that, after going through all of this with the gasoline ordeal, that finally, at last, gasoline could be delivered to people who were willing to pay for it at the time that they needed it, instead of being delivered in the night through some arrangement of some kind person that you didn't know and haven't ever seen again. And it was a beautiful celebration. Black folks just came from everywhere. Those that passing the road going on about their business stopped in. Others nearby came over and before you knew it you had this huge number of Black people over there at the grocery just rejoicing to see two gasoline trucks delivering gasoline to the place. Something they had never seen before, and we had never seen done in the daytime before. A burden had been lifted.

John and Viola McFerren emerged from their ordeal as tough and imaginative leaders. As John says, he was "trained under pressure":

Puttin the pressure on us, it educated us in a short while. It educated us what to expect and what not to expect. It helped the Negroes. You take Negroes and you put em on a plantation—and he's born and raised on this plantation—he seems to become accustomed to this and when you don't upstir him he don't know nothin else but that. Well when you stir him up and put pressure on him to run him off, he finds other ways to make a livin. And that has helped the Negroes to advance themself much more faster than just lettin him come on on his own.

The Negro must get in the economic field—get in the businesses and get in the money stream. He must get independent to get his civil rights. A person cannot demand civil rights eatin outa the other man's hand. We do not have a doctor in this county and we do not have a practicin Negro attorney in this county. And the only way we gonna get people of that category is raise our own people in that category. We're not gonna be able to get people to come in from other places because, bein the third-poorest county in the nation, there's no one that's used to livin in high society to come in and live in a poor environment and poor society. Therefore you got to take people and send em out and get em trained and bring em back in your society to change your society. That's why when the white man put on the economic squeeze ten years ago, it began our great progress. Up until ten years ago a lotta people were sharecroppers livin on the white man's place. The white man did his thinkin. But when he put the Negroes off the land, the Negro started thinkin for hisself. The Negro is being trained under pressure that makes him think for hisself.

Viola McFerren

I'm Viola McFerren. I am thirty-nine years old. I've never been outside of the South, I suppose. Not so much anyway. There were twelve children of us and I am the eleventh. We were a very poor family, but we had a loving mother and father. Much of the time we didn't have many things that were essential. We didn't have proper food and I understand that back about the time I was born and a couple of years afterward there were many times when we, along with so many other people in our community, had no food at all. We grew up in this rural community near the town of Michigan, Mississippi. That's in north Mississippi approximately twenty miles south of Somerville. We attended a one-room rural school where had one teacher with more than a hundred children much of the time.

We didn't have a lot of contact with the white community. I suppose my parents might have had a little bit of contact, but we were so isolated. You know, when you're poor and Black and have very few opportunities, you just do not have a chance to get around and see very much. You didn't have very much contact outside your own yard and the area you went through in order to get to school. It was just real poverty.

After finishing the eighth grade in this elementary school—the name of that school was Morse School—I then went to Fayette County Training School. We roomed away from home and attended the school and just before graduation I was married to John McFerren. That was about December 1950. Upon completing twelfth grade in 1951 I enrolled in a school of cosmetology. I'm a registered beautician; however I don't get to practice very much. Then in 1958 our first children came along—John and Jackie. And it was about this time that John had gotten involved into this community work of encouraging Negroes to register to vote—something we had not been able to do in Fayette County. I'll have to be frank to say that I was just scared to death and I did everything in the world I could to discourage him, because I was absolutely afraid—I was afraid of what would happen to him and what would happen to his family if he was to get involved in this kind of work. But nothing I said to him stopped him. He continued.

John had a lot more experience about some of the things that goes on in the world than I had. He had been fortunate enough to travel around a good bit. He had been in the military service and he got a lot of experience in that, whereas I had only been to this little, rural elementary school and then just across the land to this high school, and from there into marriage, and I just hadn't seen too much. I wasn't aware of a number of things that he often talked about. There was one thing he talked about an awful lot and that was the condition of Black people. He seemed very worried about how things were going.

We were farming at the time—eight acres of cotton and very little more than that of corn. And our earnings were very slim, but he always managed to hustle enough to keep two people going. He used to cut logs and haul timber where he could find it as a sideline. And I remember quite well he returned home one night and said he'd been cutting some timber on a white man's farm in Mississippi. He said that he didn't realize that there were Black people who were practically uncivilized in this part of the country. And he went on to tell about the Black people that came out to see him while he worked.

He said that they lined up and just stared at him, and if he looked around they would run behind trees and peep out at him as if he was not a human being. And he said that they just didn't, they looked like they were not civilized at all. And they reacted that way. And he came home and he told me that he just couldn't go over there anymore because he didn't know his own people were in that condition. He just couldn't afford to go back over there. He just couldn't take it.

Pretty soon after that this Burton Dodson trial was being had here in Fayette County. Everybody in Fayette County, it appeared, tried to attend that hearing in order to see one of our people being represented by a Black lawyer. As they were trying to select a jury for this case, Attorney Estes was questioning why weren't there Negroes as part of the jury and someone in some authority around the courthouse answered, "Because they were not registered citizens." And that's why they were not being placed on the jury. It was at that time that John came home and said he was going to do something about Negroes in Fayette County not even being registered to vote. The first thing I knew, he, along with Harpman Jameson, Houston Malone, and a number of other fellows, had talked about this thing and they were getting a voter-registration drive going. In the meantime they talked with this Black lawyer about organizing a civic organization to work with. Then they set out the Fayette County Civic and Welfare League, Incorporated. The organization was put into operation in 1959. During all this time I was frightened to death. And I was home most of the time with the twin babies. There wasn't a lot I could do cause I had to take care of the children, but I had time to be frightened to death.

The tension was really high then. Things was rough. At that time people were being forced off of land and they were being denied the opportunity to purchase various essential things. It was just a horrible thing. I remember quite well that John had gone into Washington, DC, to testify before the Civil Rights Commission on the conditions in Fayette County. When he arrived home there was a Negro that came to inform him of some real effort to kill him.

At that time, everything was beginning to fall in on us. Negroes that were active in the movement were just being tossed around—frightened and threatened. Some other Negroes who were not involved were being done the same way because they were relatives or friends of some of the others that were active. And there were other Negroes who perhaps were not being pressured, but they were afraid of pressure. So, having the whites turn completely against us, we had many of the Negroes that seemed afraid of us because of what was happening to us and other Negroes who were being active.

It was at this time that this so-called blacklist was being circulated. These lists were even carried into other counties and adjacent towns. And I remember quite well, one Black, elderly lady told me of going into town to see the local doctor that she had always gone to. And she said that when it was finally her turn to be called into the office that this doctor came out and she noticed that he looked at her and then he walked over to the wall inside of the nurse's station and he just stared up on the wall. She couldn't figure out why he looked at her and then walked over and started staring up on the wall. Then he came back and told her, "No, I can't help you." She found out later that he had this list up on his wall that he could look up on after seeing who came in to see whether or not to treat the patient. She was refused and she left.

Things got so rough that people couldn't even get gasoline to run their automobiles with.

Then finally it was the farming season. The Black farmers didn't know where they were going to buy seeds to plant their crops. At this time John's brother was operating a small grocery store, but the pressures began to get so heavy on him he decided to move away. Before he moved away, the companies that he had been doing business with came out—for instance, the ice cream company came and took away the ice cream box that they had put in the store to refrigerate the ice cream products. The oil company came out and took away the tanks and the pumps that you run the gasoline through. Took all of that away. His place was just stripped completely down. At that time Robert became so discouraged. He said, "Well, I'll just leave. I just won't stay here in this." So he moved away. It was thought by the white community, we found out later, that Robert was the instigator of the movement. They felt that with him having more education than John, who went up to eighth grade, he had to be the instigator because John didn't have enough knowledge to do a thing like this. Therefore, Robert really got it and he left.

The store was closed down. That left Negroes without any place at all, those that were being pressured, to buy a match, milk, or anything. We would drive way into Memphis to buy homogenized milk for the babies. If you wanted a popsicle you had to get out of Fayette County to get it. We were in the process of having our babies. We had to drive into Memphis to a hospital when it was delivery time. No medical attention, whatsoever, could we get out here. We had this black '55 Ford that we had to use for everything. John spent all of his time out in the community and out on the road trying to help people. He said he felt responsible because he said he felt he had gotten people into this predicament by encouraging them to register. He felt obligated to just go, until he couldn't go, trying to help them.

Then he decided that he would try to open the store. He rented the store from his brother for fifty dollars a month. And it took a long time to get it set up to the extent that we could even open it. Then we couldn't get any deliveries. He would take this '55 Ford and put a basket on the top of it and go into other towns, Memphis being one of them. Many of the wholesale houses would not sell to him, but he knew quite a few other Black people who were in business and a lot of times he would get this Black person to get certain things through their store. Then he would come at night and pick these things up. Sometimes he could catch company trucks out on the road or in some of these little alleys while they were making their deliveries to other places. Then he could buy off of these trucks. He could not buy anything by going to the wholesale houses where the trucks came from. This went on for quite some time.

And I remember, finally things were so tough, each morning when John would leave home I just knew that he wouldn't return. This is how I felt. When he would arrive at night I was always glad to see him, but I just knew, when the next morning came and he was off again, that this was the last time I would see him. This is just how serious things were. So I had to learn to live knowing that anything could happen at any time, just knowing what was going to be the final result. I had been too afraid to sleep at night cause I had always read about mobbing and lynching and had been told stories about what happened to Negroes when they do things that whites didn't approve of. I just waited for the time when this type of thing would happen to us. I had gotten so nervous over thinking about what was going to happen, until I wanted to sleep, but I certainly couldn't sleep at night. And during the day, after he had gone off, and I had prepared myself to get the news of his not being able to return home alive—I would work hard and get all my work done and get the babies to sleep and then I would get a nap during the day. But I couldn't sleep at night. I didn't want to sleep at night. I wanted to stay awake, because I could just see in my mind this mob, I could just hear the same kind of mob that went out to kill Burton Dodson. Everybody, as I have been told, was shooting. This huge mob, and they were all shooting. From treetops. And this man and several sons inside of this shack. All the trees were covered, and horses and everything else all around the house and body blazing away. I could just see that kind of mob coming to do us in at night. Finally, it almost got me down. Through the day there were just parades of cars driven by white people that would come past our house driving very, very, very slowly. Then at night they would drive into the drive and turn around on the gravel. You could hear them turning around and this was a constant thing. And this was something horrible to live with.

Then I just became so depressed. I just gave up. For a while I thought, when John is not here I'll go to somebody's house. But I found out that everybody is afraid and it seemed they felt better when we weren't around. That didn't leave many places for me to go. My parents were living in Mississippi which was too far to go. And the children were very small babies and I just couldn't take them out all of the time. It was a difficult thing to live with and yet I was afraid to be home.

Finally I saw I couldn't get away from the thing. I had nowhere to go to get away. John had to be gone; I couldn't be with him every place he went. I decided I would just pray about the situation and just leave it completely up to our Eternal Father. I just remember all times of the day and night when I would just get on my knees. Whenever it came to me, whenever it dawned on me the conditions that was existing, I would just stop right then and there, regardless of what I was doing—whether I was putting diapers out on the line in back or if I was doing the laundry or whatever—I just stopped right then and I would pray. And I asked the Eternal Father to please remove the fear that I had because I couldn't live with it—it was about to get me down. And I was so sick and nervous. I couldn't eat anymore. And many of the people that I had thought were our Black friends had turned against us. I guess they were afraid; they felt we had done something that was a great harm to the Black people because whites were retaliating in all these different ways. There was hardly no one left at that time that you could call a friend—even these people that had been to your home and were with you and thought you were a great person and all. They didn't think that way anymore. And this is why I had to pray—because there was hardly nobody to turn to.

Finally, all of the fear left. All of the fear of harm being done, of staying awake at night to listen, to hear what's coming upon you. All this left and I was able to go to sleep at night. And I was so tired. I just went to sleep at bedtime and I didn't worry anymore. I didn't feel tired, worried, and dragged out again. I was able to go about my business. And it was at this time I decided to work hard in the movement. I knew that regardless of what other people feel or say, that this struggle is right. There's no reason why people shouldn't be free. There's no reason why people shouldn't have an opportunity to register and vote. This is not wrong, and even though whites is reacting in a way that is saying that you're wrong, they have had these privileges and someone has to take a step for the Black people. And if our lives is going to make it better for all of the thousands of Black lives in Fayette County, then what is it to lose five little lives? I was thinking in terms of my husband's life, the three children, and mine. So I just got a new determination and I've worked hard and I've done everything that I could possibly do to promote progress in the interests of the people here.

THE JAMESONS

Harpman and Minnie Jameson have worked alongside the McFerrens in all of the many stages of the civil rights struggle. Even before the movement began the two families were extremely close—Minnie and Viola are sisters; Harpman and John have been friends since childhood. The demands and dangers of the struggle in Fayette County have drawn them still closer—together the McFerrens and Jamesons form an extended family bound tightly together by absolute love and trust.

Harpman Jameson

I was almost nineteen years old when we were shipped over to Pearl Harbor and we taken about six weeks marine hiking and rifle practice there. We were shipped outa Pearl Harbor to Guam for our first invasion. Now durin the time we were takin this trainin in California and Pearl Harbor the white and Black worked pretty fairly together, but after we got overseas and the first invasion was over we begun to pick up on the first spot of Jim Crow. There we was hung out there on this small island—island was forty-nine miles wide, thirty-nine miles long. The officers was havin their big parties. They had Red Cross women comin in. Of course, they was white. Later on the nurses begin to come in. The officers put the Red Cross women down and picked up the nurses. Well, the Red Cross women went to the white marines. Well there the Black men stood with nothin in hand. They couldn't go just for a social dance. And there was the whites—they was haulin em all up and down the road by our barracks, in jeeps, back of trucks, goin swimmin, all kinda parties—and there was me. I had nothin.

I lost my grandfather while I was overseas there. I went to my Red Cross chaplain—he wouldn't even talk with me. Also, talkin about the Red Cross—we was on a troop train goin through some parta Texas. Ahead of us was several coaches of white soldiers. And such a funny accident—when we got up there where the Red Cross served donuts and coffee, it was time for em to go. I may be speakin too much about the Red Cross, but the Red Cross sure gotta do somethin for me before I turn a hand to try to do somethin for the Red Cross, because they ain't never done nothin for me.

But let me tell you about comin back from service now. This is what I saw. There was four navy men. They'd been together overseas about two or three years. And this was three white men and one Black man. And they'd slept together, ate together, played cards together all the way on the ship back to the States. And they got on the train together—they'd taken two seats and that's where these four slept on the train, it looked like for two or three days. But somewhere along the line comin back from California to Nashville, somewhere they discovered they crossed the Mason-Dixon Line. And two of these whites had been with this Negro all this time—them jokers got up and stood up all the way to Nashville. And when I mean they stood up, they stood for two days and two nights instead of lyin back down with this Negro—and they'd been with him three years. And you know, I think this got away with me. You know, I've been thinkin about that ever since.

When I come back from service, I'd left a few things here such as a few calves and cows. And I'd left the old car. When I come back all this was run down. I found the old car. It was parked somewhere else. I pulled it together and got it to runnin. The few little cows was scattered. I got em together. Now I had a little musterin-out pay. I brought it back and I began to buy wire to go around this farm of my grandmother. We was able to draw outa the GI benefit somethin like ninety-seven dollars a month for about a year or so. So I got on this farm program and I did that. The next year we had this farm class. So I signed up in this class and I was able to draw some benefit from this class. But the farm was so run down—the little amount of money, I really put it into the farm, such as buyin land, seeds, wire, and some plow tools. I bought two or three mules and horses to get started back in farmin. I thought that was the only thing to do at that particular time—I had my grandmother and mother with me and also my little brother. It may look like to some people it might've been a big amount of money, but the ninety-seven dollars, it wasn't nothin at all to put into a farm.

I was married in 1948. I guess I thought I had saw the world and done some of everything and figured the next thing was marryin. I married a young lady—at that particular time her name was Minnie Harris. I knowed her so long before I married her I'm ever ashamed to tell that. I met her before I went in service. We'd known each other about seven years before we married. We was walkin, comin from a neighbor's house of hers across the woods there one Sunday evening, and I asked her to marry me, and she didn't say much, she didn't want to talk too much. I hadn't prepared no speeches. Just somethin she said made me—and I asked the question. And she looked at me and she didn't say nothin. I said, "I know what the answer's gonna be." And she said, "You do, huh?" So it went on for, I don't know, two or three weeks until she would finally tell me that she would. She said she would, but she had a lotta unfinished business she had to take care of before we really got married. She was teachin school and I think she wanted to carry out that school term she had started and so on. And I think I agreed to everything she said. And finally got married two months after that. So then she moved up to Fayette County and started out as a farmer with me. She saw we wasn't gettin no way there and she done a little sub work. She went back to college for another quarter or so—she was intendin to get better in the teachin field by takin these courses. While school was out that fall, when she come home, everybody had registered around here and we got on her about registerin. So she decided she would go and register. And after she registered she ain't never got another day's subbin in this county since. So we depended on the farm—as much as we would make out of it. When OEO (Office of Economic Opportunity) come into the county she got a job with OEO. And she been workin there till they cut back on funds last year. She seems to be real dutiful about her job. Anything she's a parta, she wants it to be the best of all. She likes for things to go right and she likes to get around to the poor people and really get down to earth with em and help em to make a better start and help em to do better for theirself. And that takes lotsa hard work.

I've known John McFerren all my life. In those days we lived across the field about three miles apart. We often visited and used to walk by that way goin to school. John's mother and my grandmother was good friends and also my mother. John was good with machinery. He had a small motor—it was a washin-machine motor—he had it on four wheels and it would run and pull itself. And John was real interested in that. It was a gasoline motor. John at that particular time was doin good blacksmith work. He didn't ever make one like that, but he begin to make a lotta other things. If John had had an opportunity to work with motors and things he probably woulda made a real somethin, sure enough.

Back when we were young men we wasn't thinkin too much about conditions of the South—we was thinkin just about tryin to make a livin in the world. Back then I had lots in mind that I would try to do. First thing I had in mind, I wanted to grow horses. I love horses. And I wanted to be a big horse trader. Anyway I traded a few and I growed a few. But the price fell out on em and I quickly got outa horses. Then I wanted to be a big farmer with a lotta sharecroppers, but after I got over in there that didn't seem to work out. So then I began to pull closer to home to make more offa the acreage I had at home. Me and John talked this close—about what we could make a livin outa and what we couldn't.

On down to where I first got interested in registerin and votin. I and John was in Somerville courthouse durin the time they begin with Burton Dodson's trial. Estes, the Black lawyer defendin Dodson, was callin for registered citizens for grand jury. I and John was around there and we wanted to serve on the grand jury. And we found out you had to be registered before you could serve on the grand jury. So we listened close at the trial and durin that day at lunch Estes wanted somebody to raise the money around there to pay a lady to record the trial that evenin. So I and John started to raisin money around the cafe there to get the trial recorded. That was about the first organized part we done. We raised this money—I forget now how much it was—and we turned it over to the lawyer and we began to get acquainted with the lawyer. So then he spoke about how come there weren't any more registered people down there. So then we got interested in registerin and getting our people registered. We stayed close with the Dodson trial until they made sentence on the man for ninety-nine years, I believe. And then we began to register to vote.

At that particular time we started off it wasn't but about twenty-eight Negroes registered in the whole of Fayette County. This trial was held the last of March and the first of April. In June we pitched a big registration rally down there which about three hundred Negroes got registered. July we pulled another big registration day there which about 380 got registered that day. We only had one day a month that the registration office was open. So next registration day they began to move the registration office. Or the registration officer not in.

And we began to get a whole lotta junk then and up through the years. There was one day somebody got up on the courthouse and sprinkled pepper down on the people. Red pepper! And they got up there paintin one day and they were throwin paint down on the people in line. And we have had a tough time gettin registered all the way on up through until now. Now we still don't have but just a Monday to register and the hours don't fit the workin people. The hours is from eight to twelve and from one to four. Well everybody's workin durin the day. If they ain't gonna have but one day, it'd be more benefit to have it on a Saturday. But these hours is hard to change. I have an idea it's to hold registration down for the Black man.

A lotta people we spoke to about registerin—they afraida losin their jobs, they was afraida losin their homes, if they owned somethin they was afraid it would be taken away from them, and some of em was just plain afraid to register because there was some people talked so far against it. After we got the registration started there was a number of people did lose their homes, but right today everyone I talked with say it should've happened ten years before it did. We have one fellow lived in this district—he had been workin sharecroppin and rentin for, well, all his life. He's about fifty-seven years old now. At that time he had been there about thirty years. He didn't own much but two mules. And less than two years after he'd been put offa this land he worked hard and saved what he could and bought him an acre of ground with a cheap house on it. And since he bought his house he's owned about three new trucks and he had never owned a new truck before. He's livin happy. He had added an extra room to his house. And it's not a fancy house, but him and his wife and mother-in-law is satisfied in there. He's warm and dry. And I would say he might even have a little money now. Anyway, he's one of our board of directors and he says that if he had to do over what he went through again, he says he'll be glad to do it again.

The year it all began, in August 1959, we went to our pollin place to vote. A good number of us went in—I was leadin the group. The officer of the election, which was Mr. Wright, told me, "Harpman, this is a all-white primary Democrat election. No Negroes is allowed to vote in it." So they turned us around. Some more of our people—Negroes across the county in all the precincts—was told the same thing. So then we come out and went to our regular meetin place where we had been kinda gettin up meetins and we began to talk it over. Then we consulted with Estes and we began to get things amovin towards goin to Washington.

There was about four of us takin off in a car drivin to Washington to see what we could do for the race of our people—how we could register and vote like a first-class citizen. And the trip to Washington we made good connections and we began to get a few things movin on the line of civil rights. This particular time we begged money throughout the county and we used the lawyer's car. We all drove. One of the fellows that went with us, he had an uncle in Washington—we left here Friday evenin and we got to his uncle's house late that Saturday night. The uncle tried to give us a comfortable place—he gave us a bed. But meantime I looked over the bed and three had already got in the bed so I got over behind the bed and lay on the floor. It was about one-thirty and wasn't long before the day. We were taken off to Sunday school and we had a speakin engagement with our lawyer that particular night. We never did wonder too much about whether we would be able to do it. We knew from the beginnin that we didn't have no education—we didn't have that speakin part that dress things up so—so we just were tellin the story just like it was. We had had experience of these things and we just only told it like it was. We didn't dress it up, we didn't undress it—we just told the straight truth and that was the problems we was dealin with every day.

After we registered they had a blacklist circlin around with a good number of our names on it. Every one of the merchants had one of these lists. If your name was on it he wasn't supposed to sell you nothin. We had one fellow, Isaiah Harris, he had a white neighbor of his'n—lived next door to him. He went down the road to Moscow, Tennessee, to buy some gas and this fellow was drivin along behind him. And he drives up at the fillin station and this white neighbor drives up there and winks at the man not to sell him no gas. We had several cases like that.

The league began after we went to vote and was turned down. We began to meet and speak. To get somethin started official we had to get an organization. We went to the lawyer that we'd been workin with. He'd taken our names and sent off for us a charter in the name of the league. We began to work close along with this charter and the rules that went with it. Then we began membership and takin in all the people. The county was already divided—it had fifteen districts. And we had a leader in each district and he had members and he made a report to the main body about once a month. We had league meetins quite often—sometimes two or three nights a week.

That first year it went pretty hard with us. I never saw nowhere overseas that American money wasn't spent, yet I couldn't spend a dime in Fayette County and I couldn't borrow a dime in Fayette County. And I couldn't see—that was in 1960—how we could live. We were sellin vegetables twenty-five miles from Fayette County—and we carried vegetables every other day—and I would buy enough gas in my truck and the cans I carried to run my tractor the next day. The next year we had made a plea to the government and everywhere for gas. That's what drove McFerren into groceries and oil—to try to supply the people from goin outa the county. I was so glad to see him with gas. I don't usually stop nowhere but there now.

Durin 1960 we couldn't borrow no money to make a crop on. See, farmers are always—well, the old tradition is usually goin into the bank, say the first of March. And they would make a loan for a certain amount of money to make a crop on. And we would pay it back in the fall. So in 1960 I went into the bank. And, well, the bank had always been nice talkin with me. The secretary asked me what did I want and I told her I wanted a crop loan like I'd been havin. So she wrote my name down and carried it in the back room there and she come back and said, "Harpman, Mr. Wilkerson say he can't see you today."

I said, "Ain't there another man I can see?"

She said, "No, he say he can't help you at all."

So I thanked her and I went on. This was in March. So I tried everywhere durin the resta March and April—to borrow a small amount of money to make a crop on. Way up in May I found a place where I could mortgage my land and borrow six hundred dollars. So I did that and I made the crop and I paid the six hundred dollars back that year and I had a little left to live on that winter. There were a lotta people had a harder time.

Minnie Jameson

When I was a little girl, we had a very happy family life, but it was a life of poverty. Quite a few of us had to sleep together. Our home was poorly heated. There were leaks in the roof. But we were very happy playin on the hills and ditches.

I think when I first noticed segregation was durin the time I was tryin to get to school. We had to walk this five miles twice a day and we could see the bright, new, yellow buses runnin by our door. The white children would ride in these buses. By the time we got to our buses we were cold—twenty or thirty miles we had to travel to school and we were still cold, very cold. We didn't have sufficient clothing—shoes and coats and things. So it was very uncomfortable. I think this was when I first noticed it. And then riding on the buses—the interstate buses or Trailways buses—when I first started ridin em, there was a curtain or somethin they would put up in the back where the Black people would be seated. It had holes through it. You would see through these little windows. You would sit behind that if you was able to get a seat. But if some white person needed a seat, you had to get up and stand up in the aisleway and they would move this curtain farther back.

I really enjoyed goin to school. I was always at the head of my class. I had a younger brother and we would always receive a prize for somethin at the end of the school year for not missin any days outa school. It was our intention not to miss any days outa school regardless of how bad the weather was.

I remember one day it was so cold and I guess I was so small my face swelled from bein out in the weather, but I didn't mind, just so I was there at school.

When I got outa high school I really wanted to go to college, but with other young children in the family this was really impossible. So I went to Memphis and I started workin down there. I wasn't able to get a good job. I had to work at a laundry which was very hard work, but I finally got used to it and grew to like it. But in the meantime my parents were lookin out for work for me to do. Many of the teachers in Mississippi had not finished the twelfth grade. So since I had completed the twelfth grade, they talked with the county super-intendent and she told em that I could get an emergency certificate to teach school and that if I would enroll in school when school was out then I could teach. So this is what I did from '45 to '48. And at that time I got married and changed counties.

The first time I saw Harpman a friend of mine was datin him and she went over where he was durin the lunch hour. That's the first time I saw him. I saw him then, but I didn't really pay any attention to him. The next time I ran into him a girl friend of mine was goin out to the movies with John McFerren and Harpman came along with him. So this girl asked me to go to the movies with em. So that's how I really met him. I still wasn't interested in him. We went to the movies together but that was all so far as I was concerned. Before I married him he came around several times. I got interested very slowly. I thought he was a nice guy and thought he was capable of supportin a wife and family with my help. But I don't know why I didn't continue in school and continue to work at that time when I had a better chance than I have now. Anyway he was farmin and my parents farmed so I guess I thought you could make it on the farm, but as mechanization and different things came into the picture—boll weevils—that I hadn't anticipated, well that cut down on the income from farmin and I saw a need for some other type of work.

During the fifties Harpman was supportin his grandmother who raised him and his mother was ill. We also had two little children of his brother's. We made fair crops, but we didn't have any help in gatherin the crops and puttin em in. It was quite expensive cause we couldn't do all of this work. Our family was either too old or too young to help with the work. So it was very difficult at that time. Our house needed repair. We didn't have electricity and the year we decided to wire the house was the year when our crop was the shortest. So Harpman took a job in Somerville and I believe he was makin four dollars a day. His mother and I gathered the crop that fall and I believe made four bales of cotton. But somehow we pinched pennies and were able to get the house wired. And I remember that year for Christmas what I wanted most was just a ten-dollar string of lights to go on the Christmas tree.

◆ ◆ ◆

We would often listen to news of the adjoinin county of Shelby—where Memphis is—and read in the papers where people were votin over there. We wondered why, with Negroes bein the majority in Fayette County, why they never voted. This question often came up and it would often be asked—"Black people, why aren't we votin?" I don't know what the answer was to this, but I do know this question was asked quite a bit.

In about 1955 I started to do some substitute teachin and I started back to school. This time I had really made up my mind that I was goin back to school in order to finish my college work. So I worked as a sub durin the school time and durin the summer I would go to school. So in 1959 I went to school that summer. I didn't know that John and Harpman was carryin on voter registration durin the time I was in school. So when the quarter ended I came home. This was on a Saturday when they attempted to vote and had been refused. I think they were in the process of settin up the Fayette County Civic and Welfare League when I came home.

I mentioned to Harpman, "Yes I'm in school and you are votin. Do you know what this means?"

"No, this won't have any bearin on you."

But that fall I wasn't called to do any substitute work at all. I did some secretarial work for the league. I haven't been called since.

In talkin to John about gettin the people registered to vote, I asked him did he have any idea how much pressure probably would be placed on him.

And he said, "Well, that goes for the professional people—they can pressure em—but they can't pressure the farmers. We farmers, they can't pressure us."

So I said, "They can't?"

And he said, "No."

But we didn't have any dream whatsoever about how much pressure could be put on the farmer because in the spring of '60 all aid was taken from the farmers—they couldn't get crop loans, their gas tanks was picked up, and they couldn't even purchase merchandise in the county. I didn't really regret it. I guess instead of regrettin we were tryin to find a way out.

I tried to register two days straight and we had to stand in line—we stood in line from eight until noon. Then we had to come back in the afternoon and wait in line and try to get registered. And it was the afternoon of the second day before I was able to get registered.

People would often come in needin assistance—needin shelter, needin food—and they reported different things that had happened to em. And I as secretary of the league would make note of these different requests and help em get the different supplies they needed if we had em. I also wrote letters and answered letters for the league and kept a record of what was goin on in our organization. Didn't any of us have any experience in doin this. We just had to do what we thought was best to do at that time.

Minnie played an important role in the league's efforts to create a community center. Like so many of the league projects in those early days, there were no precedents to follow, no models to copy. And the third-poorest county in America is not a likely place to raise money. To the status quo of Fayette County the project was yet another indication of a dangerous solidarity in the Black community. The mechanism of legal oppression churned into action, but the league met the challenge.

The first place that the movement people started to gatherin was at Robert McFerren's grocery—John was farmin at this time. And this was one of the first places to be closed after voter registration started. So the men would meet in front of the closed store and sit on the seats—they loved it so. And this is where they would carry on the meetins during the day. But the public mass meetins—it was very difficult to find a place to hold these mass meetins, and the only place we could find was the Mount Olive church. And this bein a church there was only a certain type of meetin that you could hold there in the church. We were very grateful to the officers and pastor for lettin us use the church because most churches would not hear to the league usin it because they did not want their church to get burned down. Some of the league members made a pledge to themselves that if anything happened to the Mount Olive church they were goin to join with the membership and do all they could to help this church get built back. So in the meantime, it was only one little room that the league was usin for an office and this was ten by eight—once you get a desk in you couldn't hardly get over three or four people in there. We kept wonderin what could we do. We didn't even have a place to store the groceries and clothin that was bein sent to help the people in the county.

There was a suggestion made that we build a community center—a buildin that would be large enough to hold our mass meetins and where we could have an office. But this was only a dream and we never—well I won't say we never thought it would come true, but we knew it would take a lotta hard work to get it through. I suggested that we build the community center.

It was very difficult gettin the money. Mostly at first it was just a dream. The league purchased two acres of land. And even the land, the price was much higher than to people who was buildin homes, but we thought it would be worthwhile to purchase the land. When the two acres of land was purchased we only had twenty dollars left in the treasury. We was hopin to build this twenty dollars up before we started buildin, but in the meantime the county was to be zoned into residential, industrial, and farm land. We felt that this zonin was takin place to keep us from buildin the center. So we had to get started on the center with just twenty dollars. And we could only buy steel to go in the footin and poured the footin for a forty-by-seventy buildin. This was all our money at the time. In the meantime Virgie Hartenstein, a civil rights worker from the North, was visitin in the county and she suggested bringin students into the county on workshops to help build the community center. This idea was accepted by the league. Students would raise some money and then they would come and stay a week, maybe two weeks, and live in the homes of people in the area. And while they were here we'd work on the community center. We raised money also, locally, as much as possible. Maybe five hundred people contributed what little they could spare at the time to help, even if they were not members of the league.

We started usin the buildin as we built it. We sponsored talent shows on the grounds with no top to the buildin. We found that if we could bring people out to the center to see what we were doin, this would bring more interest and helpin to finance the buildin. We had a ground-breakin ceremony on the land when we were ready to start buildin and at this rally I think we raised sixty dollars.

Now the center is used very much by the community. I believe some of everything has been carried on out there except a funeral. We have had weddin receptions, and parties of all kinds, our business meetins, mosta the public meetins of the OEO is held out at the community center—the Somerville courthouse hasn't been used very much for integrated meetins. Whites come to meetins out there as well as Blacks. An adult basic-education class has been out there for the last five years. It's integrated and whites are attendin the basic-education program.

James Jamerson

The movement was not a part-time thing. The pressure of events touched all members of the family. James Jamerson was just a child when the movement began, but it soon had a crucial effect on the shape of his life.
Minnie talks about James:

James was with us when it all began and he was very much interested in the movement. He took part in the marches. Whatever was goin on at the time he was ten years old he took part in it. He marched on the city to integrate public facilities and he was in the attempt to integrate the schools. And he sometimes would leave school on his own to go on marches. This we tried to discourage because we didn't know if he'd be hurt and we would like to have known where he was all the time. But it seemed that when the others left he just had to go. So we tried to understand and he was never punished for leavin school.

James attended our meetins quite often when it didn't interfere with his schoolwork. He really knew what was goin but sometime when it was at its worst we tried to keep some of that away from him. Before the movement began and James was young, I didn't tell James that there were places that he couldn't go in, some things that maybe he couldn't do. I remember a little rockin horse in front of the theater when James was small. James loved horses and he loved to ride horses and whenever he saw this horse he would like to take a ride on it. So James didn't know that he wasn't welcome to ride on this horse and I didn't think that I should tell him at such a small age. So when we would be in town he would run on up in front of me and jump up on the horse and take a ride. Bein small I knew he wouldn't let me get too far from him, so I'd just keep on walkin while he took a ride. If I'd get a certain distance from him he'd jump down and try to catch me, but first he enjoyed his ride on the horse.

Lookin back, I just wonder why the TV had such a bearin on me. In 1959, after we registered to vote, things wasn't too tough at first. So Christmas we bought a television—took out a television on installment plan. I think our payments were about twenty dollars a month. If things had gone as usual we could have paid the twenty dollars a month easily. But '60 was when all the reprisals was placed on the people who registered to vote. And merchants stopped sellin to us and they picked up gas tanks and everything of the farmers and we weren't able to get a crop loan. James had been discouraged to goin to the movie because of the situation in the county at that time—we didn't think we should sit segregated in the balcony, so we just stopped goin to the movie. So the television was all the recreation he had around home because he couldn't go to the movie. And James enjoyed watchin the television very much, but he didn't know we couldn't get a crop loan that year. My husband and I would ride all day long tryin to find someplace to borrow the money to make our crop that year. And when I would return home James would be watchin TV. And when I stopped in the room where he and the TV was I would immediately have to leave because I knew we wouldn't have the TV long and it made me very nervous. I just couldn't stand to watch the TV. However, I wouldn't tell James about it. He was enjoyin watchin the TV and I wanted him to watch the TV. But it would make me sick to see him watchin it knowin that it soon wouldn't be here.

Harpman talks about James:

James come into the family—well, he always have been in the family, just about. He's my brother's son. I raised him. I've been havin him about here since he was about six months old. He looks to me as daddy and to Minnie as momma, but he did know his mother and father. They is separated and James end up with us. He seemed to like it and my brother and his momma wanted him to be there. He been with us so long—well I always have looked upon him as mine and still do yet. I think my brother do too now. He never have tried to get him away, or nothin of the kind. And when he see me he asks me, "How is James?" and so on. So James, he is a son of ours. He's been with us all his life. He still has a key to the house, just like sons do.

James:

I was raised by my uncle and aunt. I moved in with em at age four. I had been stayin with em from time to time before that. At the age of four I didn't know too much. That's when I started farmin cause they weren't my real parents and I don't think they really had to take care of me and I guess I just felt like I had to do somethin to earn my keep. I think I started workin in the field before I started school. After I started school I still did my share in the field. It didn't look like fun, but I felt I had to do somethin. We lived in this field—a mile from the road—and there wasn't any more kids around. There were one or two, but everybody had to do somethin—make sure you had enough to eat. In the beginnin I had my sister and she died when I was seven. After that I was the only child in the house. When I was goin to school I had to get up early in the mornin, five-thirty or six o'clock, and do certain chores like feedin chickens, milkin cows, feedin pigs, and things like that. And after this I had to walk this mile to the main road just to catch this bus and go to school. One or two fellows at that time, back there in the field—we'd walk there together. Fifth grade, I think, they moved out and I walked myself.

I really don't know when I first knew there was a civil rights movement. I was nine or ten. I know we were in the field choppin or pickin cotton and Mr. McFerren come by the house. And he called my uncle off by the side and they talked awhile. And I discovered the whole thing they were talkin about was registration. Before that I don't think there had been too much registration in Fayette County among Black people. Later on that fall they begin to have meetins so a lotta times I was left at home by myself. I was supposed to go to school the next day and the meetins lasted a long time. Like it would be anywhere from twelve to two o'clock before they got back home. And I was back there in the field with no one but my grandmother, scared to death because I realized—I began to realize—that the white people in my area might be out there in the field. And I always wondered would anybody try to come to the house and break in while they were away. I was out there by myself.

My uncle and aunt never had to explain what they were doin. A lotta times I would go along with em. Like if the meetin was on Friday night and I didn't have to go to school the next day. People would come in and make speeches and try to decide what they were going to do and how they were goin to get people out to vote, and tryin to get the idea of registration over to the people. I would sit in and listen to the meetins and speeches. And I just learned what was goin on. I went out to Tent City twice and I could see there was some real poor people there. The idea of Tent City struck me too because I didn't think it made too much sense for a man to have to move offa his land, move outa his house, because he registered to vote. I didn't know too much about registration and votin then, but the idea of a family with eight kids havin to move out—it didn't make sense.

My uncle and aunt told me to stay outa the highway because a lotta white people are runnin Black people offa the road. They also told me I didn't have to say "yes sir" and "no sir" to white people. It wasn't that Aunt Minnie was teachin disrespect for older people, but the Black people's way of sayin it was "yas suh," "no suh" and I don't think she wanted me growin up to be afraida anyone.

Right after registration everything got hot down there. We used to go into Somerville every week—maybe we'd take some eggs or chickens or somethin— and we'd go into this market where we could get cash for em, cash to buy other goods with. And after this voter-registration drive started, this man who owned the supermarket refused to do business with my uncle. It was durin the fall of the year and I only had one pair of shoes and they was tearin up on me. So we went to this shoe shop to have em fixed so I could make it through the winter with em. This man who owned the shoe shop knew my uncle very well, but this time when we stepped in the door—before my uncle said anything—this man said, "I'm sorry, Harpman. We can't do business with you." I think that contributed to me gettin another pair of shoes that year. It seemed that my uncle knew all the white people in Fayette County. It seemed that he got along with all of em, but after he registered to vote they seemed to treat him like he wasn't anything. They didn't know him. Just like he was dirt or somethin. They refused to sell him groceries, gas, refused to do work on his machinery, his car, anything like that—refused him everything. Had to go outa the county just to get food to eat. Memphis was forty or fifty miles away and he had to go all the way to Memphis just to eat. Before '59—that's when this registration drive really started—we were receivin this government food, but after we started registerin to vote they quit sendin this food to Fayette County. I guess they quit sendin it. I know there weren't Black people receivin it any more.

I didn't really know what was going on in the beginning. And really it kinda upset me. At that time I was kinda a nervous wreck. I didn't know whether we were gonna eat the next day, whether we were gonna get run off the road—I didn't know what would happen. We were back there in this field. Isolated. We didn't have a neighbor within a mile. And, like I say, a lotta times I was left there with no one but my grandmother. I never knowed what might happen. Like when Uncle Harpman and Aunty Minnie go to these meetins, I didn't know whether they would get ambushed on the way home, cause back in the fields once it rains the truck stays out on the road because it's too muddy to get the truck through the fields—and I didn't know if they would get ambushed walkin through the fields or what. I was always wonderin what would happen. I did the walk alone comin home from school. But one thing about comin home from school—it wasn't dark. I could always see. But still I was afraid because I didn't know whether somebody'd be in those woods or what. I was always hopin that there wasn't. It seemed that some of the students—I was in an all-Black school at the time; grade school—and it seemed that some of the Black students turned against me. The teachers there were afraida the movement because they were afraid they would lose their jobs. I shouldn't say I was afraid, but I was always on my toes because I didn't know what would happen. A lotta times I would walk out with Aunt Minnie at night and I would take a gun with me because I didn't know what I might see. I was twelve then. I would imagine where the ambush would come. I guess I thought if I passed a certain spot on the road I didn't have anything to worry about. But I'm not sure that was true.

It was really rough goin to school. They wouldn't talk to me that much. The instructors seemed to be afraida me. They would punish some students more severely for makin the same mistake—as though they were afraida my parents or somethin. Where I really got interested in the movement was after I got to high school. They had a few protest marches and I would always leave school the middle of the day to march on the courthouse. Maybe march on the movies or somethin a Black kid couldn't get into. When I was young we all had to sit in the balcony to go to a movie. And the balcony was really torn up. They had rats, roaches, the seats were cut up—you couldn't find decent seats. We couldn't sit downstairs because that was reserved for white people only. And there was a place called the Hut—Black people couldn't go in and sit down. Black people had to be served outa the back door or back window. But I guess what really got me was when this man couldn't fix my shoes and I knew my parents couldn't buy me new ones. They did anyway, but I didn't feel that they could. I knew they weren't rich people. Before that, durin that winter, I was only seven years old, I had only two pairs of pants and I worked in the fields and at home trying to preserve those pants to wear through the winter. They was just light flannel jeans. And I had two shirts. And one pair of shoes. And when this person wouldn't fix my shoe, I knew, at least I didn't really feel that my parents were able to buy me any more. And that hurt me. And anytime we had to go outa the county just to purchase food, I think that kinda upset me too. Like I said, I never knew where my clothes were coming from; I never knew where my next meal was comin from.

THE MORMONS

The movement caught people by surprise. Wilola and Square Mormon were working hard to make their farm support a large family when the civil rights struggle opened their eyes to new hopes and a new and difficult life of political and economic confrontation.

Wilola Mormon

My name is Wilola Mormon and I was born in Fayette County in 1923 and I'm forty-eight years old. My father farmed all the time. Sharecroppin work. Not too much schoolin as a child. We lived a long ways from the school—a long ways to walk. I got through the sixth grade. After I finished school I married. I was eighteen years old. I believe I first saw Square down here in 1939—down in District 10. I was on the way to get some cows—to drive my cows up. And that's when I gave him a date. Well, I thought he was a pretty good boy when he was talkin—he was nice the way he was talkin. He was fine. He sure was. He'd come to my house and sit home with me. We'd just sit down and talk. Talkin about school and different things. He would get all dressed up. My parents were at home too—sittin right in the room. In those days we had but a room and a kitchen. We didn't have no front room or nothin like that. No courtin room. I sure was nervous. I was a little bashful. I sure did hope he'd come again after he left. It was about five days and he'd be back. It was three years before we married. In the summertime we'd be outdoors in the yard—under the trees, shade trees. No, I wouldn't tell my parents about all the meetins cause they couldn't see where we'd meet under the summer shade trees, you know.

When we got married I hoped I could get all my children schoolin and a good education. I always wanted to be in a fine house furnished all nice. Didn't think about civil rights then. Wasn't much goin then. I'd wake up about six o'clock. Then children had to be at school by eight-thirty. Sometimes I would cook rice or oatmeal or I'd churn. Some mornins were cold. You had to get outa the bed, build up the fire. Sometimes the wood would be wet and it was hard to get a fire. At night I had to wash clothes and hang em outside for the children to wear to school the next day. I washed clothes in a tub. We didn't have no washin machine. I'd go to bed ten or eleven o'clock. Sometimes it'd be twelve. I sure would be tired. I have ten children—little David, C. R., S. M., Bertal, Mayal, Edna, Melvin, June, Essau, Mildred Lee. I mothered twelve in all. Two died. A girl and a boy. They died at birth.

I first registered in '60. I heard about civil rights a year or two before. At first I was worried when my husband participated. And I prayed to the Lord to let me not worry about it. But I didn't want the old days. It wasn't too good then. It sure wasn't. Waitin for Square to come home, sometimes I'd feel lonesome—when he wouldn't be there, you know. I prayed for him a lot. One time he got beat up and never let on that he was hurt. I'd ask him about it and he'd say, "No, I ain't hurtin." He kept it to hisself. Long time before he told me. About two or three months. Sometime he'd be hurtin so bad he'd be restless at night. I'd ask, "Why you keep turnin over for?" He'd say, "You know, I'm just restless."

Square Mormon

This is Square Mormon from Rossville, Tennessee. I'm forty-nine years old. They told me I was born at twelve o'clock in the day. My brother was down in the field listenin to me cryin at twelve o'clock and at the time I was born they couldn't go to the house to eat. So they told me, "You were trouble when you got here." I told em I was boycottin when I was born cause I wouldn't let em come in the house to eat. That was my first boycott when I was born.

We was brought up real tough. Sometimes we made a pretty good crop and we ate pretty good. When I was twelve years old, then I began to think of the difference between the Black and the white opportunity. I mean why do the Black people have to work so hard and why could the white people ride around in these cars? And the schools. So I began to think of that in my early days and wonder why it seemed we were so far behind. It seemed like there was this difference in the opportunity of the white and the Black. I begun to think about prejudice. I wondered why we had to be like this, why we had to be a slave, you know. Anyways, my father used to go down and trade and we all would get out and make great big crops—cotton crops and corn and so forth—and end of the year we would be able to pay our debts. But after we paid our debts and bought a few clothes we ended up with no money and in the same shape. It seemed to me if workin was the cause of you becomin rich and well-to-do, I think my brothers and my father should've been rich because we really worked. But it seemed like it was impossible for em to get ahead. I wondered about that. I have seen some white peoples—some poor peoples were poorer'n my father was. They would move into a place and I actually have known em to go out in the field and gather wild onions, you know, and eat em. They're just about as poor as you could be. And all at once this particular man would be able to purchase some land. And first thing you would know he'd have a car and a tractor and all at once the fellow'd be ridin around in a hurry. And he wouldn't only do the work that a Black man had to do and couldn't get ahead. So I wondered about that.

But later on I could find out as I growed in age and started to do things myself. I married at the age of eighteen. I began to work a little crop on the share with my father. Then I began to deal with the merchants. Let's say I take up half a barrel of flour from the store. Take me up some lard. Maybe just a little packet. It would be ten cents or fifteen cents higher than it would if you had bought it cash. So I found out it was unfair dealin with the merchants and that's why it was so hard to get ahead. It seemed to me that the white man could get ahead because he could get a fair deal with the power structure easier than a Black man. I don't think he knowed no more and by his works he weren't valued no more, and so it seemed like to me like he would get more by a look.

I didn't know too much about Burton Dodson until the trial. I had a friend by the name of Lew G. Shields and so we says, "Let's go up and hit this trial." Actually, really what made us to go up—we heard they had a Negro lawyer on the trial. It was the first time in Fayette County history that I ever knowed a Negro lawyer to be in on a trial. So this was the main thing—we really wanted to hear this Negro on trial because this ain't happened. Estes, he was a real good lawyer. We listened to him. This was amazin to us—it was so hard to find a man you could really trust for justice. We decided the next day we'd go back and listen to him again. It was a good while before he was able to set up that jury. We found out that with a jury—if justice is gonna come out—you had to find the right kinda people. So finally he got the trial started up. So he begin to fight hard all the way through. He'd question guys and found out a lotta things a guy would say, he would prove to the jury there was somethin funny about it. So on down through that trial. I think that all the Negroes that were listenin to the trial, they could hear from what everybody said that Burton Dodson didn't kill the white man. It was clear to us that the way the white man got shot was they was shootin at Burton Dodson and one of his own men shot him. Like Estes told em, "I know it was this way because you went home and got your Ku Klux together. There shouldn't but two mens or one man should've went to arrest Burton Dodson." What he was sayin was

Burton Dodson didn't consider it was nobody comin over to arrest him. He considered it was somebody comin to kill him.

This was the first thing that really give me and lots more people an ideal. They discovered through Estes that truth was a thing you brought out through the people, and the main thing—that people need to stand on their foot and as a man, that truth could be found and justice could be found somewhere. It would give a lotta confidence through us discussin. We seen that because a man stand up and speak for a right that—you know, before the trial it looked like the peoples in Fayette County was scared that somethin would happen to em if they'd stand up, and I think they become convinced through Estes's actions that that wasn't true. You could protest. At that time I think Estes, you know, was sort of threatened hisself to come back on that trial. And he said, "Well, I'll be back tomorrow at ten o'clock." At ten o'clock we could see him walk in there and there wasn't no guards round him either.

After the trial John McFerren went to Washington and he wanted to know why a Negro had to be treated like this and why they don't have no better opportunity than they have. He was told in Washington that the reason we have this kind of trouble is because you don't have no registered Negroes down here. There wasn't nothin but whites. John come back and set up the league. In Fayette County we got fifteen districts and every district in the league needed a chairman.

The first time I heard about a mass meetin—they gettin people registered in Somerville so they'd have a right to vote for justice—well, I couldn't get there fast enough. I'll never forget, the first night I went to a mass meetin it was at Mount Olive Church and June Dowdy was the speaker. And he was makin so much sense, you know, telling about what's goin on. And John, he got up there and made a good talk—tellin about why things was like it was. It was so interestin to everyone that heard the speakin from that meetin that we all come back in our communities talkin bout the things that we heard. Our eyes had just come open. Those that were there would come home and explain the news. Then after we went and got registered the districts started havin their own mass meetins and we'd be invitin different ones to come down and make a speech. And so we got organized ourself. The Negro really started the movement in Fayette County hisself—they had their own breed.

Before then I could discover some unjust things, but I never thought it were nothin like that bad. See, a white man raised my father and he give him a lotta good teachin. So anyway, we would just come up feelin that—I still feel that we got good white folks here. We do have people that desires to see things go on better than things does now. But what happened—when we were beginnin to start to register, that was when I discovered all this hate in the white man. This is what made me really anxious to register. I never will forget, before I registered I went to the Production Credit Association and I was tradin there. We made a real short crop and we was needin some money—Christmas was comin up, so we needed somethin like a hundred dollars. So one day I took my wife and went up to Somerville and I walked into the office, sat down.

And he said, "Well, Square, what can I do for you today?"

And I said, "I have my children and they're all small. We need somethin like a hundred dollars to provide for winter."

He said, "A hundred dollars!"

I said, "Yeah."

He sort of stretched out in his chair and looked at me. He said, "Well, I don't know, Square. We got so much mess goin on around here. You been involved in it?"

I said, "Been involved? Like what?"

"Oh you know what happened," he says. "You know what's goin on."

"I don't know what's goin on," I says. "I stay on down by Rossville. What happened?"

"They just got a lotta mess goin on. Haven't you heard about folks movin and throwin peoples out?"

I said, "I heard a little somethin about that, but, I mean, what they doin?" I just played it a little easy, you know, because I wanted him to express hisself to me. I knew what was done and who was doin it. I was very interested. I just wanted to see what he gonna say.

He said, "People's out tryin to raise trouble around here. Things been going along all right. Ain't you been going along all right?"

I said, "Well, I don't know. I been still livin."

He says, "What I'm tryin to say is you got a big family, Square. You realize this and you gotta eat. And so when you come here you always got what you asked for. Well now, you wouldn't want your family out there starvin would you?"

I said, "No."

He says, "Why I'm sayin it—you don't get involved in this mess of stuff goin on round here, it may be possible. I gotta wait and see what you all is gonna do."

I said, "Mr. Paris, now you explain somethin to me. What you mean by this? What is the folk doin? I want you to tell me somethin."

He said, "Don't get involved in that and you can do like you been doin all the time. Just do like you been doin."

I said, "You mean like registerin or somethin?"

He said, "Yeah, that's what I'm talkin about. I ain't tellin you not to register, but you see how the folks comin out and what's happenin to em."

I said, "I want to know this—is it a crime? I mean why, why all this gotta happen? Is it against the law to do this?"

"No, Square, it's not against the law, but. . . ."

I said, "Well, what you mean by this?"

He make a point to me. Here's the point he made. "I got a family. Let's take you. You know how to drive. If I were to tell you to take my family to Memphis, you could take em down there because you know how to drive. Well, here's a man here who don't know nothin bout how to drive. He would be a bad man to take my family down there. He doesn't know the rules or regulations or nothin. And this is how they is. We're not talkin bout the people that really know, we're not against that. But there's so many people don't even know who is who. It is a bad consideration. And this just should not be."

So at that time I asked him, "Don't that apply for white as well as the colored? I know a lotta white can't read, can't do anything. Will that go for both sides?"

And so he said, "Well, maybe it do. Yeah, quite naturally it do. But what I'm sayin, get me straight, I still ain't tryin to tell you what to do. But I just told you you got a large family—I don't forget that—and you need a hundred dollars—don't forget that. So these are things I'll tell you about. When you make up your mind, you come back."

So I left, I left then and told my wife, "Let's go. They can have my hundred dollars." That day we went—registerin day was that day. And I told my wife, "It must be somethin for the Black man for this man to be so concerned about it." That's what really made me want to register. You know, if the white man had really knowed the psychology of the Negro—if he would've told us, "You all should register"—why no Negro in town'll register. But he was so against it. And anytime the man tells you what to do in the South—the same thing that he'll tell you not to do, that same thing you should do, because that is what psychology you read on him. He'll tell you nothin, I mean, that'll help you. Anyway we went right out from his office and we went right over to the courthouse and I said, "We're goin to register today and when we go back we're going to tell this fella what we done done. Cause there must be somethin that means a whole lot to the Black person who registers."

After we went forth and registered and come on home. I made a crop and went back next fall to pay my money. I reached in my pocketbook to get my money out and I had a plastic bag.

And the same man says, "Well, what you got in that plastic bag?"

"Oh, I got my registration card and driver license."

"Well, it's good if you got that plastic bag because when they find you out in Hatchie River they'll find this and know who you is."

So I says, "Large as I am, they'll know me anyhow."

So anyway I come over to Viola and made out an affidavit. We sent the affidavit off and I reckon some guy come in and talk to him. And when I went back to get the hundred dollars afterward he acted so quick it popped out like that. So I found out then—I was only makin room for my own self by standin up on my foot. So from that loan I see that he wasn't really tellin me that would really happen if I should vote. He was only tryin to keep me from doin somethin where I would not be counted as a citizen. Some kinda way I ain't never been too scared a guy. My father wasn't that scared of names. The only thing I ever been scared of's when I thought I was wrong. When I thought I was right—I ain't too concerned what a guy say he gonna do.

I can't forget these things what happened. At Tent City—those were days I had to weep sometimes. I would go to the tents and there were little children standin out there sufferin. Even in my house where I was livin at—I mean it seemed like I was livin in Tent City too. To see you out there cause of somethin you wanted to do that was right—to want a voice in government. It was worryin me—what kinda world was I livin in? What kinda county was I livin in? What kind people was I livin with? These were the things that kept runnin through my head. I was wonderin why don't these peoples do anything about Jesus? Is they goin to church? Now we don't have all perfect Negroes. We have Negroes with prejudice too. And we have Negroes involved with ignorance. And if they hadn't been we would be further than we is now. But I don't think we have Negroes have the kinda prejudice the white man have. The white man sit up all night long tryin to set a plan to hold the Negro down. Negro sit up all night long tryin to set a plan to come out where he can be counted as a citizen, where he could get a equal share. And so this happen—there's a fight. In the places where we in this county are fightin one another, if we had been thinkin together and really doin it we could have been a rich county. I know a lotta white men is just plumb poor and everybody's goin out of business.

The persons in Tent City seemed like a child somebody give away. An orphan. A child that was put out. He still was American, but he was put out. That's the way it appeared to me. I would walk out there to see. And at that time I was annoyed enough to know what could be done if justice was flowin. The men outside there was punished and used as a person that weren't human. Like they was some kinda animal or somethin that shouldn't have no right to say anything about what he would like to be done. I think people have in mind that if they can keep you hungry and keep you on your knees that this would be a good way to make the poor Black man be quiet. I think that really is the psychology of the white man in Fayette County—just keep the Negro hungry, keep em on their knees, don't allow him opportunity. Tent City was shot into by a passin car and this really boomed things off. They put a child out there in the orphan home and then go shoot at it. That helped, you know. Anytime a person get treated real bad, a Black human, it helps. I mean that helps the movement, it don't help the individual. That's sad to him, but for the movement that builds it because it makes everybody get more ambitious—there's more care and more meanin. It should not be like that. I remember in the movement I'm always hopin that nothin like that's gonna occur, but when they're tryin to break the movement down that builds it up.

After, the people could see the pressures of white peoples—how they would do the Black person out there. It made em see it as I see it. It made em ambitious to get with the voters. They could see there was a wall up. Weren't no way around it but to go through it. If you didn't go through it you'd be left on the other side. And those that did stand out and walk farther, they helped train the ones that come along behind. So Tent City was a show and by attractin attention all over the land, from one coast to the other, it brought other people in to look at the conditions and share with the people their sorrow. That gave hope to the Black man—he did have a friend. People began to send clothes in here and some food and began to come in and sit down in late hours of the night and have meetins and help get ideas. That gave hope. We seen we did have white friends, white brothers, and that every white man—just because he's white—wasn't against the Negro, wasn't against the poor man.

THE HORTONS

Robert Horton has worked in the civil service for years. During the difficult years in the early sixties the Hatch Act kept him from active participation in civil rights activities. This did not hold back his wife, Maggie Mae. When the movement began she was ready and raring to go.

Robert Horton

We used to have a lotta fruit trees over here and Maggie Mae and another lady used to come over here to get some fruit. I never have been too talkative of a person, and they came over, and the lady she was with, she had all kinda mouth, you know, she talked a lot and she was with us. I think Maggie Mae kinda liked me—she come on to me more than I did to her. And when after that, really the next time I met her was at church and I was drunk and we kinda got together more than the day when she came over here. I would have to walk two or three miles across the fields to see her. Whenever we had a little chance, when the daddy or mother, you know, had their back turned or somethin, we might get a little sugar or somethin like that. You know, kissin. You didn't have no long hours or all night to stay there because around nine o'clock that old man, he'd get up and said, "Bedtime." You know what that meant. It was time for you to go then. And if he went on back in his room then you had another chance to get a little more kissin when you're leavin. Then I had to walk two or three miles home across the field. You didn't get the chance, couldn't visit, like durin the week—you couldn't run to this house every night cause this girl's got to work and she got dishes to clean and stuff like that and you been here a little too often, you know. Like if you were over there Sunday, you wouldn't go back until about Wednesday. Then maybe if you got the chance you could come in maybe Friday night cause maybe they weren't workin Saturday. You'd go there maybe two or three times a week to visit. Me and Maggie, we married in December 1942. And, I don't know, I just thought she'd make me a good wife. I didn't know she was gonna be involved in all this civil rights and different things like she are now.

Maggie Mae and I discussed civil rights in so many different ways. We got in heated arguments. I told her, "Just drop the whole damn mess and come on home with me and forget about it." But I found out one thing, that Maggie is amazingly dedicated to the movement. I believe she's more a civil rights worker than she is a Christian because I think she's more dedicated to Black people than she is to the church. I don't care what time of night it is, what time of day—she's more dedicated to the Black people than she is to me. I'll say that.

Maggie'll get up outa her warm bed—I don't care if it's midnight or five o'clock or two o'clock or what. "I'm leavin here," she says. "Sally called me. Her boy's in jail and she wants me to get a lawyer and get him out. I'll see what I can do."

I'll say, "Maggie, why don't you lay down. It's early in the mornin."

"I can't stay here."

She'll get out and leave me layin in the bed. That's how I know she's more dedicated to the movement than she are to me. And she's a real fighter. When Maggie's teed off, boy oh boy. You didn't see what a couple of bombers can do. She's like an atomic bomb fallin on somebody. Quick. Move. Wooo. Man, trash flies everywhere, children have to leave home, run, and do everything because she's explodin. You ain't seen nothin, brother. If I ever sat Maggie down and said, "Maggie, you gonna have to quit the movement," you know what Maggie would do, she would be willin to give me a divorce. I'm not playin now. I'm real serious. Maggie is dead serious with the movement. If I said, "Maggie, you gonna have to quit the movement and come on home with me and just quit foolin with them people out there and just forget about civil rights," if I told her that today, I'll bet she'd give me a divorce just like that. I know what I'm talkin about.

Maggie Mae Horton

My name is Maggie Mae Horton. I'm forty-eight years old. I've been in the movement about twenty years. I have twelve livin children; two have been in the service and both are out now. No job cause it's still Fayette County. Nobody will hire em—they're connected with Maggie Mae Horton. They been to every factory, I guess, about eighty miles around. They been in those factories and put in applications and—"We'll call you, we aren't hirin." And they hirin every day. The people that walk in the streets with those boys get hired. Still mine have no work to do. It is pretty bad to be connected with Maggie Mae Horton, especially if you want work. We have a factory here in Rossville, I think it's a frozen-foods place—all of my children have went there and put in an application. Irma Jean and Emmet were about the first to put in their applications here. Irma Jean was there when they opened the door. They still haven't found a job for em. Every young Negro outa school in Mississippi, Shelby County, La Grange, Grand Junction, is workin in the place, but they haven't found an openin for Irma Jean yet because she's Maggie Mae Horton's daughter. So you see it's pretty hard to be Maggie Mae. And yet we live. Somehow.

Way back when we first begin registerin to vote—that you gonna have to ask me about because I've forgotten. I forget because it scares the hell outa me.

I started my first protest about 19 and 41. You know, I was quite young then. I started gettin all the Negroes to get sick to raise the pay for cotton choppin. At that time cotton choppin was somethin like seventy-five cents a day and pickin was fifty cents a hundred. So I pushed it up to three dollars a hundred. Way back in the little one-horse movement. Nobody was doin this but me. Everybody had some kinda contagious disease and they stayed at home. It was a strike. That's what I would call it now, but then I didn't even know what a strike was. The thing we was doin then was just everybody get sick, but that was just the plan I had. Tell the boss man the next mornin and start droppin off one by one and he don't know what's wrong. He scared of Negroes anyhow. He don't wanta catch our disease. That was the first start—me and the movement.

The next thing that started me off—Ray Russell was the justice of the peace. You don't know what law enforcement is here—I'm white and got a badge on I can beat the hell out of you and get away with it. So this man come along and beat up a very good friend of my father's—his own mother didn't know him. And I stated that day that I would never take what I had seen done, that I would never stand for a white to beat up a Negro. I couldn't take it. So it's just been one thing to another since then. You don't think of things, you look and see. Even a dumb person see how one-sided it is—seein what the white was doin and seein the Black fallin before their wives and children. White man just walk out and tell em where to get off at and cursin em—that started me wantin to do this. I didn't know about no movement. I just knowed that I would never live under no grief. I've been free for all my life—ever since I been big enough to remember. I got the daylights swatted out of me from my parents but nevertheless I didn't give in. I do what I wanta do and say what I wanta say—to anybody. That's just how I feel about it.

The movement got in progress in '59. That's when we first started to register to vote. So I think that's when the movement opened, but God-oh-me I had done many things up until then. I was raised in a white house and here's what they say—"That's what you get when you raisin one of those damn niggers. You give em too much outlet and too much thinkin among emselves." I been told that from the white man that raised me, from his parents. My mother died when I was six and these white peoples had little children and naturally that's what Negroes do—they go raise up the white man's children to beat the hell outa you when they get to be fourteen years old. So that's what I done. I was livin in the white house enjoyin all the pleasures. So I wasn't brought up under the same pressure that my peoples were. And that has put me way ahead of them. And one thing—that white lady that raised me, she left no stones unturned. Now she taught me well because they don't want you around talkin any kinda way, doin any kinda thing with their children. So once you learn it, there ain't nobody can take it away from you. So I used it to the best advantage, of course. Now the white peoples that raised me, I've never had no trouble outa em. This particular white man has never showed in no way that he's against what I'm doin. He's never showed he's with me either.

The movement made a big change in two ways. In one way I disagreed with the way a lotta things was run and, I guess it was because I had experience, a lotta things that they was tryin to get. Not disagreeable, but a lotta disagreein with certain things. But it was a great pleasure to have other Blacks out fightin for the things that I was. Although they didn't know quite where they was goin, neither did I. We was goin someplace, just gettin information as we go.

The voter registration was when all hell broke out. Durin that time they had a foreclosin on us—on our car—they wanted it all at once. No fussin with the insurance—they said that it was canceled. And I went in to see why was the insurance canceled.

The man said, "Well I don't know."

I said, "I registered to vote, didn't I? I'm gonna yet drive my car and if you cancel my insurance I want every dime I paid you."

He said, "Well they ain't gonna return you money."

I said, "Well I'll bring a lawsuit."

"Well just keep my name outa it. I live in Shelby County. What you all do in Fayette County, you all do it. Don't blame me.

"Well you gonna be the first named cause you got my money."

And then they took our tractor. They give us a chance to pay for it but we let go of it. And then we had fifty-three acres of ground that Robert's mother had deeded over to him. With all of the economic squeeze we had to sell that land. That's when trouble started happenin to me, when they started foreclosin on me. They shot at me, run me off the road, they shot at my house—oh God, what they haven't did to me to harm me. And I haven't a scratch on me from what they've done. So I know about that, they don't really mean to hurt me. I think this is just mostly to scare me. I've called in the FBIs and so on to do somethin about the harassment and they all have come in here and looked and go back. I decided not to trust them anymore, much as five years ago. I needn't tell em what's happenin to me, I just go on with it. We got three old shotguns here—I doubt if any one of em shoots. And everybody, they got Winchesters, and everything else. And I invite the sheriff and everybody else, I say, "I'll tell you what you do. If you want me just come on out to my house and we'll shoot it out." They ain't done a damn thing to me.

Dedicating Land for
Community Center
1961

The Original Fayette County Civic and Welfare League board at the groundbreaking ceremony for the League Community Center with guest speaker Benjamin L. Hooks, 1961. Seated left to right and top to bottom: Reverend V. L. Smith, Benjamin Hooks, Shirley Hobson, Reverend Massey, Earline Dowdy, Reverend June Dowdy, Houston Malone, J. A. Carpenter, Harpman Jameson, Levearn Towles, E. B. Parrott, B. T. Rosser, Joe Baskerville, Robert Scott, Square Mormon, Minnie Jameson, Richard Waddell, Elijah Cleaves, unknown, Isaiah Harris, E. V. Braswell, E. Z. Shaw, Reverend Boston Bledsoe, John Lewis, John McFerren, Viola McFerren, Shephard Towles Sr.

Richard Yarborough and his family, evicted for registering to vote

Tent City, 1960

"Tent City was a miserable life. The tent was sixteen by fourteen. . . . My wife and four kids livin there. We had to cook in there; we had to sleep in there; we had to eat in there. And mud—when it rained in Tent City it got so bad on Tent City ground you had mud almost up to your knees."
—Early B. Williams

The first child born in Tent City

Support from the people of Philadelphia

Food distribution at McFerren's grocery

"We hardly had anything to eat.... We caught a ride to Somerville and got out there. And there was gobs of food and gobs of people. It was wild."
—Venetta Gray

PART II

"GOIN ON TO REGISTER"

1960–1961

The speakers in this section were among the hundreds of people who responded to the first call for voter registration. Without the determined support of these people there would have been no movement. They understood the danger involved in defying an oppressive system, but they despised the false security of passively accepting a way of life that cruelly exploited them. Most of the speakers who follow were well into middle age when they voted for the first time. Their memories of the distant past should give some idea of the kind of world these men and women now sought to change.

E. D. Liddell

E. D. Liddell is my name. I wasn't here in slavery time, but I wasn't too long comin after. I'm over two hundred and some better miles from my native home, down in Mississippi, called Sugarlock. I left there as a six-year-old chap and was raised in Tennessee. I got this far and I had been settled down here to make eighty-seven years old if I don't die by my next birthday. I come along from where woman cook hominy in ashes, cook bread in ashes—called em ash cakes. We had to make meal with a piece of tin that had holes in it to rub the corn on it thisaway to cook your bread. I et em and had to do it or not have nothin. I lived in pine country. My father was a shingle maker—outa pine. Drawed em with a draw knife on a bench. Covered houses. And he was a sorghum cooker—cooked up all the sorghum in that country and after he died I took it up.

We been longin and pullin for many a year to try to learn what we could about our own race. But still we can't learn it now because confidence is hard to find. A true speaker is hard to find. The way I see it and the way I live it—I would like to have equal in law; I would like to have what I sell get as much as you; I would like you to speak to me and recognize me as a colored man if I come to your house, and I recognize you if you come to mine. Well, the white peoples looks at it thisaway—they thinks that we are wantin their race of people. Marryin em. But we already got white niggers in our country. I'm talkin plain now. We must love and care for one another regardless of color. If the white man wants my daughter he'll take her. He does do it. But if my boy ties up with his girl—why here come the Ku Klux and take him and put him in the river.

God created every man equal—give you as many bones as he give me. Me bein dark for the disobedience in the sight of God. That's how come me's Black. Look out there—you didn't laugh, I did. Civil rights and equal. A lot of em don't know what equal means. We're human we're supposed to have equal part in law; we're supposed to get what the white man gets for his stuff. We're supposed to get it too because we're labor.

I'm down here in the South and I've got to stay here and sleep and eat. Mr. Nixon now, he's goin on with his people, but now, you see. He's like a sloppin machine. He's up and down thisaway. He's been bought into and he have to do it to live. The paper quotes enough to let us know that he's got to satisfy his people and he's got to blindfold the other race to stay in with them.

When I registered in 1960, they stalled it and we couldn't get no whereabouts. And they were all just sittin there. When we voted they said, "Now you get on outa here. Don't let me see you talkin to this one and that one." The man that was masterin the vote said, "Don't you be standin out there talkin, go on off by yourself." I thought I was a free voter. If I was capable of votin I'd come to be a citizen. That's the way I figured it. But he drove us out.

We want equal in law. We'd like to have it. If I have a cow to sell, I'd like to have as much as Mr. Charlie did. That's what I'd like. Of course, the white people don't look at it in this country thataway. We can go to their house if we have any business, even if we do have to stand out there on the back porch. I've had to sit on the woodpile. We're not lookin for equality on this side of judgment.

I'm still readin what dissatisfaction there is betwixt the races, not only us—it's in foreign countries. One race against another; one nation against another. Time has come, time has come to make a change. That's what makes me talk so. This voice'll close sometime, and I won't have nothin to say and can't have nothin to say. I better talk while I'm here. I talk, read, and study, and ask questions.

Porter Shields

My name is Porter Shields. My age is seventy-eight years old. I was born and raised here in Fayette County. When I was growin up, why it was rough here in Fayette County. When I was quite small, I remember we couldn't have any shoes to wear in the wintertime. When the weather got bad I had to stay in the house. They had quite a time keepin me in there cause every little chance I'd get I'd run out there, even sometime out in the snow. No shoes on. There was eight of us. Fourteen in all, but some died real young. There was just one room and a small kitchen. We et just common food. The parents'd go eat before us and then we children would get around the table. Some of us would sit down, some stand up. There was a big bunch of us, you see, and whilst the rest of em'd be talkin and forcin over the food I'd be eatin, and by the time they get down and quiet, by that time I'd eat up all the food.

We had three months of school—that was two months in the winter and one in the summer. That was all the school went on in Fayette County. Well the white children, they had nine months of schoolin. We worked in the fields the biggest time. We'd start in the early spring cuttin corn stalks and knockin cotton stalks. We'd start plowin the last of February and along in March we'd start to plant. After I got large enough to plow I did have shoes, but when I was growin up, you see, I didn't. I was paid fifty cents a day. In the mornin we'd wake up round at four o'clock in the mornin. We'd go to the fields by five o'clock, stay in the field till twelve o'clock, then come out, and at one o'clock go back in the field, then we'd stay in the field until sundown. That's twelve or sometimes fourteen hours. That's fifty cents a day, four cents an hour. The white people were friendly all right but they didn't care how they pressed us and how we had to work. It was kinda hard. The days were kinda dark. Sometimes we'd get ahold of some money and sometimes we wouldn't. Then we would have to go to the merchants to get feed stuff for the winter. They'd let you have just what you could make out on—just enough as to get by. No, no, you couldn't borrow any money. Instead of lettin you have money they'd let you have clothes or shoes or somethin like that—but the money you couldn't get. You didn't get enough to save any.

About '58 a few people registered so that they could vote and those that did register, well, they had a hard way to come. It wasn't easy. They don't have nothin in the county. They had to go elsewhere to get whatever they needed. They couldn't even sell their cotton. They was evicted off the farmland that they was on. After they was evicted they was determined not to leave the county and so there was one man who had a farm and he let the people put up Tent

City and people lived around there for quite a while. When you get an interest to do somethin, if you a steady person you stay. I am. I make up my mind to do somethin—whatever I get within me, I do whatever I can to see it to the end. After I come to myself and I seen my people out there strugglin, I said, "Now why would I sit back? Why would I hold back?" And so I'd say, "Well now, first I believe I will tell my landowner I'm goin to register." I said, "Well no, I don't have to tell him anything. I don't have to tell him anything. I'm a man and goin on to register."

So I went on. The first time I went the polls wasn't open that day. They even locked up the rest room and everything. Just to make it hard. The next two days I went back. I reckon there were two to three hundred there to be registered that day. (*From Square Mormon*: Please excuse me. Remember when we was tryin to go out and register then—they not only locked the rest rooms but they turned the heat on. It was already around about eighty or ninety degrees and they turned the heat on. We had some old ladies in the line, from fifty to seventy-five years old, and all of they's stewin down under the heat. Some of em fell out. We picked em up. And after em havin got up we said, "Well what you wanna go home?" And they said, "No, we gonna be all right. We goin back down there." And myself, I went and got Eunice and some others and carry em way down out in back of Somerville in the thicket to be excused and brung em back cause the rest rooms were locked.) The next day we went, well then I got a chance to register, but we had to stand on line. We waited so long. I got there early in the morn and stand in line until two o'clock in the afternoon before I got a chance to register. I felt that I would be sent off my land but I didn't care. I felt good. The landholder he changed. He let another family have our house to live in and he hadn't even told me nothin about it whatever. Well then I come on down here. I went and built here. I been here ever since. It was time to get out.

We had our mass meetins and organized and got district leaders. Probably, we'd meet in somebody's house if there wasn't a church or somewhere's we could meet. In the beginnin we wouldn't get but very few, but after we get organized and get to work, get the experience movin from one to the other, well others would fall in. We'd say, "In what way can we work for our freedom? What steps should we take?" And usually someone would give a suggestion. And from one to the other, you see, we'd work things out. We'd do this at night, you see. We'd work in the day and have our meetin at night. I told you before, when I make up my mind to do somethin I'm not gonna rest until I get it done.

Sometime the problem would be kinda tough. Our own people would say, "I ain't startin that mess. I got to live somewhere and Mr. Sam say, 'We always got along with one another.' And he good to me. Yeah, so you all go ahead on in this. I ain't gonna do anything." I'd say, "Well, listen we are citizens here and you won't be counted a citizen unless you register to vote." I'd say, "See now, listen, we have been in the dark and asleep long enough and it's time to wake up now and be counted." Well some of em, they'd turn their heads still. I'd go back again. And they would go down.

I don't get angry very quickly. Nonviolence is the way. You can't take fire and put out fire. You can keep treatin me all kinda ways and I won't fight back, why real soon you'll get to the place where you'll say, "Well now, there's somethin wrong. I just can't fight this person." Nonviolence is the way. Just think of our Lord Saviour Jesus. On the cross why he turned to his Father—"Father forgive them, they know not what they do." They crucified him with charges made against him. And he is our example.

George Bates

George Bates is my name. I was born in Fayette County in 1909. After I come up, to grow up and be my own man, and could kinda sorta look into things—I worked for near fifteen different white peoples on their farm. Sharecropper's what we call the tenant. And I worked for em for years and years. And as the years ended up I still had the same thing I had when I started. I wasn't accumulatin anything at all. We really worked hard. And the white people would gimme credit for real workin. You know, one of the top best hands. "And anything you want, you can go up there to the store and tell em I said let you have it." But when the crop ended you took up. You got all you had comin. You had less now than you had. "There ain't nothin comin to you, but now we gonna let you have a little somethin. You can go up to the store and get anything you want. We ain't gonna give you ten or fifteen dollars, but you go up to the store and get anything you want. Just say, we say let you have it." We was up there tillin, workin, and they let you have it. We could buy a common somethin or other—you know food or workclothes, somethin like that. No payday. We would pick this cotton, carry it up there and gin it, and throw it all up, and go on back home and go start pickin another bale. We didn't know when it was sold and how much it brought—we didn't know what they got for it. Nothin. The boss—what we called him—the boss would go on up there and sell it. All we'd do is the pickin and carry it up there, and throw it up, and go on back pickin. And when we got through pickin why he'd give us what he wanted us to have. Maybe thirty dollars or forty dollars or fifty dollars or somethin like that. You know, outa the whole crop. And that's all we ever knowed. That's all we'd get outa the whole year. That's what he said we cleared outa our crop. "Why you cleared fifty dollars outa your crop." And that's all we got. We weren't resistin in no kinda ways and whatever he'd say that's what was done. He was always kind cause he wanted you to stay on more and keep on workin for nothin. He'd try to talk to you and treat you kinda nice to keep you from leavin off his farm and goin to the next man's farm. But whichever way you go you went to the same thing. You wasn't goin to get nothin; you was workin for nothin. I remember how I made ten bales of cotton—just the two of us, me and my wife. About a week or two weeks afterward, the man we was livin with, Mr. Sam Dunne, said, "Well come up to the house now, I'm gonna settle with you." And I went there for my settlement and thought I'd get two or three hundred dollars. He said, "I done sold your cotton and I'm gonna settle up with you. You cleared more than any hand on the place. You cleared fifty dollars." He said, "Get that and walk on."

Afterwards I quit farmin and worked for a white woman for two years for fifty cents a day. That was somewhere in the early forties. And I just had to live outa that fifty cents a day—me and my wife. I seed I wasn't getting no further there than I was farmin. If it ain't one thing, it's another'n. So I sharecropped for twelve years. Just about the same thing there—make it and they get it all, make it and they get it all. That's just the way it went, you know.

So when this here whole thing started I said, "I been workin all these years. I ain't got no stronger than I was. I'm a little older now. Look like this here's somethin to change somethin, change somebody." So I took a part in this movement. But after I took a part in this movement, they didn't have no more work for me then. I lost all of my work. I wasn't the same man. I was a stranger. Somebody they didn't know. No sir, that end me up for bein their nigger—that's why they always called us, "My nigger." I wasn't no more longer me after I took a part in this movement. After I took a part in this movement and they found out I wasn't no more their nigger, I found out that were right smart of me. I was workin myself to death and wasn't getting nothin so I might as well's not be their nigger and get some rest.

From that time on I took a deep part in it. I was doin my business with a Mr. Farley. They locked up some civil rights workers in jail and about eight of us went down to protest at city hall. That's when they really put the heat on. And so when I went back next month for my forty dollars Mr. Farley said, "You owe me twenty dollars."

I said, "For what?"

"Well, you got this three years ago."

I said, "Well I got a receipt here. Every year I pay back every penny I owe. I ain't got no backtime here. I paid and I got a receipt to show for it."

"Yeah, but this here's a bill we overlooked, we hadn't found. You owed it but we hadn't found it. And you got to pay it."

I said, "No, I ain't got to pay it less'n I know I owed it."

"Here's your fifteen dollars and that's all you gonna get. You owe us the other."

I said, "I don't owe it. Ain't no use you tellin me I owes it. You may take it but I don't owe it."

We been disagreein from that day on. I said, "I just don't do that kinda business."

Mary Sue Rivers

My name is Mary Sue Rivers. I'm a native of Fayette County—born and raised in Fayette County. Runnin, and hidin, and dodgin—that's what it was like as a child. You couldn't do nothin. In my childhood days comin up they was workin my mother. There was two girls, no boys, but we had to work boys. Fifty cents and twenty-five cents a day. Bring us outa school when we shoulda been in school. They do all this for Mr. Man's fodder, pick this Mr. Man's cotton. His children was goin to school and we was out there in the field gatherin his crop and makin his livin for his children. And it stayed like that all of our growin-up days.

As a little girl we was pickin peas, pullin fodder, plantin, pickin cotton. All was farm work. I never have done anything but farm work. There never was no jobs in this county. Pickin cotton, you gotta pick it off, put it all on your back, then you gotta put it in your sack, then you gotta go up to the man in the wagon, and then you gotta shake it outa that sack after you has weighed it. Some of em sacks had eighty to a hundred pounds. There was too much in pickin for me. Pickin it, pullin it, then shakin it out, then not gettin more'n a dollar fifty cents a hundred. That's right, I'm tellin it like it is. And right now farm work is nothin. These folks'll tell you they getting eight and nine dollars on the farm and they ain't gettin three. But now they got to say that to stay in their house. They must say that to stay in their house.

How'd we get along with the white boss? Well, I remember he'd come on across the field and tell you what to do and keep ridin. And you'd do it. And that's how we'd get along. I know more than that. I know some white men on their fields they'd ride the whips on their horses and whip the folks in their fields. That wasn't the Civil War either. That was the first of the forties and the last of the thirties.

My mother ran into a lotta stumblin blocks with these white folks. She never got what she asked for; she always got to get what they wanted her to have. You know they had a law in here the government put out some years ago. The white people could get their money from the government but the Negroes couldn't get that loan, cause my mother tried and she didn't get that loan. She tried so hard to get it and couldn't. Then during Mr. Hoover's time they brought in what they called the soup line. And that bread they had then was blacker than anything you wanta see. And they sold that bread! They didn't give it—it was sent here to be gived, but they sold it. That's right. It's been hard times ever since I been in Fayette County and it's still hard times.

When my mother got up into middle age she began to feel if she don't have it and wanted to get it she was gonna be her own woman. Then she went to sayin, "If I don't get this I ain't gonna do nothin." And standin out on her own, man, that made us a little bit more standin out ourselves you know. So we didn't just do just like a lotta children had to do.

I was fully a grown woman before I got to the place where I could tell em what I wanted to do. I got tired and I told my mother, I said, "Momma, I just can't go; I can't work for em." So I went out then tryin to go out some for my own.

I registered in '60 in November. Lots had been ahead of me. They started in '59. I lived way out here and they didn't have no precinct for us to register round in these areas. You had to go over to Somerville to your registerin. And the persons in the rural, they didn't hear about these things as early as the persons right in the city. I was workin in a cafe in Somerville at the time this civil rights movement come around.

The day of the votin John McFerren comes down to vote and they wouldn't let him vote. He said, "I'm gonna see somethin about it and I'm gonna fix it so's everybody can vote. I need a little help," he said. "I need a little money to go in this thing." So my husband gave him two dollars and I gave him two dollars and lotsa more men and women on the street was interested and helped him that day. And he came there and told me, he said, "I ain't a gonna stop fightin. I'm goin along with it." And I said, "Well, if you ever need anything else, come back to me, cause all of us need to be registered voters." Well at the time I didn't know why it was so important. He knew more about it than I did, because if he hadn't've he wouldn't've wanted to fight to get it through.

I didn't feel scared votin. But a lotta em did. And I know they did but I didn't because I figures, "What was for me, I want it."

"I'll get you what you want," that's what the white man tells us. But you don't ever get what you need. [That's why] if you don't stand out and say somethin you still in the hard-time category and they push you around and kick you around just like they wish to.

June Dowdy

My name is June Dowdy. My age is fifty. Born in Fayette County. Growin up was very much on the complicated side because we grew up the tough way and we got our schoolin the rough way. Sometimes we were in one grade for two or three years because we didn't have but six months of school and we could complete only about a month and a half or two months because we had to come outa school and go to the field. Cut wood, bust rails, get ready for the summer, knock stalks with long sticks, cut corn stalks with a hoe or somethin, patch the fence for the cows, and so on. So we didn't get a chance to complete a full school term. Books, we didn't have em. Used the same clothin for a solid week. We'd come in, pull off, and mother would wash em, dry em, and iron em, and then we'd put em back on and go back to school. We wore those overalls until we just wore em white. Finally I did finish the eighth grade in the public school. I wanted to go to high school but my father was not able to send me. I always did love books you know. So I had to work all the time.

My daddy worked sharecrops and boss man would ride around. I didn't like that so well, but I always tried to do a good job so when he did call he would give me as many compliments as he could. That's what I worked for all the time—tryin to please the person that's in charge of the job. With all this labor I was puttin out I wasn't gettin what I call a fair deal. So I worked hard but we couldn't seem to ge a fair share as a result of our labor.

Our labor was goin other ways ruther [than for ourselves]. We would work what you call "on shares," "on halves." I worked the crop and gather it and the boss gets half of it. But he furnished the chain, the plow, the seed, and the whatnot. But I work it and gather it and so forth. He paid his hands by "the dribbles"—not money, at that time—some was gettin money, but very few. But in that day they would give your order to the grocery man for five pounds of meat, and four pounds of lard, and five pounds of sugar, and half a bushel of meal, and a sack of flour, and some fatback meat, and so forth. And then that's your week's ration. You'd get told maybe once a year, "Here's a little money to get you some garments so you can go to church." So we wore one pair of pants for our Sunday clothes and they were washable. And we would wear em this week, wash em, and go back to chuch the next Sunday mornin. This was parta the rough way.

So that was in my youth and comin up through my manhood. So when I got out to myself, then I come to beginnin to accumulate somethin. Doin very well. Wasn't hard. And finally the idea of Negroes registerin was beginnin to get into the minds of the Negro people. Some few had attempted to register and they were allowed to vote. But to me it was controlled because you'd have to more or less vote for the ticket that they want you to vote. You voted for em, not for yourself. Then, on and on, we made a move to kinda register. Then we were beginnin to feel pressure and people began to sound around among Negroes, "Don't register." However, we thought it was the best thing to do to help ourselves and we went about to try to get registered. Mr. McFerren was sorta spearheadin this. Resentment was all round among the white folks and they had gotten together to slow this movement down or stop it. There come out a decree, you might say, "If you register, you have to move," and all that sorta thing. We were beginnin to form lines once a week to register. It went along pretty good. The line got to be so long, Negroes seemed to be so interested, until they begin to apply pressure. The boss men would watch the line, see whether or not the Negroes made any disorder. One time Mr. McFerren told me to go up and sorta seek the place. You know, they'd hide the registerin place. They'd be in the bottom of the courthouse one time and they'd be in the first floor the next time, and maybe the next time they'd be upstairs. So I was walkin around there tryin to find the place to register. Looked like the white folks were laughin inside because they knew where it was and we didn't. So I walked up to some white peoples in the basement and asked em where the Negroes registered at—I mean where the peoples registered.

They said, "Yeah, I can tell you."

I said, "Where, sir?"

And he said, "In Hatchie Bottom."

So I told him, no I didn't want to register with them. There's a little river north of Somerville and that was little Hatchie Bottom and this was the place where they used to hang folks. That's why he told me this was the registerin place for Negroes. I didn't want to be registered in the hangin crowd. That was the rough side of life.

I was once pastorin in this county durin the movement and before the movement—I was one of the only ministers that would speak out on these issues. The other ministers would always have the shut-mouth. Some would say, "It's good," but mighty few of our Fayette County ministers would take sides on the issues. And I found myself bein moved out of Fayette County. So as of today I don't pastor in Fayette County. Somehow and someway the church declared the pulpit vacant. I was pastorin north of the county here and I went away one Sunday. And when I got back another local preacher had got among my people and before I knew anything they sent me a letter the pulpit was empty.

In this county the pastors didn't control the congregations, the congregations controlled the pastor. The peoples was poor, they couldn't pay nothin, they didn't have no jobs, and seemed that somebody was tryin to keep em in that state. Mr. John loans the Negro minister money and he's a deacon in the church—and so now, he'll ease up to this preacher and tell him, "Now don't do this or don't do that." Now the preacher'll look back and say, "Well, he's payin money to me and he's gettin me my conveniences and so forth." So he'll yield. This is one of the things that make him shut up and don't talk about this thing. At the time of the pressure over registration the preacher was subject [to it too]. So he couldn't come in and get in the line, or be uptown when the peoples were registerin, or lead his congregation to the polls for em to vote or register. Preachers didn't do that, you see. They would call that politics. Their people, their friends, would tell em, "That's politics. Stay outa politics." He'd just believe that this is the wrong place for him. So I always thought that to comfort your people, to help em—if you can't help em to be a good citizen, you don't help em to be good Christians. The reason the Negro minister was holdin out was because they likes to have a pulpit to preach—they didn't want nobody runnin em around when they go home the next night. This was the way of life at that time.

I don't ever believe in violence. I ain't had a fight with nobody since I been grown or since my boyhood days. My brother used to whip me and when I got big enough to whip him I whipped him once and that broke up the fight. I haven't had another fight since. I just don't believe in violence. Of course peoples uses this sometimes, but in the long run it won't pay. I really think that if there's anything worth anything, somebody got to give somethin for it. Life is good, but sometimes somebody's got to die for it before it can be felt. I always believe in the Bible: "He that seeks to save his life will lose it; he that loses his life for my sake will find it again." And makin people good citizens is righteousness and nothin else. This is the way of life the Lord loves.

Early B. Williams

My name is Early B. Williams. I was born in Fayette County, Tennessee. My age is thirty-six. I have six children. In the fifties I was a sharecropper. I worked on shares. I worked this crop and boss man I lived with, he gets half, half of everything I make. I didn't never make enough money. Hardly had enough to live off of. From March, that's when we started gettin our money to make our crops—we got twenty-five dollars a month until July. When July come, we didn't get no more. We had to go out and try to pick up a little job—any kinda job, just to try to make a livin till harvestin time.

In '59 I went up to register to vote. I wasn't one bit scared. After we went to register to vote I asked my landlord—I had been hearin people say we had to move because we registered—and I asked him about it and he told me. So that's when Tent City began. I went up to see Mr. McFerren. He was head of the thing; he organized it. They got the tents out so we moved up. There was about fourteen tents at the start, I believe. A lotta families livin there and nothin to do. They was there because they was evacuated from their homes, because they did the same thing—they registered to vote too. One man—they set his furniture out on the highway, set it down on the road. McFerren had to go and get it—took a big truck over there and got it and bring him down.

Tent City was a miserable life. The tent was sixteen by fourteen—that was the size of the first tent I lived in. Sixteen by fourteen. My wife and four kids livin there. We had to cook in there; we had to sleep in there; we had to eat in there. And mud—when it rained in Tent City it got so bad on Tent City ground you had mud almost up to your knees. McFerren managed to get food. We'd sit around outside. Nothin else to do. I was never sorry I registered. I figured we'd overcome someday.

I thought I had to live my life in a tent. One night I was layin down on the bed. I was sleepin, about twelve or twelve-fifteen say. We never worried too much about anybody botherin us. We figured we wasn't doin nothin to cause anybody to bother us. So we was layin in bed sleepin. Boom! I didn't know what happened. It just shook the whole tent, the shot did. So I got up. I don't know what had happened. I got up. I was just listenin. I didn't never know I was shot. So blood started runnin down my side and my wife, she said, "You shot." So I looked at my arm and blood was runnin down. And my brother lived in the tent beside mine and she yelled through the wall and he turned out and they took me down to the hospital and had me fixed up. Came on back, so the next two or three nights someone came back and shot again, but it didn't hit nobody. I hadn't did nothin to nobody.

My tent was sittin facin the road. It wasn't much further from here to that wall. I'd say twenty feet from it. And there was a bank about this high, I'd say car door level. When I woke up I heard a car pullin out. I didn't feel too much like revenge, you know, like fightin back. I always liked this nonviolence. Somethin down inside.

We was there in Tent City twenty months, I believe.

Venetta Gray

It was nearin '59 and things were gettin real rough for us. We'd been havin bad crop years. We had lost a lotta what we had. My husband's nephew had tried to sue him. We had tried to borrow money. And by the time all the action started in Fayette County we were really down to the grit. We didn't have anything hardly but this place and we were tryin to hold on to it. My husband was drivin a tractor which had really put us into it because we owin on this tractor. And we had these children. And by the time all this stuff came up—Tent City time—I had gone up and talked to Viola and told her what a time we was havin and what the problem was like. She was havin pretty much the same. We hardly had anything to eat. And I remember they were givin away this food over at Tent City. I said, "Maybe if we go over they'll give us some food." We caught a ride to Somerville and got out there. And there was gobs of food and gobs of people.

It was wild. It was. And we couldn't hardly get us to the store. We had to park way down the road. And eventually I found out Viola wasn't at the store; she was at home. And I went down to her house and I talked to her and told her the condition we was in. She said, "Well I don't know what we can do right now. We have plenty of food but it's at the store." She said, "But they're issuin it up there. By the time you go back I don't know what'll be there. It'll be issued on out for today, I believe. The truck will park there and they will just hand it offa the truck." My children didn't have any clothes. Viola went back in her house and got up a box of clothin and stuff. It seems they were some old clothes that had been sent to her children—Little John or one of em. She gave em to me.

And after that I became interested because she had kept in touch with me to tell what was goin on. So I started attendin the meetins. My husband and I went when we could catch a ride to go to some of em. And that year of '60 I was pregnant with my last child. I started standin on line on the courthouse lawn tryin to get registered. I think I made—I don't know how many trips. I know I had to go for about two weeks. I went practically every day. There were some days I was just too tired bein pregnant. I was just too tired to go, but I kept goin back. That last day, I had almost given up. It was so hot standin in that sun. They weren't registerin over two or three people a day, but I did get registered. A big line, big line all the way out. All the way from the door that you were goin in completely out to the sidewalk. And there were people standin everywhere. Some would just get tired standin there on the long line and would just lie down in the line because it was just so slow. I was proud to see that line. It just made me feel great. There were lines all the way around the courthouse, all along up the steps, and then on inside the buildin along up to the office. And then the last day I got up real early and got there and I got on line and I finally got inside the door. That helped a lot because I was out of the direct heat. And I eventually got there. When I got almost to the door they told me—they didn't tell me anything—this lady just got up, I suppose to get a glass of water or somethin. Takin an aspirin or anything—they would just take all kindsa time. But eventually I got registered.

After registration our names and the others that had registered at that time were placed in stores. And if you went into any store to ask for anything, before you was waited upon they went through this list and if your name was on this list there wasn't any eatin. A blacklist. This list was just us Blacks. And they would tell you, "You don't buy here. We don't serve you. We not gonna sell you anything."

After attendin meetins and becomin involved, after becomin a member of the Original Fayette County Civic and Welfare League, and workin with it, and seein things as they really exist here in Fayette County, made me more determined. We stuck it out to the point that we would attend meetins and stay until twelve or one o'clock tryin to get things worked out, tryin to understand some of the things that needed to be worked out.

Gyp Walker

Gyp Walker's life is unusual. While the other speakers in this section struggled to make their way within an oppressive system, Gyp spent most of his life traveling the road as a free man. Gyp's story might seem to move away from the political events of the early sixties, but the spirit that kept Gyp on the road— the desire to think and feel and live joyfully and freely—is surely relevant to the civil rights struggle. When it came time for the people of Fayette County to support these values by lining up to register, Gyp was right there.

I'm William Henry Walker. I'm sixty-four. Born in 1907, September 2. Yeah, I was born in a little shack in Fayette County, not too far from Moscow. On the old Moscow-Somerville road in one of them old Tennessee log cabins. Still stands. No tellin how old it is. Was around when I got here. They call me "Gyp" for a nickname cause the gypsies stole me one time. Yeah, they stole me. I was out there playin and the gypsies stole me. I was out there in front of the shack and they run down there and got me. They was travelin the road, you know, in covered wagons. I wasn't no baby, but I was a little boy. They didn't get very far with me.

I got on the move around here in 1927. I got close to the freight train where I could get a free ride so I hopped a car. Oh, it was easy ridin. Knowin how to catch it, see, that was the main thing. Catchin and ridin. If you could catch it you didn't have no trouble. Catch it right though or you're liable to get your head cut off or arms or a leg. I didn't work. I started workin later—goin to Arkansas to pick cotton. I was doin all right—seein the world like I wanted, that I wouldn't have never seen if I hadn't have gone out there on my own. Bein in one place, you know, you can't find out what's goin on out there. Yeah, I've traveled more than anybody around here. I was born travelin. Always travelin. I was supposed to travel. I was ready for it.

The first hobo trip I taken was outa Memphis. I didn't know where I was goin. I hadn't never been to Mississippi. I thought I'd go on a hobo trip through the country. I went to Crenshaw and I found out all the trains stopped there goin and comin so I just stayed around there all the day until late in the evenin I caught one back to Memphis. A one-day trip. That was the first one.

When I hoboed I didn't take too much. I don't know, whatever I had on. Wasn't much need for it in the jungle nohow. Jungle is the place, you know, where the hoboes camp, where they get off and rest. Not too far from the railroad tracks. Bushy area. Plenty of wood. They have cans where they make coffee, make mulligan stews. Every nationality out there. Wasn't just Negroes. Everybody. Everybody ridin, goin. Some were sightseein, some were lookin for work, some were just ridin. Yeah, all ridin. No prejudice. I went anywhere I wanted to go. A sheriff would stop us sometime—I always had news for him. I told him I knowed where I was goin and I was goin where I was goin. I wasn't stealin nothin, I wasn't tryin to break in nothin, I was just ridin. He'd say, "Well just ride on." But no fights. It wasn't too rough with hobo camp. Everybody was all right. I'd get along good. No rough stuff goin on in the jungle. At night we'd talk about everything—where they'd been and where they was goin. Yeah, all kinda hobo stories. They'd tell all about the road and where you'd have to be careful. Some places in Pennsylvania was rough, you know, they'd try to shake you off the train—make you jump off.

My trips? Down to New Orleans. Been down there seven times. I've been to Baton Rouge two times. I've been to Scottsdale and Greenville and on to Baton Rouge. I've been down 61 Highway six times into New Orleans. I've been up North. Been to Chicago, oh, about seven times. Been to Cleveland many times. St. Louis—I lived in St. Louis five months after I came outa the army.

I don't know what everyone else was doin. Some of em goin mad—I don't know what they were doin. I didn't feel like settlin down. No, no, I'd gotten started—no settlin down. Yeah Lord, they was plantin corn and me ridin. Ridin, goin to see what you want to see—well it was fun. Didn't worry about bein poor. Always gonna eat so I didn't think about it. Wasn't no money to be made here nohow. If I was gonna work I'd've been workin for nothin, so I just as soon do nothin and enjoy it. If I'd come to a house I'd say, "Here's a hobo needs a feed."

I been singin since I been a small kid. First time I heard anybody singin I sang. Beginnin of World War I plenty of singin'd be goin on. I just picked it up. Most people don't sing cause they never tried. You don't know what you can do until you try. You got willpower to try, you can break down anything. No matter what it is. No such thing as can't. "Thy will be done—where there's a will there's a way. In the jungle we'd sing all kindsa songs—blues, hillbilly songs, cowboy songs. Sing along the way. Sometimes ride and sing all night.

No, I never had enough of it. Traveled the road until the war come up. I'd just gotten started when the Crash came up. Then everybody was ridin. Every train that run, somebody was goin on it. They didn't talk about the Crash. Goin where they were goin, been where they been—I don't know what other people were talkin about but there wasn't any business talk. We were hoboes, that's all. We didn't know what the others were talkin about. Only thing was the war was comin up and some of us hoboes joined the army. I met a lotta em in there. They'd been around.

The army, it was all right. But see they always—in the army, you know, you're supposed to do what you're told. And if you don't do what you're told—you best just don't be there. You stay there—you gotta leave if you don't do what you're told. Ain't nobody gonna whup you, but they can punish you. I took a good number of trips from the army. I left cause they snitched too much. The soldiers that snitched, you know, they got stripes. They'd run and tell the white folks, the company commander, everything. I didn't like that kinda stuff so I told them they could fight their war by theirselves. I stayed away thirteen months one time. I don't know if they came lookin for me. They didn't find me if they did. Wasn't smart enough to find me. Naw, no. I wasn't in Fayette County. I passed on by Fayette County that time. I didn't like snitchin. See they'd tell any kinda thing to get a stripe on their arm. Do anything to get a stripe. I knowed I was breakin the law, but it was much better to go cool off than to stay there and kill somebody. I would have killed someone to keep all the snitchin from goin on. They'd make up stories. Let em fight emselves. I showed em I'm not dumb. I stayed off so long, when I did show up there they put me out again. They said, "Well you too smart. Ain't gonna send you overseas cause when you get over there you'll run off over there and nobody never will find you." That's probably what would've happened if I got over there.

I started readin the Bible when I learned how to read. I done regular readin in that through the years. Bible is nothin but only tells you about right doins. Whatever you do, do right, cause you won't do no trouble. It helps me prophet some. See there's no trouble to prophesize. You have to remember what have been, just as it was, and you have to see the present, just as it is, and then you can tell what the future will be. You have to have a good clear memory. Strong memory. As long as you don't get in no worryin stage you can see things like prophets. To see things you can't have no kind of botheration. You've gotta have your mind clear. A child ain't old enough to know there's a world out there—there's so much unseen trouble they don't see. You can't see it all with the natural eye. You've gotta look over it in the mind. And you've gotta know the truth to see. The truth will set you free, you see. You've gotta learn the truth, carry the truth, and live by the truth, and keep the truth by you all your life. And when you learn the truth, you can see. Satan ain't created nothin. God created all the creation. Satan ain't made nothin. But he's a big liar, I can tell you. He puts the thoughts in your head that tie your mind all up. Pray to the Lord and he'll show you what's goin on. But when you don't watch for him, the Devil'll show you somethin. That's his business—to fool you. I don't have no trouble with him now cause I know how he operates.

Peoples for a long time have heard about the world comin to an end, but they're lookin in the wrong direction. See, the world is the movement among the people, among the nations. And that evil-doin among the nations has got to come to an end. It must come to end. That world is gonna be destroyed. Earth ain't gonna get destroyed. Leaders, buildins, towns—all that changes. They're renewin towns up—twenty years from now you won't know where you are when you get back here. More streets, new buildins, and everything. No change in the Bible. It's all written. Means somethin to everybody. People live selfishly and don't pay attention to what they're doin. What's goin on is a sign of the times—you can tell that from the Bible. It says, "Hypocrites will see the face of the sky, but they will not see the sign of the times. Stars will fall from Heaven. Wars and rumors of war. Fathers will be against sons and sons will be against fathers; mothers against daughters and them against mothers." When the stars fall from Heaven, the hour of redemption is almost here. And redemption means man will be redeemed from sin. See, by disobedience sin came and by sin death came. And there'll come a time when death will go away. But it's not until you believe that God's able to it away. Man would never've died in the first place if he hadn't've disobeyed God's orders. You die from worryin yourself to death. You worry, worry. "Let not your heart be troubled." You read the Bible, you find out what troubles you. Worry in the heart and the mind causes sickness and diseases and death. See, a merry heart works better—sing and be merry. A merry heart is better than medicine. A merry heart can do it better than medicine. You see nothin's gonna do no good if you don't have no faith in it. I kept from worryin when I was a hobo. I had nothin to worry about. I kept watchin, prayin, and kept goin. You get off one of them trains and run down the side of the tracks and get the next train ride. I knowed how.

Back when I was hoboin I was in Shelby County and a guy asked me, "You all registered to vote in Fayette County?"

I said, "No."

He said, "Well vote. You're workin on those roads and payin those taxes.

I said, "I ain't never worked none yet."

They tried to get me to vote. I said, "Uh, uh." I'd be gone again. I was hoboin then. I couldn't stay in one place six months. I had my freedom. When I settled here, then I registered to vote. Been votin ever since. Well you see all the people that registered to vote, they put up a boycott not to sell nobody nothin that was registered to vote. So I didn't know if they had my name on this blacklist, they called it—a black sheet of paper and everyone's name printed on it in white. The list come out—a picture of it in *Ebony* magazine. I got a microscope to see all the names on it—my name, my mother and father, everyone that voted was in there.

When I was young and never been nowhere I was livin in dreams. That's what started me goin. I'd dream about all the places everywhere and decided I'd see if I could find em. I found em. Yeah, I found the things I dreamed about. I don't feel sad now. I've traveled. I'll get up and go again if I want to go. See, when you've traveled and you do settle down, you have plenty to think about— people you've met and places you've been and many things. Things that are unbelievable to the people that haven't never seen em.

Viola McFerren speaking at Mt. Olive church

"Finally, all of the fear left. All of the fear of harm being done, of staying awake at night to listen to hear what's coming upon you. . . . And it was at this time I decided to work hard in the movement. I knew that regardless of what other people feel or say, that this struggle is right. There's no reason why people shouldn't be free. There's no reason why people shouldn't have an opportunity to register to vote."
—Viola McFerren

Newly arrived civil rights workers from the University of Chicago singing "We Shall Overcome" with community members

"I think the Black people were just real happy to know that there were some white people in the world that cared about their condition and wanted to help. And I think the Black community accepted them with open arms."
—Viola McFerren

Getting out the vote: Cornell University voter registration project, summer 1964

John McFerren overseeing voter registration

Voter registration on a hot day

"They weren't registerin over two or three people a day. . . . A big line, big line all the way out. All the way from the door that you were goin in completely out to the sidewalk. And there were people standin everywhere. Some would just get tired standin there on the long line and would just lie down in the line because it was just so slow. I was proud to see the line. It just made me feel great."
—Venetta Gray

Determined to register

Waiting and waiting to register

"I said, 'Mister, this is true, the white peoples don't know we exist. If you think they do you go count the jobs what they got. Go in there and see how manty Negroes you find. And when you get outa there go in all the stores—all the various places where whites are employed for better than $1.25 an hour. See how many Negroes you find there. And you come back and tell me if we exist in Fayette County.'
"He said, 'Well, if you put it that way, I have to agree with you.'"
—Maggie Mae Horton

PART III

"A FEW MOVEMENTS
TO IMPROVE THINGS"

1963–1965

At the end of 1960 the situation in Fayette County attracted national atten-
tion. In New York City a series of newspaper articles by Ted Poston of the New
York Post and publicity on Barry Gray's WMCA radio program brought the
league's activities before a large and concerned audience. The Tent City crisis
stimulated a massive drive for food and clothing. In mid-January of 1961 a
convoy of seven forty-foot trucks carried 150 tons of food and clothing from
New York to Tent City. This staggering response came just one week after the
Department of Agriculture denied that there was any reason to send surplus
food to Fayette County. The decision was based on reports filed in 1958 by
local white officials who claimed that there was no need for federal assis-
tance. In fact, over seven thousand people were eligible for aid. Only after the
Kennedy administration took office did the people of Fayette County receive
material aid from the federal government.

During these difficult times there was no other place in the rural South
where the civil rights movement had become such a central concern in so
many lives. In 1963 when student activists began to set up summer work-
shops to encourage voter registration and to stimulate indigenous leader-
ship within various communities, the Original Fayette County Civic and
Welfare League and its supporters had already been working on its own for
three years. The people of Fayette County did not need their political educa-
tion brought in from the outside. The cumulative daily experience of living as
oppressed people was enough to instruct them; this was enough to bring out

the extraordinary capabilities of ordinary men and women. As a result, when college students came down to Fayette County they came to take part in what was already an on-going project. A Quaker-sponsored group arrived in 1962 and another followed in 1963, but it was during the summers of 1964 and 1965, when large groups from Cornell and Wisconsin arrived, that the most determined registration drives took place.

Each of the county's fifteen districts elected a leader who supervised reg-istration activities within that district and met with other district leaders to form the decision-making apparatus of the league. White civil rights workers were distributed throughout the districts and shared the homes of families who could find some extra sleeping space. Each day Blacks from the district would pair off with whites and visit people at home to encourage them to register and to arrange for transportation to the registration office. Altogether forty-three hundred Blacks registered, enough to dominate the coming elec-tion for tax assessor and sheriff. The election was stolen at the polls. In one district fifty-one whites and eighty-eight Blacks were counted voting, but when the votes came in the white candidate received 201 votes and the Black candidate 72. Across the county tallied votes bore little relation to the real vote. On election day angry pollwatchers made numerous calls to the Justice Department, but almost nothing was done.

Whenever the league takes aggressive action in pursuit of its goals, the McFerrens are confronted with all forms of harassment. As leaders they have come to expect this. Their narratives here focus on the obstacles raised to thwart a league victory in the elections. Only occasionally do they talk about the intense pressure they felt from the hostile white community.

John McFerren

Mosta the voter-registration drives has been organized in each district of the county and has used my small store for headquarters. I have one pay phone in my small store and I do my contactin of each group leader through the telephone. This is the largest area county in the state of Tennessee—it's 704 square miles. However, our phone stays outa fix a whole lot. And I have a strong reason to believe the phone is tapped because I took two paper sacks and put one inside of the other one and put it over the receiver and hang it up. And all of a sudden, outa the deep blue sky, the phone'd ring and I'd go there to answer the phone and the operator'd ask if the phone was outa fix. By havin the paper sacks twisted over the receiver they couldn't hear no sounds outa the store and that's why they would call up and ask if the phone's outa fix.

We have had any number of elections, but in my jurisdiction we haven't had one single honest election without some friction in it. I haven't seen one that carried out the state law or hadn't some federal violations in it. We filed a suit against the Democrat committee in 1959 and also we have filed all kinda complaints to the Justice Department on irregularities in elections. We have made some progress but not as much progress as we know we should've made. They have slick ways to apply pressure on you. We don't have any votin machines. We have ballots. And mosta the places do not have private booths to vote in. Now you take when you have a table to mark your ballot on and I can stand off twenty feet or thirty and tell exactly what you're markin on your ballot because I know where the slot's at—they can put pressure on you if you don't vote the right way. And that makes folks afraid to come out and vote. It keeps em always afraid to take part in the votin.

We have one Negro on the Election Commission here—he was appointed this year. And he don't even know when they have an election meetin, less knowin bout the business what's goin on. I was talkin to him and askin him about why wasn't there some booths at the votin places and he said he didn't even know when the election was even called. That looks to me like they got this one Negro just to color the milk. That's all it looks to me. Just to color the milk. And I can't see any service that he's doin because he don't know what's goin on. Now how can he be on the commission and don't know when the election's called, don't know why they ain't got no booths? He's just a figurehead on the commission. I been complainin with the organization for a good many years now bout the ways the elections was handled, but I'm sure that the state, federal, and local is not too interested in havin honest elections like they would claim because the Negro would make too much advancement if they would have fair elections.

Viola McFerren

After the first registration drive there was a lot of tension. The white community was angry, hostile, and very disturbed that Negroes were becoming registered in order to vote. And it was at that time when we began to have difficulties in getting registration days straightened out. We had one day a week which was on Wednesday at that time. Often we would have just hundreds of people in town to get registered. Several people would get registered and then a note would appear on the door of the registration office saying that the registrar was out for coffee or that the registrar had come down with mumps and various little stories of that kind. Anything to interrupt the registration. There wasn't enough people working in the registration office to take care of the people—even if they hadn't gone out for coffee so often and come down with the mumps. These people would stand on line all day and we would try to find out why the registration had stopped and why some other people could not be employed to carry on this work. There were times when the registration office would be moved from its usual location. I remember on one occasion it was carried up on the second floor around a lot of hallways, nooks, and corners that made it kind of difficult for people to find. And it was sort of a spooky-looking area that it was carried into. It was a little bit frightening to people who knew they were not wanted to be registered. When you look in the faces of these horrible, angry white people and then you had to go around these dark halls and corners, it wasn't such a pleasant ordeal.

We constantly had telephone calls. We had—well there were many nights when you couldn't even sleep. The telephone'd ring and when you answered the telephone there would be profane language used and telling that they were going to kill you. For the most part there were men's voices on the calls that I answered. Telling you that you better get out of town if you didn't want to be killed. And there were a lot of horrible noises and sounds made in the telephone as if a person was struggling for his life. And you'd hear this as if this was the way you're going to be sounding. There were calls saying that at a certain time they would arrive and kill John and they were going to burn the house down. And this was a constant thing. It wasn't anything easy to hear. It didn't comfort you at all. But finally I got to the point where it didn't disturb me as much as it did in the very beginning.

I remember one night John was coming from Memphis and he said he was being chased by another automobile and he took some back roads and made several turns and finally shook this automobile off a little bit and then he drove on into home. He was driving so fast when he drove on into the drive—it frightened me; I wondered what was happening. He stopped the car and he and another young man jumped out and ran behind the house and sort of hid out to see if this automobile was going to drive into the yard after us. But the automobile kept passing. It didn't come in.

Another time on a Saturday night we were at work in the store and I left a babysitter with the children. It might've been eleven o'clock when we got this telephone call that someone had thrown something into the house and a car had been heard pulling away. And we dashed home and the children were so frightened—they were just scared, scared terribly. The babysitter was frightened out of her mind almost. And there was this huge rock lying on the floor that had been thrown through the window on the front side of the house. Luckily it didn't hit anybody. We called the sheriff's department and the sheriff came out. And well, there wasn't too much that he did do. I don't remember him making fingerprints. I do remember him asking do we suppose that the babysitter's boyfriend might've thrown it through the window.

A little bit later, about 1964, I remember a large group of civil rights workers that came and helped us with voter registration. This was a group from Cornell University. And I can remember other groups coming through the years. The Black people were just real happy to know that there were some white people in the world that cared about their condition and wanted to help. And I think the Black community accepted them with open arms. In my opinion they were just like being a part of their family—those that lived in with various families. They were very proud of the young people. I really think there was a good relationship between the students and the Black people of the community. There were some Black people who did not take a part and there are many who do not take a part now, but Fayette County Black people were very happy to have them and it was sort of like a shot in the arm to have someone else with so much interest and energy to really help you get out and get a job done.

"A HELPIN HAND"

The arrival of white civil rights workers was felt by both Black and white citizens of Fayette County. These three brief accounts give some idea of the various responses their presence stimulated.

Minnie Jameson

One of the first students to come was Charlie Butts from Oberlin College. He stayed around quite a while. This was my first time to work with a white person and I didn't know if he could be trusted. Our little office then was across the street from McFerren's grocery. Someone had sent us an old mimeograph machine and we had an old typewriter, but these things didn't mean anything to me because I didn't know how to use em. While Charlie was stayin there he taught me how to use the mimeograph machine and how to get started with the typewriter. We set up a little newspaper at that time called the *League's Link* and this was published twice a month. Things went quite well with Charlie, he was a lotta help, but at first I was afraid to cross the road with him to go over to the store. I don't know if he knew it or not, but I always would find some kinda excuse to keep from goin across the road with Charlie. But after he stayed with us quite some time then he became as one of us—we wouldn't think about his color.

I wondered why it had to be the way it was just because we wanted to register and vote. I didn't know people could be so mean—not even white people—until this happened. At that time I was thinkin that all white people were of that attitude. But after students started comin and givin us a helpin hand at a time we really needed help, I had to think about that again and reconsider.

Square Mormon

What we do here in District 10, at time of election we call a meetin and sets up the people that go work at the polls. We know how many cars we gonna use at each poll precinct. Two cars or three cars—we have em. All day long they bring peoples and carry em out. At the end of the day you can bet for sure we have found our people in our precinct. We learned that you can't wait for the people to come, you gotta meet the people. If we finds some people on the way to the poll we say, "We'll come back and pick you up" or "We'll pick you up now."

We found out it's more important to get the people at home. We can give an education to em and let em find out what it's all about. I know some districts don't pull up to this. Some districts fall simply because the lead people don't put emselves to enough trouble to really go in there and get the folks. You really gotta get with the folks to get somethin put over. You gotta deal with em. Anyway we been successful. In our district we win all elections. Anybody in our precinct if he run—there's no joke about if he can win.

You have to be willin at first to do anything. When we first started registerin, we would bring the white civil rights workers along and start goin to the people's house every night, every night—knockin on the door and tellin em, "Why you haven't registered?"

And they would say, "Well, why I haven't registered—I have no way to go to Somerville."

I would introduce em and say, "This here's Bob Galbriner from New York and he's a civil rights worker and he's out workin with the registration."

Bob'd say, "Well, I'm not gonna try and get you registered. I'm just workin now if I can be of any assistance to you. I'm not here to compel you to do it, but I would like for you to."

Anyway, they would tell their story about why they hadn't registered and he would say, "Well, I could take you in the mornin if you like."

We left and come back home and I told Bob, "Well look now, there's one thing I want you to stop doin—you stop tellin them bout you weren't down here to compel em to do anythin. You is down here to help em, I know that's true. But see, our folks is a little upset bout you and from now on you just say, 'Now look, why haven't you registered?

So Bob said, "OK, I'll do that if you say I should."

See, the folks had got an impression that Bob was FBI and, not that I wanted to play a two-way trick on him, but me I was tryin to move em. So I told him not to explain where you stand, you just tell em, "Why you haven't registered?" They know the white man have somethin ready and they gonna be so scared to tell em why they haven't registered and they gonna come runnin to register to keep from speakin to the man.

The next week Bob comes up to me and says, "Hey Square, the rumor's out that I'm the FBI."

I says, "I'm tellin you what I would tell myself—if I hadn't registered, I sure in hell would register now."

So I just left it right there. And man let me tell you, the news got out that the FBI's out to get folks registered. And everybody say, "Square, come and get me registered, come and get me registered."

We had peoples at that time would be scared for me to come into their house. This is why we went at night. It was my idea. Bob wanted to go out in the daytime to the fields. I told him, "No you can't do that. There some peoples there—if you go out in the fields and talk to em and the boss man's sittin over there in the car, they will act like you was the boss. They won't talk to you. They will worry bout what's gonna happen when you leave. What we want to do, we don't want to upset em. At nighttime the boss'll go home to eat supper. So we will go round just at sundown and talk to our people, not because we're scared, but for the sake of our people."

Bob said, "I give you credit for this. I think you got the right idea. The folk acted a heap better; you could really see the difference in em."

You see, I knew how people were.

Kathy Westbrook

In the beginnin we first began to start registerin people they were afraid. They were afraida white people in the neighborhood, they were afraid that they couldn't go to the merchants and get their food and clothin as they used to, and we had a problem gettin em registered. We had to come in, sit in their homes, and talk with em a long time. We just had to sit down and convince em they wasn't goin to be hurt. Some people was really afraid.

A lotta people love to call me a big troublemaker. And I begin to ask momma and em a lotta questions. I wasn't really old enough to do a lot, but I begin to ask a lotta questions about a lotta things and stuff.

They begin to talk about, "You can't do this and can't do that."

I said, "Why you can't do it? I mean, like I heard on the news yesterday that you can do this, that, and the other. And you all go up there to votin. People haven't to go up there and be pushed around just any old kinda way."

Then they'd say, "There's not anything we can do about it."

I'd say, "Well, there's somethin somebody can do."

I didn't like the idea of bein pushed around by anybody. In the first place they used to go to vote where the white officials was runnin the place. If your vote come in and they throw your vote away there wasn't anything you could do about it.

Then Vicki, and Bob, and all of the civil rights workers come down and talk about it. I became interested. I'm nosy. Vicki she told me one day, "You're too young to vote and you can't be at the votin place on votin day." So they began to tell me little things that I could sit down and do at home like maybe call somebody or take somebody over to vote. Well that's the way it began. We wasn't really doin anything very much but get the people used to goin, and the few people that were goin, we'd try to get em up there and have em vote. Only a few had enough courage to go up and do somethin. And then comin up to the next election we began a few movements to improve things. I was interested in this. So we began to make simple ballots to illustrate so that people would know how to vote and people who didn't know how to read could use those to go by. And that's how I got started. I didn't know what to do or how to do it, but I knew there were things to be done. We had mass meetins which were really sorta dangerous in those times—the time of the Ku Klux Klan and all the resta em—and I used to like to go and listen in and hear what would be said.

After we began to get in the movement and some of the things were beginnin to look kinda good—you know, some progress—the white people became furious and they begin to go round and make threats and they begin to talk with the older people. These people was afraida em, they knew it, and they begin to talk with em and tell em, "If you don't stop foolin with those white folks who come in here from up North tellin you all this trash I'm not gonna let you have no more groceries outa my store." Somethin like that, you know. And then sometimes the people that would come in here to help us, they would get threats every once in a while. You could tell when it was gettin dangerous.

It started from that. It really seemed to start from a little somethin and it began to rise into somethin big.

"INTEGRATIN THE HUT"

Although the league's primary goal was voter registration, there were numerous sit-ins as well. For the most part, the participants were high school students and white college students, but Maggie Mae Horton was not willing to sit back and play it safe.

Maggie Mae Horton

We were havin sit-ins at cafes in town. I knew Herbie Bonner was a tough man, but even Herbie ran that day. Danny Beagle, a civil rights worker, was walkin the streets beggin somebody help come find his brother Pete. Well nobody would go in the Hut to find him. What Danny didn't know was that I was in the place when Pete got hit. I was in the place with Pete and he didn't know how to crouch that all civil rights workers know to go into. Well Pete didn't know how to do it and that's why his head got bursted. When they burst Pete's head I ran out on the street with all of that blood on me and I couldn't get him up and he was just out. And two white mens come walkin up and I says, "Call the sheriff, call the police, do somethin." They said, "Let em kill the sonofabitch." Oh, I went screamin then for someone to come. So two or three come in—Mr. Leslie, he's a bad sonofagun, he was standin with his bat drawed back and I just moved the bat over and I went in the door. Then Danny come to the door and when he did I said, "I'll help you carry him." None of the Negroes—everyone was afraid. It wasn't a Negro to help pick Pete up. I helped carry him to the car and then several more pitched in. Mosta our boys was integratin another place.

After we got him in the car and carried him to the doctor, Danny was all upset and said, "Come on, go in and help me integrate this place. My brother got killed for goin there."

His brother said, "Well I'm still around and I'm gonna stay around, but I can't go in with you."

I said, "I'll go in with you."

We got almost to the door and Danny said, "I'm scared, Maggie."

I said, "I'll go in first and when they hit at me you be in."

We went in and they didn't bother us. After we got on the inside somebody come runnin and said they saw Robert Horton and that's my husband. When I come out I was mad two ways. I didn't want Robert there because Robert work for civil service and when you do that the Hatch Act says you can't be in no kinda marches or nothin. But all he wanted—he wasn't marchin, he wasn't integratin—he went in and got a cup of coffee and got it poured on him. This same man that beat up the Hobson girls—Julian Pulliam—he poured the coffee on my husband. I stood outside that door and begged and hollered and cursed. He couldn't get outside. I couldn't get in cause they locked the door.

Robert Horton

There was one time when they was integratin the Hut. That's a cafe in town. The Hut. Some white civil rights workers were in there. I went in where they was.

Me and Danny Beagle, Debby Ribb, I forget who all was in there. We was in there just havin a cup of coffee, coke, and it was segregated to the ground, man. And old Julian Pulliam came in and told the lady to give him a cup of coffee. And she asked him, "Cream or sugar?" And he said, "Black." And I wasn't even payin him any attention and he went and dumped that whole cup of coffee right on top of my head. Hot coffee. And brother, I don't know what I woulda did if it hadn't've been for Tim Hall. He grabbed me, Debby and all of em ran over there and grabbed me. Said, "Cool it. Let's go." Then they grabbed the door and held it. Debby got hit over the head and they stabbed James Gray in the hip. Then we went on over to the courthouse—what's that little old guy's name, that CIA man, he was on the police force then? Blackwell. We had a big rigamarole.

This little old deputy, he said, "I'm gonna have to arrest you if you don't quiet down. Threatenin me and sayin things about me."

I said, "You all saw that man."

"We don't know who that was."

I said, "You all saw that damn old man go on walkin back to his cleaner's store."

"You keep on makin these wise threats, we're gonna have to lock you up."

I said, "Well you lock me up."

TWO MAGISTRATES

Although Fayette County Blacks failed to win a countywide election, there was some success in another important area. The main governmental body in Fayette County is the District Quarterly Court. Each of the fifteen districts of Fayette County elects two magistrates and each of the five towns—Oakland, La Grange, Moscow, Rossville, and Somerville—elects one magistrate. The County Court, as it is commonly known, convenes at least four times a year to rule on financial allocations throughout the county. In many ways this financial leverage assures the court far more power than the separate mayors and sheriffs of the county. Harpman Jameson can give you an idea of how this power can be abused:

The magistrates in the county can run the value up on property. They select certain roads that they will blacktop a year or do some improvement on. You take where Negroes own a good bit of property on the same road. When you turn off the main road onto this particular road where Negroes live—if it's gravel it's probably just a half-gravel road with deep holes all in it. Haven't no bushes or trees been cut back from the sides of the road for years, and you're just goin down a little muddy pass. Well go back to the main road just about a mile further, turn off where there's pretty nearly all white livin down that road. Well the bushes been cut back—well not only cut back, they been pushed back—the road's been widened out and they haves a blacktop down through there. That brings the value of the land up. Now you take this other road we're speakin about—the land is valued on the tax about the same, but when they go to sell it it will not bring the price of the land along this blacktop road. All the roads that I know that Negroes live on, the biggest of winter you can't hardly get over that road. And this difference is made in the county court by the district magistrates.

The land like it's standin, no road in there, it probably don't sell for over maybe a hundred dollars an acre. But you cut a good pavement road down through there and put a blacktop through there—that same acre of land will start at five hundred dollars an acre and keep on goin up. That is one way of keepin the Negroes' property down at a lower price level until the white man get it. Then he gets the county court to go in there and here come the pretty, smooth pavement road. He probably bought the land for a hundred dollars an acre. This pretty, smooth blacktop road come in there—the land gonna start at five hundred dollars an acre and go on up. It's an old tradition in the South—the white man clammin up on the Negroes' property.

Voter registration was not uniformly successful throughout the county, but a few districts that were well canvased were successful in electing Black representatives to the County Court. For a few years there were six Black magistrates. This was hardly enough to significantly affect the court's prejudicial use of its powers, but enough, at least, to place witnesses and vocal critics within the structure of power. Today there are no longer any Black magistrates.

Gladys Allen

I'm Mrs. Gladys Allen, age fifty, and I was born and raised in Fayette County. All my parents were here. We was always afraida white people. I don't know what the idea was. We were never told to be afraida em or anything but we just had that instinct. I remember years ago, when we were children, if my parents weren't home and we saw white people comin up—of course, they were always comin to buy cattle or somethin—we would run all the way in the house and upstairs and close the door. We were just afraid to come out. And they would be down at the door just knockin and hollerin. They never knew nobody was home. I don't know what gave us the fear. I never heard my daddy say he was afraida em and I really don't think he was. But it was somethin instilled in us. We always felt we was under the white people or somethin. We really were afraida em. Of course, you take these days and times, my grandchildren aren't afraida nobody. I mean, they'll meet you at the door and start talkin to you right now. They're not gonna run because—well like I say, I don't know why we were that way, because we never was taught to be afraida em. You know, no one never did spell it out—"Now you better be afraida white people." There was just somethin in us.

I think after I got grown and started workin around whites I come to know em a little better and I just wasn't afrada em. And I may be gettin a little far advanced, but after I got really grown and understood em I felt like they weren't anymore than I was in no ways, because I worked with some of em over six years and I did really know that I was just about as much as any of em. I didn't feel under em no ways, shape, or form cause some of em was a far lot eviler than I am.

I worked with one lady for nine years and she was almost like a sister to me. And I started really likin the white people then. You know, I know that some of em—they're not all bad. Really. Cause she was just a wonderful person. And I helped her raise two of her children, and I raised em just like I raised my own children. When they needed discipline I spanked em and when they needed lovin I loved em. My own daughter was jealous of the little girl for a while.

I think the movement affected my own life more than anything else. Nobody had never threatened me in no way at all. I've always been a person that loved people. Period. And after this registration drive started was the first time that I was really aware—the people that I had known and lived around and with all my life, they just turned against me. When we'd go in the store they'd act like they was so crazy about you and all of this—and then when this happened they started bein so indifferent. And I felt, a little, I don't know what it was—hate. I don't like to say it. Hate. Because I felt somethin creepin in my heart that wasn't really love and I didn't like that at all. I'd never been a person that'd want to hate anybody and I had never hated anybody. But I just got to this place where you couldn't feel the way you had been. Just to watch em, to see the way they acted. It let me know that they wasn't like me. I wasn't like em at all. I just didn't feel inferior to em anymore. I didn't feel under em at all. I just felt like I was above em in some ways. And I think there was a whole lotta people—they had love and respect in their hearts, even for the white people. But after some of these things happened somethin else started creepin in.

Well, I was elected as a magistrate in August of '66 but we were not really recognized among any of the white magistrates. The only time they recognized any of us was when one of em wanted to be elected and then they'd come speakin to you and tell you to vote for em. But other than that, we'd walk in the courtroom and they wouldn't look at us. They don't consider us one way or the other. We're just there. They have a man that does the prayin at the beginnin of the meetin and, unless there's some white ladies there that's bringin their reports in at the quarterly meetin, in his prayers he doesn't even mention ladies. He says, "Lord, help these gentlemen . . ." to rise to some sort of conclusion or somethin. And I said, "That prayer didn't even get outa his mouth, cause I don't think God heard it." Oh, I could put up a much better prayer, a more sincere one, than he does. Like I say, when some of the white welfare ladies come in there with their reports, then he says, "Ladies and gentlemen." But I'm the only lady there now. The other lady that was there, the other colored lady, she moved outa the district, so she's not there anymore. But even when she was there he didn't mention "Ladies and gentlemen."

I ran because they just couldn't get anybody else to do so in our district. In our district they had to beg, beg. They tried to get men to run and they wouldn't. Only one man considered it. At that time everybody that'd start wantin to be anything—they were tryin to bomb our homes or set the houses afire or somethin. But I wasn't afraid of any of that. I don't know, but I felt like they weren't goin to bother me at all. They didn't. I'm not a politician. I couldn't be a politician. But I felt it was important. And we really needed some Blacks on the board. And still we need a lot more. Mosta the places we done our campaign was colored churches. We didn't even go in no white community at all. It was strictly the colored people because we have more colored people registered to vote than white in our district. I had to do a lot of thinkin. Actually I wanted to do all that I could. But there's just nothin we can do because there's not enough harmony. There's thirty-six magistrates and only five colored. We can't carry no votes no way.

Just recently we tried to elect a man of our choice on the school board. They were goin to elect one because the courts had just about ordered em to and told em they had to have a colored man on the board. So in place of em talkin with us, the rest of the magistrates were tryin to get some kind of hand-picked man that they could just tell what to do and what not to do. And then when we chose a man, just the five of us voted for him. Just one white was the only one that voted for him. The other white magistrates voted for their hand-picked man and voted him in. So that left us out on that again. They elected the Black man themselves—a man they wanted, a man I'm sure they can control. In other words, nothin that we have asked for has winned before em. We've tried to get a road out here, several times, and they won't even consider it. I've written to Judge Luck, I've written him three letters, and asked him to put it on the agenda where we could talk about it in the meetin, and he has never put it on the agenda yet. They won't even talk about it. I went personally to the road commissioner and he always say that he can't do nothin. They don't have any money, but still they can fix—all these white people that just build little subdivisions out around—they put blacktop roads all the way into those subdivisions, and here these roads have been here for years and years and years and they're not blacktop yet. And there's so many people down this road—it's like a city. So it's just one of those things. Really, we haven't been able to do anything because there's not enough of us to do it. I know that's the problem because if we had enough to carry the vote then we could do somethin. But they all stick together. They're not goin to help us. They listen, they sure do. They don't do nothin. They just vote it down. When it's brought to the table they vote it down. Whatever you ask for. We haven't been able to get anything through.

Cooper Parks

Cooper Parks is my name. I'm forty-five. It was rough growin up as a child, but it got a little rougher after I grown up to be a man and done things on my own. When I started standin up for my rights, that's when it got hard for me.

When I ran for magistrate, what we were really doin was tryin to get people registered. We was fightin at the ballot box, that was the only way. Most people that did register that were livin on some white person's farm—they would have to move. They would have to move and would have no place to go. I guess you heard about Tent City. Boss man would tell you, "What you gone register for? You don't know what you doin." But we still kept carryin to register.

We had a lotta em said, "The boss said I can't go."

I asked em then, I said, "Ain't the boss man registered?"

And they'd say, "Well yes, I guess he is."

I said, "Now don't you think if that's good for him, don't you think it's good for you?"

"Well, I don't know. I got to live and you can't carry me home with you."

I said, "No I can't carry you home with me, but I'll do the best I can for you."

"Well, suppose he make me move. Where'm I goin then?"

I said, "Well there's always a way out. You always know you can find some-place to live."

And a lotta em, really they would slip off. You couldn't go on Mr. Charlie's farm, just pick up a bunch of em and carry em up there. They'd tell you to meet em out on the road somewhere. I remember I carried some real good friends of mine to register and we come back into town—I had some civil rights workers with me—and we'd get near about the town and they'd say, "Put me out because I don't wanna ride through town with you all." It was just they was afraid.

I knew the magistrates in Fayette County is the most important thing in the county. We makes the law. And if we had enough Black magistrates we could do a lot better. We don't have but five out of thirty-five now. See now, the majority of people in Fayette County is Black and if we got enough Black magistrates we could rule this county. I think the magistrate is more important than the sheriff, because the sheriff—no matter what color he is—he can't do nothin without the magistrate givin him authority. He doesn't make the law; he just enforces em.

I run for public office as magistrate in '67 for Fayette County and this guy I ran against, he been magistrate ever since I been old enough to know there was a magistrate. He was a white fellow and I beat him about two to one. The week after I won the election I got a letter sayin that I didn't qualify to public office. I went to Somerville and I wanted to know why. So they told me they had a letter from a citizen of Fayette County in District 10 claimin that I had been in jail and had a criminal record. So I asked for a photostatic copy of this letter and this lady wanted to know what I was goin to do with it.

I said, "I don't know what I might do with it."

And she said, "Well, I can't give it to you."

So I said, "OK. Well, if you don't I'll get my lawyer to get it for me."

She said, "Well the letter wasn't to you anyway."

"No, it wasn't to me but it was about me."

And she said, "Well I'm gonna give you a photostatic copy. You make sure you know what you're doin."

And she give it to me. After that I went to Somerville with my attorney to be sworn in and everybody in the courthouse told me and my attorney that the judge was out and they didn't want to swear me in. All the time the judge was back in the little room. And my attorney went on back and pulled him outa the room. He come on out and swore me in.

The affidavit accused me of stealin cars on three occasions and wasn't none of it was really true. Some guy was usin my name and anybody else's name he could get. And they said they got this from the sheriff's department. I got my attorney to go down there and clear that up. And I also got this guy that was usin my name. I carried him to Somerville and he testified it was him, it wasn't me. It was a frame-up from the beginnin. It wasn't just a human mistake. It was the white people right here who'd been seein me all my life—they knew me from a kid on up. They see me every day; they know that I hadn't been in jail. They knew I hadn't been nowhere new. They tried to frame me up because I was Black and they didn't want me to run for public office. Some of the white people asked my older brother to talk me outa runnin, which he tried. I guess he was afraid too. But I didn't listen.

Was I worried? Well not really. But now my parents, mosta my people were worried—they were afraid for me. It didn't bother me. I just said Fayette County was my home and I was here to stay. And I felt it was right. I was gonna register. And that's the way I feel now. This is my home and I will live here and I intend to stay.

Things are not fine now. We have some people around here now—they're still afraid. If you stand up for your rights like I did—well, we have some cops here now. They come over to my bar and arrest boys and say they're drunk and really they don't be drunk. They come over here one night, just after I got my beer license, and you're supposed to stop sellin beer at twelve o'clock in this county. But it don't say anything about stop sellin food—I could stay open all night. So the sheriff department man came by one night about ten minutes to twelve. They went up the road; they parked their car and stayed up the road till about five minutes after twelve.

They came back down here and asked me, "Cooper, why aren't you closed? Your beer license says you're supposed to close at twelve o'clock—have your doors closed."

I said, "No, my beer license doesn't say anything like that. I'm supposed to stop sellin beer at twelve o'clock and twelve-thirty have the bottles off the table."

He said, "No, you're supposed to close at twelve."

I said, "Well I'm not gonna close."

"Well if you don't close I'm gonna carry you into court."

I said, "Well that's what you're gonna have to do cause I'm not gonna close."

He said, "Well meet me at court tomorrow mornin at nine o'clock."

So I told Judge Luck my story and he told the sheriff's men, "This man don't have to close as long as he's just sellin food."

And then the sheriff told me, "Well, Cooper, why I want you to close is cause we don't have enough men to work this county. If you stay open some of my men will have to work all night."

I said, "This is not my problem. I'm down there tryin to make a livin. If this county needs some more men you might have to hire em, because I'm not gonna close as long as somebody wants to buy some food."

But now if they don't get you one way, they got a way of tryin to get you. What they do now, they gott a roadblock down at the end of this road and they got men sittin at both ends of the road. When people leave this place, they's checkin em for drivers' licenses and anything that they can find. They don't bother me too much here, but when they stop people comin into my place or goin out, that's the same thing.

PART IV

"IT'S GONNA TAKE BONE DETERMINATION"

School Integration: 1965–1967

Public school integration did not begin in Fayette County until twelve years after the Supreme Court decision. McFerren and the league brought the school authorities to court and in 1966 the Board of Education was ordered to integrate its schools. Edward Gray and James Jamerson were two of the first Black students to graduate from an integrated Fayette County school system.

In the past, great economic pressures and a tightly controlled system of advancement kept most Blacks from pursuing their education past the acquisition of basic literacy and simple math. Most Blacks in the county stopped their schooling after the eighth grade. Venetta Gray's account recalls the difficulties of a family determined to give their child a high school education. Her struggle was surely a source of strength for her son Edward.

Venetta Gray

In '65 John McFerren along with some other plaintiffs filed a desegregation suit in federal court against the Board of Education. My oldest son, Edward Gray, was at that time a junior.

The next school year '65–'66 he was to be a senior. That year he was enrolled along with James Braswell and a few others in the integrated high school. Anyway, James and Edward were very close friends and they enrolled in the previously all-white Fayette High School. I was not only treated very rude by the whites—I was misused and mistreated by the Blacks because I had the principal of the Black school come to me and—he didn't say in so many words that "I hope your son flunks this year" but this is what it all summed up to mean. He was upset Edward was taken outa the Black school—his school, so to speak.

Edward had a very rough year. He hadn't gotten too good an education at the all-Black high school. And Edward had to study real hard. We had but this one heater and Edward had to study at night. Bout January and we had a big snow. He would wrap himself in quilts and sit around this big heater in this open space out there in the hall and try to study. After goin up there he told me, "Oh, if I had only been here at least a year ago. I lost so much. Momma, I wish you could just go up there and visit and see how the children study." He said, "I have to set there half-scared and frightened and try to grasp what I can. The teachers they're tryin to teach up over my head where I can't get it. But I'm determined. I'm not gonna let you down. I'm gonna get it." He knew the principal had made this statement about him flunkin and this really stuck out. It made him more determined.

And havin to walk down this road. We had this tractor. My husband would get up in the mornin time and take him on the tractor down to the road. And this is the year he built this raft to get em across there. Every day meant so much to Edward.

And there was a time there was a fight—some white fellows jumped on Braswell and Edward. And I remember, well, they were callin Viola and tellin her what was happening up there. But I think the boys took pretty good care of emselves. The entire year was just a frightful year. And how he studied outa all that turmoil. Even the janitors jumped on him. But outa all of it there's come some good. I remember the first year he went away to college he told me what he would've faced had he not gone there that last year. He believed he wouldn't have been able to make his first year in college. Oh, I was so proud. At the graduation exercise Edward and Braswell were the only two that finished off that year. There was quite a few that started off—I think about seven—they started but they began to drop long around Christmastime. They just didn't make it. But James and Edward did graduate and Mr. Braswell and I attended graduation and were so proud of em.

I think the worst thing that could've happened that did happen was to have friends around em to look down on em, to tell em that "you think you're white." To have your Black friends tell you, "You think you're white because you're goin to the white school." These are the things that will hurt you. And I can see now why the integration is so hard on the whites still in the public school system. I see and understand how hard it is for em to have a few friends of their own race because I know what it was like for my own son to have friends of his own race. They had friends that they thought were friends that just turned away from em and closed the doors on em because, like I just said, "You think you're white." And the same thing happened to us as parents.

I sure have hopes for my children. Edward, he has done one year of medical school and he's now workin on his master's degree. Financially he just wasn't able to stay in school. He's in the Air Force Reserve and he's goin to go ahead and go in—this is what he told me over Thanksgivin when he came home. But he's determined to have finances—we don't have it—so he's goin into service with the hope of comin back to medicine. Hugh, my second son, he transferred and done his last year at Fayette High and he graduated in '67. He had his BS last year and his hope's to be an attorney. I hope for him—nothin to offer him but high hopes.

In Fayette County I'd like to see a change of heart. That's the only hope I have here. I don't see anything happenin in Fayette County unless people treat people like people.

Edward Gray

My name is Edward Gray. I'm twenty-three years old and I was born in Shelby County near Memphis, Tennessee. The reason I was born there is we didn't have a hospital in Fayette County—there isn't a hospital still. At the present time there isn't a hospital. The reason I was born in Memphis is that I was the first child and they thought at the time there may be some complications. Memphis is about sixty miles from my home.

With me I started to work helpin my father out around the farm real early. Seven or eight years old, man, I was parta the program really. It was nothin unusual to go to school in the mornin and then come back home in the evenin and go to the field. Say, for example, in the summertime you'd come back home and spend three or four hours in the field helpin your father who's out workin choppin cotton or whatever had to be done. Not only the cotton—there was okra to be picked or whatever. You was parta the family and you was a parta the group and this was one of the ways the income was made and you was a parta it. Though you was goin to school, you was also helpin out at home, right. This continued not only in the summertime, but in the fall when you started pickin cotton and so forth. A whole lotta kids—they didn't go back to school. The school started in September and they wouldn't get back to school till January—till all the cotton or whatever got to be picked. It was harvested before they got back to school. Not only would they be behind from that year, but this was a constant thing for every year. I mean every year was like this. And one of the factors I can see—they were stayin on a white man's place and he said that they had to have this cotton outa the field if they wanted to stay on his farm. And there's no other way for the farmer to get it out unless he has the help of his children. And he knows if he don't get it out he's gonna have to move somewhere. So this is just one of those things, you know. The white man needed someone who could pick some cotton and get up and work when he said. The education—heck no, man. He figured if his sharecropper could read his name well enough to read his scales and weigh his cotton—that's about all he needed. That's about the way he considered decent education.

As far as sacrifices are concerned, I know my mother and father made extreme sacrifices for me and my brother to go to school. And not only then. They're makin sacrifices today. But, say now, some of this stuff it's gonna sound funny. Like when it rained. If I went to school and it rained hard while I was at school I knowed—we lived off the road like—that I was gonna get wet as a dog goin home. Cause I was gonna have to walk across this little bridge if the bridge was still there. Water maybe washed it away. And if I went around to the other road I couldn't go across that way cause that's where water was comin down under the bridge. So I knowed there was gonna be water any way I went. So the best thing I could hope to do was get through the water, keep my books from gettin wet—because if you lost a book, man, you wouldn't get another book, man. You'd be charged with that book. You'd have to pay for that book at the end of the year. You done just lost a book. The best thing you could do was try to keep your books from gettin wet and hope to get home before you got pneumonia. Like I say, it was a rough thing. In line of sacrifices—if it rained at home that day—durin the wintertime it was real cold—if my father didn't bring us to the road on his truck he'd bring us on his tractor, or else we had a wagon and he'd bring us in the wagon, or we'd ride the horse. He and my grandfather used to bring us when the water was as high as we was. I would say I was eight or nine years old. He would meet me there in the mornin or the evenin when the water was up and he would take me and put me on his shoulder—walkin through the water hisself, and I'm on his shoulder, to keep me from gettin wet. That's right. And if it rained hard I just knowed there'd be somebody waitin on me to take me across that water in the evenin. Cause man, if I went across I'd've gotten drownded. The water was just too deep. You know the bridge—it wasn't nothin unusual for my father to have to fix that bridge, put that bridge back in shape, and repair those planks on it, five or six times a year. First big rain, man, it's gone. The planks are gone down the stream here and there. That's the way it was. Right. I mean I know there was a whole lotta sacrifices. And still I'll be amazed. And this is one of the things—it motivates me to go ahead on and try to do a better job as far as education is concerned. It's kinda hard to believe some of the things I had to go through, but it's the truth—every bit of it.

Another thing in regards to schoolin. I never missed any days outa school workin at home or pickin cotton at home because I had to or somethin like this. My mother and father thought that education was a primary thing that we needed—that we had to have. And school was just one of those things that we just didn't miss. We just didn't miss it. If there was somethin we had to do—if we had to pick some okra that day—we'd get up early, say at six o'clock. At six o'clock in the mornin in the summertime there's a whole lotta dew on the ground—and man, you'd be wet, you'd get wet pickin okra, and you'd come round to the house and dry off to get ready for school and go to school. If you didn't get it through the dew you'd get it through the rain. It was nothin for me to wear overshoes and boots down to the road where we caught the bus—and there's this big oak tree, it's still there today—I used to stand behind that tree and change my clothes after I walked across this creek and leave my clothes there till I went back home that evenin. So when I got back home at evenin, nine times outa ten I'd have two sets of wet clothes.

When I really began to know anything about Tent City—I used to attend the mass meetins. My mother or my father—there was always one of us who'd go and someone always stayed home cause I had an aunt then at the time and we had to burn wood to keep her warm, especially in the wintertime. And someone had to go with whoever went—to walk to the road. It was the customary thing. Me and my brother Hugh we always went. Another factor that brought Tent City out is the fact that other people in other places began to be concerned about Tent City and sent relief and food and aid to the people in Fayette County. That's when you can say, "If other people feel this way about Fayette County"—they've never seen it, you know—it's the kinda thing that makes me to wonder, "Somethin's really going on in this place, you know." That's when I really began to focus on Tent City.

As far as food on the table, I figured there probably wouldn't've been as much on the table if it hadn't've been for food bein sent in. And clothin. Especially clothin. One year I'd run outa pants. I remember, it was near Christmastime. And my mother'd run into Somerville that day where the supplies and stuff would come in—at McFerren's store, that's where it was—and we got some shirts and pants. I remember these pants really distinctly cause I felt like a sissy wearin em. They were made like girls' pants—in front they didn't have no pockets, they didn't have no pockets up here. And the pockets in the back—you'd drop your hand in your pocket and it'd be way down here on your leg. They weren't like normal pants, you know. And I felt kinda funny wearin those pants, you know. And I had to wear em for over a year cause that's all I had. But that's one of the things I feel proud of in a sense—that through all of that I was still able to overcome the things that was obstacles in my way, things that seemed to pop up from here and there. But through all of it, with the help of my mother and father, I come out all right, determined to keep on pushin.

After goin to these mass meetins you began to see how other people in the county—the McFerrens, the Mormons, and people like them—began to express their views about it and how they felt about the situation. You began to develop mental pictures in your mind—you began to say, "Well, here I am, I'm lookin at things. I can see what my mother and father and other people—what their goals are, how they're tryin to stick together and obtain these things that they feel we should have. Yet still I can see the white man, on the other hand, is workin against us. At the same time knowin the white man is the person when I need somethin, he's the person I got to go to to ask for this." You get two or three different mental views in your mind. This is when I really began to develop a sense of hate or disrespect for my fellow man—especially the white man especially in Fayette County. You really have to experience it to know what it's like. I can sit here and tell you about it all night, but to experience some of these things is really seein it like it really is.

As far as integratin school is concerned there's so many things I can tell you about that. It was 1965 when the first integration program in Fayette County began. The freshman and senior class went to the previously all-white school. There was about 500 to 530 students there and I think there was about sixteen Blacks. When it first started you didn't get on the white bus that came by your door. You'd get on the regular Black bus; you'd go up to the all-Black school; they'd pick you up up there and bring you back down there to the all-white school. This went on for a while. You didn't get on the bus at first with the all-white school. I think this went on for two or three weeks and then you was later put on the bus with white students.

That first day, man, it was just like—it's hard to describe. It was a rough day. Like the teachers—you could get the sense that they didn't want you up there—"Man, we got these niggers comin in our school and we don't want em there." But a whole lotta teachers, you could see that they would try to act nice to try to hope that maybe you'd be satisfied and after this year you'd go on back to the nigger school and not worry about this no more. "If you find out we're gonna treat you all right—maybe you just wanta find out how we gonna treat you—if you find out we treat you all right maybe you not gonna come back no more."

Back to that first day again though. On the bus you had a special place to sit. It wasn't at the back, it was at the front, but it might as well have been at the back because you was isolated—there wasn't anybody else up there with you. They'd always try to figure a way where they'd have a seat between you and the other white kids sittin behind. They were always causin harassment. Like it was nothin for you to get thumped beside the head, or slapped beside the head, or throwin coins—this guy done got on with a pot full of coins that day and he got on and throwed coins from the time you got on the bus till you get to school. And a whole lotta times the bus driver'd see it and just ignore it. They acted like they didn't even see it, you know. A whole lotta times it'd be their children or their grandchildren'd be doin it, you see. Or their next-door neighbor, you know. And they were whites like they were. It didn't mean nothin to em. The only reason he's drivin the bus is for the salary, for the money. So he didn't give a damn. So he didn't want you on there nowhere.

Well, back to that first day. We got to school—I can speak of my situation—I went in there that day and, man, they looked at me like I was a guy that walked in from Mars. You see, I was the only Black student in my homeroom. Man, they treated me like I was a—they didn't have nothin to say to me. That's number one. The only one that said anything to me was my homeroom instructor. My homeroom was where this lady taught Latin. So they got up there this first day and recited the Pledge of Allegiance in Latin. And that was the first time I had even been in a classroom where Latin was taught. I stood up—that's about all I did do that day cause I didn't know nothin about no Latin whatsoever. When the teacher had us stand up and introduce our name and all that stuff, when I stood up man they'd "Huh-huh-huh-huh-huh-huh-huh—they got a nigger standin up here." Guy who's chair was next to mine, he moved his chair all the way almost out middle ways of the floor to get away from me, you know. It was a hell of a thing. Not only did you develop a sense of—you know you wasn't parta the group, see. There wasn't no doubt about that. You knew you wasn't parta the group. But you develop a sense of hate. Well not necessarily for them, but you'd hate you was in the situation. But yet and still—I tried to keep this point in mind—I knew that I was doin somethin was gonna help somebody else, see. Because I knowed that this wasn't somethin that was gonna last but one year and be all over with. OK.

Now they had us separated so that some of us would eat one time, some of us would eat another time, some of us would eat no time. And they had it set up so that you would seldom run into anybody—another Black student—durin the course of changin classes. Only time you might see em would be in lunchtime and then you'd be gettin showered by pennies—they'd throw pennies at you the whole thirty to forty minutes before the next class. It wasn't nothin for you to be able to collect your lunch money for the next day offa the flood—nickles and pennies—we didn't get many dimes and quarters, but we got our share of nickels and pennies.

This was a thing that didn't let up. This went on for nine months—this kinda stuff. It wasn't nothin for a guy to walk into you in the hall and call you a nigger. You get to the point in two or three months where you didn't pay that much attention. For a guy to hit you—they'd hit you in the stomach. You'd walk down the hall and somebody's hit you on the side of your head with a piece of chalk, or stuff like this. Or they'd walk up to you in the corner and elbow you or somethin like that. That wasn't nothin. You was accustomed to every pressure. You didn't know what was gonna happen the next moment. You really wasn't relaxed to study. You felt, you knew you wasn't relaxed—you knew you was outside, you wasn't really a part, they didn't want you in the system. That was one thing that was against you—they didn't want you. It may have been better if you figured your teachers was for you. You really wanted to have somebody on your side, see. You knew you was a minority student there. If you coulda felt that out of all those guys there, that maybe five or six teachers was on your side, you mighta felt better. But there wasn't nobody you felt was on your side because he wanted to be on your side. They may have just done that because they wanted to keep their jobs. There wasn't nobody that was on your side because he felt that integration was a thing that they believed. There wasn't no such thing as that. Like I say, in your classroom there was animosity, in the halls there was animosity—I really didn't feel free.

Like when I went about my studyin. I can't study in the day. Like when I studied in school and college I'd get up two or three o'clock in the mornin. It's nothin to get up two or three o'clock in the mornin to study on until I get up to go to class. Man, you couldn't study at school cause somebody's gonna call you nigger and they'll be throwin chalk at you all the time. Just the fact of sittin there knowin—you readin and you know you might get hit on the head—you not comprehendin, you just lookin at words. It's the fact you knows you was always the center of attention and you know'd you was gonna get attention some kinda way. Now what I mean by attention is a piece of chalk or corn some guy had shelled the night before. Or pennies. Now outa nine Black seniors there was only two that graduated that year—me and James. These people dropped out. They just quit. They didn't come, man. Things just got too wild up there—they couldn't take it. So it definitely worked. With guys goin against you, bein the minority student in that school, and knowin the teachers were like they were, and knowin you'd be put in any situation that provided an evenue for failure, for your downfall—it was tough. In gym, man, you'd change clothes and when you'd come back somebody done throwed water on your clothes and throwed your books outa the rack where you had em, or pulled the shoestrings outa your shoes, or somethin like this.

Like I said, you wasn't studyin at school—that was just a place you made an appearance for the sake of it. You wasn't studyin, you wasn't learnin. That's one of the reasons I think a whole lotta the Black students didn't make it see, because when you got home at night they had other things to do. I worked when I got home. I didn't drop down at no desk and start studyin. I got home and worked till seven o'clock at whatever I had to do and went to bed around eight. My senior year in high school I didn't watch no TV. If you asked me what come on TV after eight o'clock durin the week I couldn't tell you. I didn't know cause I'd go to bed around eight o'clock and I'd sleep till one-thirty or two. Then I'd be done got up to study. It's hard to describe. You'd wake up and make a fire to study cause the house is cold. You woke up, you're damn right, cause when you hit that cold floor you sure woke up. But the thing about it was tryin to make yourself to stay on up to study. That was a hard thing. Once I was up I didn't go back to bed. Around two-fifteen I'd be hittin the books and I wouldn't go back to sleep.

Then in the mornin we had to pick okra around six o'clock. My mother called us around seven-fifteen to get us ready for school and while we'd get ready for school my father would come on over from the okra field to take us on down in the truck to the bus line so we wouldn't be late. That went on all the time. You did this because you was aidin the family in survivin. That little bit you was doin was helpin. If you went down in the okra field and you picked two crates of okra by the time you left for school—at that time okra, I think, was sellin for three cents a pound and a crate of okra was about twenty-eight pounds. OK. Then you picked about fifty-six pounds while you was down there. Then three times fifty-six—see, you done earned a couple of dollars. Say, for example, if there's five of y'all and you picked that much. That's a nice little chip in the pot. And the longer it stays in the field the larger it gets and the lower the price. You had to be there to do your little share. It might not seem like much at the time—to you—but you was doin your share. When you're poor everything counts.

James Jamerson

I was in the second group to integrate the school. The first day I was kinda shaky, but didn't too much happen. It seemed the white students had gotten kinda used to bein around Black. But still they didn't want you. The first day I didn't have any major problems with the students there except for the bus I was ridin. I was the only Black kid on the bus. The first day I got on the bus I sat about middle way not knowin I was supposed to sit on the front seat. That was the seat reserved for Black students on the bus. They did a lotta talk. They didn't hit me or nothin. I guess they was just as afraida me as I was of them. After the first day when I sat middle ways all of the white kids would beat me to the bus. They made sure I had to sit on the front seat. They used to sit back in the bus and call me nigger. Sometimes they'd take two and do this. One fellow would say, "I smell a gar." And the other one said, "A ci-gar?" The other'd say, "No, a nig-gar." That didn't really bother me because I wouldn't let it bother me. I didn't take it seriously.

I almost got in a fight one day with some white guys. One mornin I got on the bus. I wasn't feelin too well—I didn't feel like goin to school but I went on anyway. This fellow started throwin paper, he was cursin me, callin me names. And so we got offa the bus and walked into school—I kinda shook him up a bit. I didn't know it at the time, but durin that time I was the only Black person at school. I was the first one to get there. I kinda shook the fellow up and before I knew it I was surrounded by white fellows. They were cursin and tellin what they were gonna do to me.

One of the fellows that did all this big talk had played with me in the summer. I had a horse; he had a horse. We both liked ridin horses. So he would come over to my house. Or we'd meet somewhere in the fields. We'd ride horses a whole afternoon. I wanted to say, "Well they're not all bad because this fellow here wants to be my friend." And the day this trouble started he was the first guy to jump up there and tell me what they were gonna do. It really made me angry because what I wanted to do, it wasn't anything nice.

One of the fellows walked up to me. He said, "That's my brother you got there. You hit him, you gonna have to fight all of us."

I said, "I'd rather fight all of you cause I don't want to kill nobody."

But mostly it was too many of us to be under the same pressure as the first group to integrate. There was five hundred in the high school and maybe seventy-five or eighty Blacks. I wasn't under any real pressure. It wasn't anything I didn't expect goin to a white school. But I guess I was under pressure because it was hard for me to study. For one thing it was hard for me to keep up with the students at the school. I was already behind from goin to that Black school. And the first day of school the instructors come in and started the class off like they had been teachin em for a whole semester. This was second semester. That kinda slowed me down. I wasn't used to that. To come into the class and start in the middle of the book really throwed me behind. I think that's about the main thing that upset me.

I don't think anyone made any gestures to be nice to anybody. Maybe in my physical-ed class. Like we would do certain sports—volleyball or basketball or somethin like that. I found that the fellows that choose teams would mostly be white—there was twenty-seven or twenty-eight of us in there and four Black in the class. They would always try to choose the Black first because they found out that the Black played the game better than they do. But they didn't really show any interest in us. Right there in the physical-ed class—there wasn't anything but boys around—they had us outnumbered six to one—they seemed to get along with us pretty well. But the minute they got on the outside with the girls they showed resentment. Since this was the second year of integration I felt that they were gettin used to the idea of Blacks bein in school. But I guess at the same time the girls they were datin hadn't accepted Blacks. Or maybe they were tryin to show they were men.

My friends in the all-Black school were tryin to say that we went down there because we wanted to be white, we wanted to say that we were more than they were. But to me it didn't make any difference. I went down there because I wanted a better education. I knew the facilities they had down there were better than the ones at the Black school. We never did have to go outside in the rain to change classes like we did at the all-Black school. I didn't mind being cut off from my Black friends because my uncle and I had been in the movement eight years by that time and I thought it was time for me to do somethin to show I was with him. At those mass meetins they would always call on me to recite a poem or help make out the program or somethin. And so I really felt that I was a parta the movement and I felt it was my duty to go down to the school. I don't think I got the full benefit of the education that I went down there for. I know my American History teacher was really prejudiced because I was Black. The way he would pronounce the word "Negro," you know, would always come out "Niggra." That was the best he could say. It was the same teacher Edward Gray had. Half the time he might say "Niggra," but most of the time he would say "Nigger."

Cleotis Williams

Cleotis Williams did not join Edward Gray and James Jamerson in the first integrated classes at Fayette High, but he did share their experience of entering a white school. His account suggests that meaningful integration—that is, lives experienced in sympathetic relation to each other—is difficult to achieve even when there is abundant good will.

I'm Cleotis Williams, age twenty, born in Fayette County. I never attended an integrated school. I graduated in '69. When I started school it was a two-room shack. That's what it was. Two rooms. And the grades were from one to eight. And I think there were somethin like four teachers there to handle all of us. When I started to school I had to walk only about a mile because the year I started my father started drivin me to the bus. But my brothers before me, they had to walk all the way. Well over five miles. White kids, they rode buses all the way. Now when the movement started I was a child growin up in the county. We had split sessions. Harvest time you'd be outside pickin cotton and you'd still see these buses going up and down the road takin white kids to school. Naturally, this scarred your mind. Makin me think, "What's wrong? Somethin's not right. Definitely."

My really first contact with white people was before I even started school. There was an old man my mother, father, and brother used to work for. He was the first white man I ever really knew. And, you know, he was the boss. He used to ride me around with him in his truck. And I used to say some pretty terrible things to him, things like, "Man you better get out there in the field with your red self and get to work." You know, stuff like this. But bein a child I wasn't aware of all the hangups of society and all the taboos between Blacks and whites. And I remember this distinctly, one day I took his gas top off his truck and threw it away. I did it on purpose because he made me mad about somethin. I don't know what it was but I threw it away. And believe this or not, he had a dog—this is a fact, my mother and my brother can back me up on it—he called his dog "Snoop," but he wanted us to call his dog "Mr. Snoop." That's a fact. *Mister* Snoop. But I never called a white man's dog "Mister."

So I guess, really, my first contact with white children would be when Art Emery and his family came here from Iowa. His children and I used to play together. When they first came, like, you know, we were all really good friends—we'd play games together and all this. But when school started we were still goin to the Black school and they were goin to the white school. The whole scene changed. After school started this whole friendship changed completely. They stopped comin around. We used to go over there, but after—you know, you could tell by the looks on their faces you're not too welcome, you oughta leave. When school first started we were still friends. Real tight. So when school started we were all standin together waitin for our buses. So naturally they were goin to the white school, we were goin to the Black school—there were different buses. The white bus, for the first two days, wouldn't even stop to pick em up because they were standin with us. And so then we had to separate, we had to go down about thirty feet away and we'd be standin there alone and he'd pick em up. And we used to be standin on the road and this guy actually, the white bus driver, actually used to pull off the road and try to run over us. And that's the truth. We used to have our books sittin close to the road—a lotta mornins the paper went everywhere. He'd actually pull over every mornin. He'd get that close.

In '65, the year I started high school, they started the Freedom of Choice Program. Now I could have gone to an integrated high school but my father was totally against that. That was my freshman year in high school. You know, I tried to talk him into it but he wouldn't let me. The reason I wanted to go was not that I wanted to go to school with white people, but was just that I knew they wouldn't want me there, and that's why I wanted to go. Sorta a protest. But no, my old man wouldn't let me.

The year I was a freshman Art Emery's family took me to Iowa, to a private school there. Art was wholeheartedly for Black people. He was so outgoin that you really didn't have to go outa your way to be nice to him. A real kind guy. He was a Quaker. A pacifist. He was against Vietnam and things like this. The private school in Iowa was a Quaker school. They say it's one of the best in the country. At that time I thought of myself as an artist. In fact, all I was doin was freehand sketches. They thought that I could really develop my talent there. There was two Black kids in the whole school.

The girl's name was Tetchya Bakaya. She was from Africa, from Kenya. And the other dude was from Cincinnati. I don't know his name. I asked a lotta questions when I was there, but I just didn't like the life style. Period. They didn't play basketball. They played hockey. Well I knew nothin about hockey. The types of food they were eatin—carrot cake and vegetables in jello—I knew I just couldn't adjust to this life style. Period. And so, ever since then I've had the realization I don't like the lifes of the white people. When I came back home, I just didn't want any parta it.

The family asked me, they said, "Did you like the school?"

I said, "School was all right."

They said, "Do you want to go?"

I said, "No! No thank you."

I just didn't want to be involved in it. I didn't want to be around. I wanted to be back with real people here, tryin to make it without all the hangups. And I stayed. I didn't attempt to go back.

Sometimes Art Emery said things, little mistakes, that hurt. Once Art got up in church down here and said that he was behind the operation, he was the brains in it, my father was the manpower. That I didn't like. I didn't like that at all. Of course my father, bein the type of guy he is, he'd never say anything. But I still, you know. And there's a lotta little things. When we were on our way to Iowa, it was just me and him and we were talkin to each other. He started screamin at me, he said, "Look me distinctly in the eye when you're talkin to me. And talk loud." You know, all this. To me it was real corny. I was just bein nonchalant. Just me and him in the car. I was just talkin to the guy, you know.

Arrivin in Iowa was a completely unique experience for me. He had sold his own house. We were stayin with some friends of his. Now this guy had a lotta Greyhound buses that he chartered. And so I had a room upstairs and he had a room upstairs. Big basement with dart game and pool and all these things. I was just doin all this crap. It was crazy. Then I went to this Quaker service. You know people just sit there—no singin, nothin. Finally one man got up and he said somethin about how he was readin somethin in a book of his, and he thought about it and sat down. Then this other lady got up and said somethin about her daughter and she sat down. And then we all stood up there and shook hands and we split. It was crazy, man. Hell with these folks. We have fun in our churches. Weird. Real weird. Frankly the people in Iowa are the friendliest people I think I've seen anywhere I've ever been. That's a fact. But there's just somethin missin. I couldn't talk with people there the way I talk with people here. I don't know. We just didn't hit it off. You just can't rap with white people like you can with Black. See the whole life style is different because they live by their set of rules and we have our set, and, oh man, wow. At school everybody just seemed like—you know, I just fitted right in with the group and everybody was just cool. It didn't look like anybody had any type of hangups at all. But I know they did. I just didn't see it. It's just in the background. Way back in the background.

I was only up there for a week. They were tryin to make it a permanent thing but I didn't want to go. Art was quite a guy. Real good dude. He'd do anything. Crazy, man.

Look at our schools in Fayette County the way they are today. Most people here, I'd say 70 percent of the people in high school don't even read novels. Probably haven't read a one in their life. See nobody's tryin to influence anything. Just get it over. I had one white teacher. In fact, he was one of my favorites. Because the guy was white and he was a Southerner, but we would discuss racial issues and everything and he would listen. He really listened. I'd tell him, "Black power!" And he'd tell me, "Brain power!" And that gave me an idea—we got to use our brains too. In the schools the teachers, they don't try to influence Black kids to go to college. I mean the Black teachers now. You'll find a few good ones in every school. But the others would try to scare you about college. Now see, I've been to college for two years. Everything that they told me in the high schools was totally wrong. Totally wrong. I make it my point, I make it my business every day to go to Somerville and see the dropouts. I talk to em and I got one guy, and I think I just about got another one, to make his mind up and go back. I do that every day. I'm a substitute teacher also and that's what I do. I don't try to teach, I say, "Raise your hands and let me see the hands of those goin to college." You know, they say, "Why?" I say, "Why not?" There's a lot still to be done.

Now the other day they had a pep session up at the high school. What they have is not integration. Not really. Well, I'll say they have integration, but no interaction between the races. OK. All the white people got on one side. All of em just huddled together. All you could see was white faces. And on down the other end, Blacks. They'd call out a guy's name—Blacks would cheer for Blacks, whites would cheer for whites. And there's nothin bein done—they got white peoples and Black peoples on the staff. They aren't doin anything tryin to bring the people together.

PART V

"IT'S A POWER STRUCTURE TYPE OF OPERATION"

Federal Aid: 1966–1971

Late in 1965 President Johnson's massive War on Poverty reached Fayette County. The various federal programs that came to the county were greeted with optimism. For the children there was Head Start; for young adults there was the Neighborhood Youth Corps, the Job Corps, and Upward Bound; for the unemployed and uneducated there were classes in adult basic education, vocational rehabilitation, and job-placement services. In addition, programs such as Medicare Alert, Emergency Food and Medical Service, and the Food Stamp Loan Program provided desperately needed assistance. Numerous members of the Black community were either elected or appointed to serve on the board of directors of the Fayette County Economic Development Commission, the governing body in charge of the various community-action programs. In addition, many Blacks found employment in these programs. Because of these positive aspects of federal aid, Blacks were patient with the many abuses within the administrative structure that governed these activities. No one really expected the power structure of Fayette County to let hundreds of thousands of dollars flow into the county without trying to exert some control over it. Even so, the first executive director of the County Economic Development Commission was a Black man and he could not have been elected without some white support. By 1968 over thirteen thousand participants were receiving over one million dollars worth of federal assistance.

Unfortunately for Blacks in Fayette County and across the rural South, massive federal assistance programs were initiated at the very time the

United States increased its war effort in Southeast Asia to terrible dimensions. The crisis in Vietnam became the dominant moral issue facing our country and civil rights was, in a sense, demoted to the status of being one of many secondary issues. For a few years many Americans had supported and even participated in the civil rights movement, but now Blacks in Fayette County and across the rural South felt suddenly abandoned. They found themselves isolated within a vicious political and economic system that had suffered some defeats but was now quite ready to mete out punishment and go about recouping its losses.

Soon after L. J. Palmer, the Black executive director, died, a white director was elected and control of the community-action programs passed out of the hands of the poor. The board of directors was packed with uncooperative whites and timid Blacks who continually failed to articulate the needs of the poor. The few Blacks committed to their people found themselves virtually powerless. Soon the executive director began to run things by herself. It is not an exaggeration to claim that her arrogant administrative behavior had nearly the same effect as deliberate sabotage. On January 31, 1972, the federal government denied funding for a large share of OEO activities within the county. Needy people lost the opportunity for adult basic education, job retraining, and a number of other valuable services. In addition, many Blacks who were employed to administer these programs are now out of work. Among the government's reasons for withdrawing the programs were that "the adult basic-education program was operating in a vacuum," that the program was functioning without a full-time director "to give a daily sense of direction, insure coordination and adherence to the system," and that the policy advisory committee that is supposed to insure community participation "has no idea of what function it could perform and is basically moribund. . . . The committee rarely meets because it has nothing to do." This was the disastrous outcome of a local program that failed to represent the poor and never operated with anything more than the shameful appearance of democratic procedures. The Black community did not even learn why the program was refused refunding until league members wrote directly to the OEO office in Washington, DC. The executive director of the local program, a person who was neither Black nor poor, did not seem to understand why the people of the county deserved to know how the federal government evaluated the programs under her direct control.

Blacks in Fayette County faced their new crisis alone. The federal government was unresponsive and the media and general public had turned their attention elsewhere.

Viola McFerren

In my opinion the league is responsible for the Poverty Program comin. In 1964, I read an article in the newspaper where people, communities, that were interested in getting funded for the Head Start Program had only two days to submit their applications. And upon reading this I knew that we needed this program in Fayette County very badly—being the third-poorest county in the nation. So I called Washington and asked to speak to someone in the Head Start Department. I talked to a Miss Polly Greenberg and she told me that it was not too late if we could get a letter of intent in to them and they could even help by sending some people down to write the proposal. But she wanted to know if there was some agency that could implement the program. At that time we felt that the only agency that could really go into it would be the Board of Education who had transportation facilities, buildings, and so forth. But they didn't feel very good about us at that time. I didn't know how I was going to talk with them about this.

Through some miracle the board accepted it. However, they didn't seem to accept it for all children in the county that were in need of it—the board implemented it only for Black children. So they set it up in the worst schools in the county. They gave very little consideration to the project and at the end of that year they were told that they could not have another Head Start Program under OEO right away because of the manner in which they had conducted this one. The Board of Education was run by whites. Now there were some Black teachers employed, but it was being implemented by whites.

Well, during that year we understood there were some people that were working to set up an organization to sponsor the Poverty Program here and we tried to find out who was working on this because we wanted to be a part of it. We finally found out there were two Black teachers that were working with several whites. When we went for information over at the courthouse we were really given the runaround—we were not really talked to as if we was human beings that was concerned. Then we decided that we would contact Washington and ask them what did they know about it and to let them know that poor people were not included in the planning stages. This is when Washington got it over to people here that poor and Black people must be included even in the planning stages. We insisted that this committee that was being set up to apply for a charter from the OEO be composed of some poor people from the grass-root level. I was one of those that were named and I represented the Original Fayette County Civic and Welfare League. From there we worked to get the charter. There were only two Black people and three whites. But it was very easy to communicate with those whites. There were one or two that were not quite easy to understand our point of view. On the other hand there was another one that seemed to have understood right off the bat. It went very well. It went better than it's going now. I remember very well, it was my recommendation that the director be a Black person and we had no opposition. We could've been voted down on that because we had three whites on the board and only two Blacks. This was in 1965.

We have many problems now. It hasn't been going well for several years now. We now have a white executive director. It is controlled by the Fayette County Quarterly Court which has a majority of white people. We have one or two Black people who came from the hard-core poor and the needy and, in my opinion, one of these Black people is nothing more than a brown-faced white person. And this is very difficult for me to understand. Her attitude—I just don't understand how she could get so far from the truth, and so far from what's real, and so far from the people who suffered and are suffering because of their activities in bringing about some changes. This person was even recommended for work in this commission, but now this person knows nothing of these Black people who have suffered through the years and have stood behind us and are really responsive for getting the Poverty Program here. It's very difficult to understand how some Black people think when they too are victims of these circumstances.

At one time, personally, I thought a lot of good was coming out of the Poverty Program, and I guess now there is some good. But really, now, it's a white-operated thing and it's a power-structure type of operation. There's an agreement in it that takes some people off the board if they have served a certain length of time—and they can't return in the future. And at the same time there's an agreement that allows the County Court, which is composed primarily of white people, to appoint people who can serve an indefinite period of time. It appears to me that Congress itself has helped to weaken the Poverty Program and to break down the representation of poor people because if many controlling bodies are like the one that I live with they aren't that concerned with the poor. And that's why I wonder how could our government discriminate to that effect—allowing some people the opportunity to serve an indefinite length of time and others having a designated length of time that they will serve. So the federal government has given the Poverty Program back to local political authorities. Absolutely.

Venetta Gray

After people like Mrs. McFerren, who were so determined, got the Poverty Program into the county, I was hired as a teacher's aid in Head Start. I was sent to school and got the trainin which I enjoyed. I had never had the opportunity to be on a college campus. It was very educational. I worked with Head Start about four weeks. At this time I knew that this Neighborhood Youth Corps would come into the county for a pilot program just for the summer. I was called and talked to by Mr. Palmer, a Black man who was the director. And I was transferred then to the Youth Corps.

I really had an experience that I had never had before in my life, because bein a coordinator I had to work with some of these white people, some of the very same people who had almost kicked me in the shins comin in the store intendin to purchase. They were some of the people we were tryin to work with because the program was to work with private groups offerin work sites for Neighborhood Youth Corps for the summer. This is where I really caught it. I had to go to these people to talk to em—some of the white people—concernin the various youths that had been assigned to me as workers. This was quite an experience. At this time their fright, I think, of money comin into the county made it overshadow me bein Black, because they were so concerned by all this money comin into the county and how they would profit from it. So this helped the situation some. Not to the point that they were really willin to cooperate with us as Black people, but to get a job done. These enrollees would be involved in chores where someone needed to get a job done. In the meantime the whites knew the money would be spent in the county.

At this point this is where I got to know and really get the feel of the white man in Fayette County. I got the feelin from the white man that the Black person is inferior, incompetent, not intelligent. The white man looks upon the Black man as bein under his thumb, and to bow to him and to submit to what he do or say. This is how the white man in Fayette County looks on the Black and this is what I got a chance to really see. I had this sharp feelin. I had never been around em—I hadn't been reared up on a plantation farm around em and I had not worked with white people other than meetin on the highway or bein picked up on a truck by one to be taken to the field. So havin this chance to stand up by him and explain my position and havin not to stoop or be ready to go to his field—this had some kinda feelin that I hadn't had before. It made me see the white man for what I think he really is in Fayette County. Maybe I'm wrong, but this is my opinion. And I still feel that the white man here feels we're inferior. I think bein a woman was some of it too because there is a role that the Black woman usually plays here—bein a baby-sitter and a dishwasher and a maid, you know, around the house.

The pilot program left after six weeks and I had to find some other job. I got a small job at the plant, the garment factory. Then I was called back to the job. I had been informed, not that I would have the job, but that this program would come back to the county. Mrs. McFerren had been workin with other people that had given her support to bring it back. On February 27 of 1967 I was called back for my first day's work. I felt not quite as shaky because I had had a chance to deal—I'm usin the word deal—with some of the whites as supervisors and I had worked with some of the enrollees and I had become a little more acquainted with the job. Havin worked with Mr. Palmer—to me he was lettin us know to be a little bit soft-peddlin workin with the white man. This I remember. It still comes back to me now. Because I think the only way we can do a job is do it as we see it, as well as we know how. I went back to work and I have occasionally had run-ins at the Neighborhood Youth Corps office. We've had our problems. I am the only one of the first staff members that is there now. There has been a constant turnover in the program for one reason or another. We have had—I have had problems with the director concernin race. Like their havin people in from the state office and maneuverin em around in such a manner that they never be able to sit down and talk about the program or talk about matters that really needs to be talked about and discuss with the staff—with the Black people of the staff. This had to be brought out and be known. This has not only happened in our office. It has happened in various offices with the Poverty Program. It bothers me to hear the white man say here in Fayette County that he is willin to work with the Blacks—to me they just want to use the Blacks to make it look like an integrated white-Black situation. It is not that at all.

Well, in every program I know of now the heads are all white. There is the Neighborhood Youth Corps—it's headed by a white, and there is the Head Start Program—it's headed by a white, the wife of one of the attorneys, and there is the III-B Program which is now on its way out, which had a Black director. And the overall commission since the death of Mr. Palmer, it's been directed by a white—Alice Cogdill. The Manpower Program, it's headed by a white too. Anyway, the hirin committee was dissolved and the hirin comes through the whites. They hire who they want to. From the beginnin of the Poverty Program they were lookin for college degrees rather than a real understandin of the community's problems.

But I think we have accomplished somethin, I really do. If no more than for me—just to have a better understandin of myself and those I work with.

"YOUR REASONABLE SERVICE"—TWO DEDICATED MEN

The next two speakers are among the few remaining members of the Fayette County Economic Development Commission who speak up for the interests of the poor. Both Elvin Jones and Hayward Brown are latecomers to the movement who committed themselves to action only after periods of radical self-examination. For both men involvement in league activities and in the administration of the Poverty Program meant the start of a new life.

Elvin Jones

I have always loved this county and I have always wanted it to be my home. When I was a child I left here, but when I was a young man I came back to this county and I said, "If I were born here I know there's somethin in this county for me, and I'm determined to see it through." I had quick plans of goin into some type of business, workin real hard. I was real crazy about tools, mechanical work. And I had a feelin that I would be able to progress and get ahead. And it looked like the more I scuffled and tried to get ahead, the more disadvantaged I was. The problems just got—it seemed it wasn't any use—and I just turned to drinkin a lot.

I was seein I wasn't getting anyplace drinkin, so then I started readin the Bible, studyin the Bible, and then I got active in church, and I still seen that I was just branded as an outcast and there wasn't any hope for me. I owed some bills in different places, and I wanted to get active in civil rights work, and I was afraid to cause I knew what would happen to me. Every time I would mention somethin about what I would like to do for the county I would be told to "stay outa the affairs of the county if you want to be protected." I don't know what protection they meant because I wasn't getting any.

So when I got some of my bills paid down to where I could kinda rule myself, that's when I began to get active in the civil rights movement. I'd come to a few of the meetins and 95 percent of the things they were doin in the county I agreed with, but I didn't have any voice because I was afraid to speak out cause of what would happen to me. I attended them off and on since 1961, but I never would speak out and say anything because I knew what it meant for me. Durin the time that the boycott was on, durin '61 I believe, most of em couldn't get food, couldn't buy from certain stores if they were registered—but I always could buy wherever I wanted to. I wasn't so much afraida my life, but for my family. I was afraid that they might not be able to survive with what food I could get for em. At that time I thought the movement wasn't strong enough to help everybody. So I just helped my own.

When I began to work myself into civil rights work they applied pressure immediately. I was arrested for gamblin. I was some thirty yards or more from a crap game. I was sittin down, me and another boy. They never bothered him, but they come and got me and arrested me for drunk and gamblin. And

I wasn't drunk and wasn't gamblin. The week before that arrest there was a man—can't remember his name—and he had a donut shop here in Somerville. A white fellow. Doin real well with it. And he was attendin the White Citizens Council meetins. He found out all their plans—that they had plotted to kill Mr. McFerren. He knew the amount of money that they had offered, and when he began to let the information out to a few people I was one of the ones that got the information and I took it to the McFerrens. This white man didn't go along with the situation that was happenin here in the county. So they throwed this donut shop out. Just overnight. His business fell to three dollars the next day. They just had a meetin and said, "Don't go there." And they warned the colored if they went there what would happen to them. They wouldn't be able to buy. So they just froze him out. He couldn't operate. And when he got ready to move, he couldn't hire colored to move him cause they were afraid. And me and a white man from Illinois and one other colored individual went there that night and loaded his stuff up on his truck and took it out to his home. He couldn't stay in town with his business down to nothin. His crime was that he found out what was going on and how crooked it was, and he didn't want to go along with it. He was born and raised in Mississippi and they felt like he was a Mississippian and he would go along with em. But he let the secrets out to just a few of us. When I went out to help him load up his truck that night people in town knew that I was there. So they got me arrested.

I've been really active in the movement for the last sixteen or eighteen months. I mean really goin at it for all it's worth. A lotta rumors had gotten out about it, about what all was goin on and what not, so I started to watch it. And I got to comin round quite often. Mrs. McFerren contacted me at first. She asked me about bein at a particular meetin. And I was there. And I started from that night. And then right after, the election came up. And I got involved in gettin people out to register. I had gotten to a financial state to where I wasn't afraid that they could take everything away from me. I had gotten most things paid off and I wasn't afraid that I would lose what I had in the house—which is not very much, but is all I have. And I wouldn't lose my automobile which wasn't paid for. So whatever I did, I wasn't so much worried about this. I felt like the league was right. Ever since then I've been workin 100 percent.

After I got active in this I found out I didn't know anything. Workin with the Poverty Program I found out all the different loans that's available. I never knew they existed. And so many other things I didn't know about. After gettin on the board of directors I still learnt more. It was surprisin to know that certain things do exist. The white power structure runs the program. It's just them that has any power. What they decide they want to do—which is the director with the aid of about two more whites—they do it. They do just what they want to do. And they have their hand-picked colored. The members didn't know when nothin was goin on. Mosta em didn't. Whatever the whites decided they wanted to put over, they put it over. You don't know about some of the things till they're already doin it. They got "Meals on Wheels." I believe it was sixty days before I knew anything about it. They chose me to represent the league on the board. But when the league would confer about things they had heard was goin on in this program, I couldn't even tell em cause I didn't even know about it. Even the new buses they got, they was bought and in operation before I knew anything about it.

Sometimes a program director will say, "Look, I've made mistakes. I'm only human." But they've made too many mistakes. I don't think they're qualified for the job. Poor people are involved. And I don't think the director should want to take all the responsibilities. I think they should want to share this with the board and rely on em for some assistance. A lotta people's involved and you don't know whether everybody feels the same way you feel or not. That's why now we've begun to cry out. But the III-B Program is already goin out. I had a chance to talk to some of the officials at state headquarters. They told me they made several recommendations that if this program was to go on, how to go about runnin it right. The program was worth a lotta money to the county. It helped the poor people. There's a book on how the program's supposed to be run. I received one from Mrs. Jameson and when I checked in on it our program was no ways near that. You don't know anything. They don't tell you anything. You find out the best way you can. Accordin to one of the representatives from the state office, he said that our director hadn't been complyin with the directives they had received from the state office. And he made this statement, he said, "We are flexible. We're not like a stick-in-the-mud. We will bend. But when we keep askin you to do somethin, we mean what we say. If you don't do as you're instructed from this office we will cut you off."

If I were runnin the program by all means I would get all my board members and especially the Executive Committee and I'd inform them on all changes and see what they'd suggest. We would come together and put our ideas together and see what we thought was best rather than just takin everything under control myself and doin as I see fit and hirin who I pleased. Cause what'll happen, you'll eventually get in trouble and it'll all be put on you—you don't have the backin of your board when somethin do go wrong. Even from the county or the state, or wherever it might be from—you don't have no backin from em because they're not informed on what's goin on. When I first got on the board, each different committee they assigned me to, I never have got any consideration of what I was supposed to do or nothin.

They put me on the Human Rights Committee and the Alcoholics Committee—and I asked about that because I had been an alcoholic and I know the effect it can take on individuals, his family, and his surroundins—and they never did call me or tell me anything about it. Every time I asked questions they'd give me some kind of runaround. There wasn't anybody to get together except just me. I was the only one appointed. And this Human Rights Committee never did function whatsoever. Then when the state program had a meetin up in Jackson for two days, they didn't encourage me to go, didn't tell me anything about it. And when I did find out about and asked em questions about it, they said, "Oh yeah, we forgot to tell you because it'll be goin on two days and it's a busy season and you're a farm laborer and you can't get off this time of season and it's not that important that you go so don't you worry about it." And then when they found out I was determined to go they told my wife, "Tell him we might be able to pay his mileage." But when I got to the meetin in Jackson and got to question some of the fellows that was there, they told me, "Don't you settle for mileage—they supposed to pay you for the time you lost, cause you are poor and you can't survive bein up here and away from your job." I learnt that I would be able to get up to fifteen dollars per day. No one in Fayette County told me that. And this Human Rights Committee was supposed to be functionin in this county. And all they did was just appoint me as bein the chairman of it—just to say so, to say they had it. But there was no committee. Just me. That's all I knowed until I went to this meetin—never knew what it consisted of, how it was supposed to function, or nothin. I went to this two-day trainin session. They gave me a lotta literature and I came back home and began to read. I haven't finished readin it all yet, but the whole program's run a lot different from what they do here.

Things don't work out in Fayette County because they want to take advantage of you. Mosta the white in this county that haven't gotten above poverty himself, he tries to buy the Negroes' labor for nothin. And if the Negro can ever find out a way to get loans or any type of money whatsoever, he'll begin to come up from under their power and do somethin for himself. As long as they can keep you blind to what rights are yours, well then you'll have to be down over there to work for em for whatever salary they give you. And there are some that I wouldn't definitely say hate Negroes, but they are against you if you ever make an attempt to do somethin for yourself. When you stand up bent over they'll ride your back, but I learnt one thing—if you stand up straight it's hard for an individual to ride you. That's what the Blacks are gonna have to do is get themselves united together. And me, myself, I want what's rightfully mine—I don't want nothin that belongs to nobody else. And in our program that we have here, if it were handled the way I see best for it, it would be a lot better off. Right now it's not complyin with none of the rules, you might say, at all. And every time you ask a question at the board meetin, if you're not careful they'll overrule it and they'll get the conversation off on somethin else.

I feel I have to do more of the work for my people than I should. Before I got on the board Mrs. McFerren and Mr. Brown were about the only two that would speak up at board meetins for anything that was rightfully due for the poor people. The others—occasionally you'd have one that would vote with but as for comin out in the open and expressin themselves, and I know a lotta em was capable of speakin up, but, I don't know, they would just withdraw. So that is why some of these things have slipped by. And I'm sure that Mrs. McFerren and Mr. Brown couldn't swing everything. Just them two. We have some other little support, far as folks motion a second. But to really crowd in, when you do that you'll be branded. Some call me crazy.

Now the white board members have got the word over to me that whenever I don't understand nothin to let em know and talk it over with em—don't write Washington. So all I reply to that is, "There's nothin for me to understand cause I don't know anything. How'm I gonna talk somethin over with you that I don't know about? You never told me any of the functions of the thing so how can I ask you what's wrong?" Nobody pays any attention to the bylaws of the Executive Committee but Mr. Brown and I. We say, "What's the use of havin it if it can't function?" And since I've been readin these different books and whatnot, I've found out what the executive board's supposed to do. It's supposed to function in between the regular board meetins and have a recommendation of things, to get the agenda made out for further board meetins. But they bypassed it. So if they can keep this power from workin, their power will still be the controllin power. Until we be able to get some poor peoples involved on this board, or somebody to speak out for the poor peoples, it's gonna be hard to control.

Hayward Brown

Hayward Brown's account of his attempt to set up a cooperative factory is closely related to the larger story of the white power structure's preempting of the Poverty Program. As in the earlier confrontations where pressure focused on McFerren's grocery store and gas station, the principle of economic oppression remains the same—what the status quo cannot control it cannot permit to exist.

My name is Hayward Brown. I lived for a number of years in Michigan. After I became mature I went into farming and was married and begin to raise a family. And after a period of time we begin to wonder what we could do to be more basic in helping people in general. During that time a friend of mine sent me a newsletter, the Haywood-Fayette County Newsletter, that was edited by Mrs. Virgie Hartenstein in Cincinnati, Ohio. It intrigued me to think of the opposition that the people were running into in the localities I'd only read about vaguely. So I asked Mrs. Hartenstein to put us on the mailing list. The next issue told about a man in Fayette County named Square Mormon who had seven children, who had earned for the year about twelve hundred dollars of which six hundred dollars was profit. At that particular time I had to have at least two hundred dollars a week to break even—to pay my debts and to set my table. So I asked my wife, "What would we do if we only had six-hundred-dollars income that we could use per year?" And this caused us to start thinking. In the Book it says, "Thou cannot serve two masters." We were either going to serve money or we were to serve God.

We thought it would be nice to tour this sort of country and see what it was like, so we bought us a school bus and made it into a mobile home. At this particular time I knew what it was to bring home a check for five hundred dollars a week. But this sort of thing gave me the understanding that there were people a lot less fortunate than we were. We spent four weeks on the road. We came down through Illinois, Kentucky, Tennessee. And I looked up this man called Square Mormon because I was interested in who he was, what kind of background he had, and the conditions he was enduring and so forth. We stayed on his farm eight days. We had quite a bit of talk, he showed me around, we talked to the people and so forth. Then we went on the rest of our tour and on back. This was about the last portion of August. We set about liquidating—sold everything we had. It was quite a sacrifice for us because we had a 120-acre farm paid for. I had made a proposed plot of it where it would be divided into small acreage. I had already had experience in real estate; I knew what it would be worth and how to promote it. We figured there was approximately half a million dollars there if we wanted to stay five to ten years to promote it. In the liquidation we took less than three hundred dollars an acre for it, paid up our debts, waited for the baby to be born in January, and in February we were here to stay.

Then we tried to find a piece of property in Fayette County. The sad feature here was that they have a natural choke on the people. That is, there was no opportunity for the youngsters and they were moving out. We have a void between the high school dropout and the age of around thirty-five to forty. The Black people only owned about 10 percent of the land and they're selling it and the white people are buying it because the Negroes cannot finance it or put the money out that's necessary to make these kind of purchases. And the white people will pay a premium for the land. Now this creates a natural choke—the old people dying, the young people moving away, and the other people buying the land and won't sell an acre of it back at no price. It wouldn't take long to have what you call a purge. So now this is the condition we were looking for land under. We could find land, but it couldn't be bought. So we finally found a man who would sell us some land. We bought three acres and I began to settle things. But we had problems there. The surveyor didn't seem to have time to survey our land, but Mr. David T. Murrill, the man that I bought the land from, said, "You move right in, put your children in school, and then when you get around to it you can pay for your land." So I put the money in escrow at the Rossville Bank and we waited for the man to survey the land. This kept going on, and going on, and going on, and then Mr. Murrill finally called him. He said we would be willing to pay a premium if we could get it surveyed. This was the magic word. Within a week or ten days he was out and surveying. Mr. Murrill had had land surveyed before. He had a four-acre tract surveyed, it cost him twenty-five dollars. But when ours was surveyed it cost seventy-some-odd dollars. Well, I wanted a title search on the tract. And asking for a title search in Fayette County is like asking for a share of the courthouse. They were giving me a number of reasons why I did not need a search as if they were going to pay for it. So when I demanded one, or there would be no sale, they said, "It will cost you a hundred dollars." In Shelby County you can get a search for seventeen dollars and a half plus three dollars and a half for each added instrument. But it cost a hundred dollars to get a search here plus the title insurance. This is the kind of monopoly they have on Fayette County.

Then I began to move in and do a number of things. I began to organize the people, I began to get our mechanism set up, I made searches on what was necessary for us to put in a cooperative. The reason I say "cooperative" is because the people have been exploited for such a long period of time I felt it was time the people had something they could own and control. Cooperatives are the only thing that I know of where the people could have the say-so—what was done and how the organization was run and who would do what with the money. The kind of preparation I'm attempting to bring in, hard-core labor can learn in a very small period of time. Punch-press operating is the main operation of this cooperative. And it only takes about a half an hour to teach a person who has the ability to drive a truck how to operate a punch press. In cooperatives you don't have a union because the people own and control it and why should they have somebody else to help them run their own business or intercede for them to make themselves treat themselves right? Now that's the advantage of a cooperative over a corporation. In a corporation the money controls the people; then they need a bumper between the management and the people to bargain for them. But when you own and control it yourself, you don't need someone to tell you how to run your business. This was the kind of thing the people were interested in, but this is not the sort of thing that Fayette County will permit. It is an unwritten law that anything that the power structure of Fayette County cannot control cannot come in the county. It's as simple as that.

We have had machinery sitting on trucks now for over nine months; we've had contracts for almost a year. These we have not been able to execute nor to use because we have no place in Fayette County known to us where we can put machinery down and put it to work. We made our first application for a rezoning six months ago and despite the fact there was no objection by anybody in the community we got a flat refusal by the Fayette County Quarterly Court. They would not give us a permit where you get your permits. We had to go through the zoning commission. They would not recommend it. Therefore, the court would not honor it. Then we went into another phase of letter writing. We went to the United States Civil Rights Commission. They had a civil rights investigation here at the Chickasaw Electric Building and we made quite a complaint. I told my story there and, fortunately enough, say coincidentally if you like, this last April they gave us a rezoning. Just this past Monday we got our first permit and now we're beginning to finish up this building that we've had all this period of time. It just sat. I've still got machinery right out there on my trucks. Well we have made quite a stir. With this kind of opposition, people felt we'd never make it so their interest died down. Now that we've got the building in the start again we hope to rejuvenate their interest.

We were warned; we were told what to expect. We had read concerning the various things—Medgar Evers had been shot; a number of the other civil rights people had been destroyed; persecutions of all kinds had happened. We knew that. Art Emery had been run out of the county practically. He had run into roadblocks when he started the Mid-South Oil Company which was just before we come down. So we knew what to expect. We have wondered that we haven't had any more confrontations than what we had—personal confrontations. The only thing is, as I see it, they've been able to control us without that. Just through the courts.

I got a letter from one of our Tennessee representatives, Mr. Ray Blanton, almost a year ago, and he said, "Under the Nixon Administration extensive investigations into the kind of complaints you make are unlikely, practically unheard of." Now that seems to be the whole tenor of the thought—the Nixon Administration is not going to do anything to any major degree to help the minority groups. I wrote to John Mitchell a number of times and I asked for closer involvement of the Justice Department just for us to be able to survive. I got no response. I got no response from the Justice Department. I know they got it because I sent it registered, return receipt. Mr. Weil, who is of the Justice Department, he called me and I sent him a packet of my problems and so forth. And no response. I've written to him a time or two since. And no response.

Let's look at it this way. When the federal judge McCrae of Memphis had a setting in on the school-desegregation case of Fayette County, he stated publicly and boldly in court, "I have been threatened, my family has been threatened, but this will not influence my judgment in the case." Now if they are bold enough to threaten a federal judge, what do you think about the small attorneys who work for us? Now you know something about the McFerren case when he was beaten up. They had hired a Black gestapo. The mayor of Somerville, the police force of Somerville in collaboration with the sheriff, and the grocers put up money to these Black folks to beat or kill McFerren when he came to town. And the police department called them when he come to town. Now if they do that sort of thing, what is an attorney? What is he? Why should he stick his neck out and jeopardize his situation?

I do not make a call or a call comes in without someone listening in on it. I don't know who's listening in on it. It's common knowledge that the phones are tapped. Also, my mail was being tampered with. Then my mail was not only tampered with—my first-class mail was cut wide open and sent to me wide open. I even got letters from New York with a Memphis envelope—a post-office envelope—on it. Sometimes my phone would go out for two and three weeks at a time. You couldn't use it at all. Complaining would not help a bit. I made a complaint to the FBI, I made a complaint to the postmaster general in Washington, and they said, "Now if you want to get smart we'll show you what we can do." Simple as that. We made a complaint to 475 members of Congress—wrote them special letters giving them the whole entire package of the way we were being treated here. Less than twenty-five out of 475 answered. I've had friends who wrote to their senators from different states and the senators said they didn't receive those letters, they have no notation on their files. Now this is the sort of thing that we're fighting—it isn't on a local level, it isn't on a state level, this is on a federal level. I thought we had security in the mail; I thought we had security in the federal government; I thought if you approached the Justice Department you would be sure to get justice.

Call it colonialism if you like; it's survival of the fittest, if you like—for those in power to remain in power. It's a matter of survival. Thirty percent of the people have been ruling 70 percent for all these hundreds of years. The only reason they can rule is because they have control of the economy. The minute that the people begin to control their own economy then you can see what would happen. That's why it's an unwritten law that there shall be no business brought inside Fayette County that they cannot control. There is to my knowledge only one existing Black business in Fayette County now that is not under control and he has just finished his twenty-fourth lawsuit in the last ten years. That's John McFerren.

Now as an example of controlled economy—during our confrontation, the first time in the history of Fayette County, the schoolteachers participated. Last fall forty of them were no longer needed. Some of them had twenty-five years of teaching experience. The school board claimed all kinds of things—they didn't have tenure, they didn't have this, they didn't have that. Had to go to a lawsuit to have them reinstated. Now this is the sort of thing. It isn't every case we can take to law. They say sue. And our question is, "With what? We're the third-poorest county in the nation. By who? We have no attorneys to represent us."

This is a perfect purge. This is going into the fifth year of nonprofitable farming due to weather conditions. There are more farms up for sale now than has been known in a long period of time. The banks are going broke because the farmers cannot pay for their land. It seems like fate is intervening. Those who have the land can't do anything with it. With the assistance of the federal government or assistance from the Federal Land Bank—through an organization outside of the county—we could begin to do things. We cannot do it with the structure in the county. That's what I mean when I say, "Having things under control by controlling the economy."

The Black community asks, "How can one man buck the power structure and do something nobody else has been capable of doing?" It is a foolish thing from their point of view that one person or a small group of people feel that they can beat the odds and overturn an entrenched mannerism of life and reform—and this is what it means—revolutionize and reform a county without going into a grave confrontation.

Well, that's the whole story see.

Now the Scripture teaches you, Romans 12:1–2: "Offer your bodies a living sacrifice, holy, acceptable unto God, which is your reasonable service. Be not conformed to this world: but be ye transformed by the renewing of your mind, that ye may prove what is that good, and acceptable, and perfect, will of God." Now, I often ask the question, "If a person will not be reasonable with God, who will he be reasonable with?" Now if you sacrifice your life—give your life as a sacrifice to him—that's a reasonable service. If it hadn't have been for that faith I would not have been here, because in Michigan I had all a common man would want.

PART VI

"BLACK MAN DON'T GET NO JUSTICE HERE"

The Hobson Incident: 1969

The white community's seizure of the Poverty Program is just one disturbing result of the rapid withdrawal of the federal government and the American public from the civil rights struggle. The status quo's reassertion of its power was accompanied by a series of violent episodes. On August 12, 1969, a major crisis developed simply because a Black woman angrily referred to a white boy as "boy." The events that followed left Fayette County more tense and irreconcilably divided than at any time since the movement began.

Vester Hobson

I am Vester Hobson. I'm twenty-seven years old. In August of '69, on a Tuesday afternoon, I had taken my mother to the wash. We were on our way back home and we stopped to pick my sister up. On the way home, in Somerville, right beside Julian Pulliam's store, his son Gerald Pulliam spun up the hill and we were right on top of the hill. While he was comin up the hill he seemed to be goin exceedingly fast. He made a bad drive. We almost collided. My window was rolled down about halfway I guess. After that I said, "Boy, watch where you're drivin." And I kept goin thinkin nothin more about it.

After I got home I got outa the car. My mother and Vernell was gettin the groceries and clothin outa the car and my little nephew Michael was in the car. So after I went in the house I locked the back door; I was comin back to help get the clothes out.

I heard somebody say, "Who was that made that damn smart remark?"

So at this time I walked down the back porch and I said, "I made the remark."

And Julian Pulliam said, "What was that damn smart remark you made?"

I said, "What difference does it make? Do you realize you're on private property?"

He said, "Why hell yes."

The next thing I knew he had me round my neck beatin my head and my shoulder. I was tryin to get loose. I didn't know what was goin on. And by this time Vernell, my sister, she grabbed him to try to get him offa me. And then Julian Pulliam grabbed Vernell and I got and broke loose. And then my mother was tryin to get Julian Pulliam offa my sister and I was tryin to get both Pulliams offa my mother and my sister. And every time Vernell tried to get up my mother said, "Vernell, run in the house and try to get the gun." And every time Vernell would try to get up to get the gun he would knock her back down off the porch. She told Michael—Michael was over there screamin and hollerin, he's eleven years old, he didn't know—she said, "Michael go in the house and try and get the gun." So he went in and he looked for it but he couldn't find it cause I had cleaned up and I had moved the gun and put it in the closet where it used to be behind the stove.

After that I saw some blood and my mother was bleedin. And I said, "Look what you've done to my mother. You got her head bleedin." And so everyone was hollerin and cryin and my sister-in-law was across the street watchin the car and she saw what was goin on so at that time she was coming across the street.

She said, "What'n hell you men doin over here beatin on these ladies?"

"I don't know," he said.

I don't know, they thought she had somethin or what, but at that time they started backin up gettin in the truck to leave.

And my mother said, "I'm gonna have all of you arrested."

He said, "That's just what I'm gonna do. I'm goin to Somerville right now and have you girls arrested for jumpin on my son."

So at the time I saw the blood in my mother's hair, William Neal and another fellow was drivin up. They said that they had overheard em saying somethin about the Hobson girls in Somerville. They said they believe that he was comin out to do somethin. So they was tryin to get out to beat him out here and see what was goin on. And my father had overheard somethin in town too. He had been down to my sister workin and they couldn't tell him anything so he was comin home too.

As the Pulliams were drivin off I said, "Vernell, you go in the house and call the police." So she went in the house and called the police and the fire department came. I don't know why the fire department came. The police parked out there and walked in, they didn't drive up. So the deputy sheriff he came up and said, "What happened?" So we told him what happened. He said, "Well you come to Somerville and swear out a warrant." We said OK and he left. Vernell, after she called the sheriff, she called Mrs. McFerren and told her what happened. And she said she would take us to the doctor. And she drove us to Memphis to the doctor.

We didn't get a chance to file a warrant that day so the next mornin my mother, Vernell, and my father, we went up to swear out a warrant. So they said they would have to have a hearin before they could post bond or even lock him up. They didn't lock him up at all and they set the trial for that Friday mornin. We employed an attorney. There were so many people there at that hearin. They didn't have it upstairs in the big court. They had it in a little small one. Maybe fifty could get in that little room. And people were standin all out in the lobby and everywhere. So I got on the stand and then my mother and then my sister-in-law told what happened. And Julian Pulliam and Gerald Pulliam they got on the stand.

Our attorney he said, "Why did you go out there and beat up those girls, why did you do that?" He said, "You did beat em?"

Pulliam said, "Yes. You think I was gonna let them jump on me and I'd do nothin about it? You think I was gonna let em be beatin all over me and I wasn't gonna do anything?"

And after the trial they gave Gerald Pulliam over to juvenile court cause they said he wasn't old enough. Then the father, they turned him over to grand jury. Grand jury came up and they said he wasn't guilty. So we had felt there still wasn't justice; we were gonna take it to the next grand jury and they said the same thing, they said he wasn't guilty. It cost us eight hundred dollars and we still couldn't get justice.

Mrs. Raymond Hobson

We had done went to the washin, went to the grocer, and were comin back home. Just as I were steppin outa the car he drove up—Julian Pulliam and his son. He pulled so close I had to go back and push outa the car on the other end. So I stepped outa the car. I weren't thinkin nothin.

Pulliam said, "Which one of you gals is drivin that car?"

Vernell said, "Does it matter?"

He said, "I said which one of you gals is drivin that damn car?"

That time Vester walked outa the car, she said, "I was the one drivin that car."

He said, "What kinda slob words that you say?"

She said, "Does it matter?"

That time he just grabbed her head under his arm—just, you know, just beatin her all over the face, and Vernell said, "You can't do that to my sister! What you beatin her for?"

That time Vernell grabbed Julian Pulliam's son and Julian Pulliam grabbed Vernell. He's just beatin her all in the face, and I said, "Listen Julian, what'sa matter with you all? What you all beatin these girls about? What in hell they did?" And that time I rushed back and tried to pull em off Vernell. He just reached back in his hip pocket and grabbed his blackjack and come over thisaway and hit me right cross my head, and I fell. And every time I tried to get up I saw blood was just flyin. He had the pistol in one pocket and his blackjack was in his righthand back pocket. He just jacked it out. It'd come back over his head, you know, and struck me. And every time I'd try to get up I'd fall. He'll just still be there beatin. He was beatin Vernell and his son was beatin Vester.

And my little grandson—every time I'd try to get up I'd fall. Pulliam'd kick me on the head or what. And I yelled to my little grandson and I said, "Break in the house son and try to get a gun." And I said, "Vernell, can't you get loose and get a gun?" And every time Vernell would try, you know, to get loose and get up on the porch he'd grab her and just knock her back down at his feet. Just beatin. And so, we couldn't get in the house to get no gun, and Jenny Rae saw what was goin on and she come runnin.

She said, "What'n hell you beatin up those poor three women? What have they done?" She said, "Do you know you on private land?"

He said, "Hell yes!"

And I said, "Mr. Julian, I'm gonna have you arrested."

He said, "That's what I'm gonna do, go right on down and have all three of you arrested."

I said, "What the hell we did?" I said, "Why did you come out here, you and your son, and jump all over us? What have we did?"

He said, "I'm gonna have all three of you arrested."

By that time the fire wagon, and, well the police did come by the back part, all them come out here as well. One of em was his brother. And so the sheriff come and I was bleedin and so he say, "You oughta go to a doctor."

And I say, "You ought have that man arrested."

He said, "No we can't arrest until you put out a warrant."

And I said, "Well I don't know what he allowed to do. You all better go on and have that man arrested." I said, "Cause we ain't done nothin to him. I don't know why he'd a dood that."

And I was bleedin so, Mrs. McFerren told me it was best for me to head on to the doctor. So Mrs. McFerren take me to the doctor and he helped me. And

Pulliam circled Somerville tryin to find me. I don't know what he tried to find, but I heard people say he circled Somerville. Went to the doctor's office and tried to find me there but I'd gone. And he ain't paid nary a penny for my doctor bill. I had to pay every penny. My doctor bill was over two hundred dollars.

Ain't nothin happened in court, nothin but they said, "Not guilty." Never did they let come the truth. Just took us way back in a little back room to some jury. And we went back there and we told our story just like it was. And they come up to the front there, all them juries come on up there and say, "Not guilty." It was six whites and four colored and they didn't know nothin. Some of em was so old they couldn't hear. They said, "Not guilty," that's exactly what they said.

And I told em, "He hit me back here with a blackjack."

And he said, "Naw, it weren't no blackjack, it was a club."

I said, "Well, it had steel on the end of it." I said, "It just went *biiing* when you hit me."

And he said, "Well clubs have steel on the end of it."

And still he was not guilty.

I told em, I says, "I haven't had a night's rest since I got this lick on my head. I can't lay flat on my back. I don't think I'll ever get over with it." I told em in court, "If my husband or my son come to either one of you white men's houses and jump on your wife and your two daughters what would you all do?"

"We ain't in it. You ain't talkin to us, we ain't in it." That's what they said.

Black man don't get no justice here. I'm tellin the truth. Black man do not get no justice here. Not here in Fayette County. They do just what they want and nothin to fear, nothin to say.

The Black community demanded justice for the Hobson family. The league began a boycott of Somerville, the county seat, and held regular demonstrations in front of the courthouse. Blacks were now refusing to buy at the same stores that had blacklisted them ten years earlier. As the strike wore on the white economic community became increasingly nervous. The sheriff deputized a force of about fifty white citizens. When one peaceful picketer informed one of these deputies that his constitutional rights were being violated, the special deputy replied, "Constitution, Constitution, Constitution. I'm sick and tired of hearing constitutional rights from you kids. I'm going to take your damn Constitution and beat the hell out of you." As the boycott continued, well over a hundred persons were arrested for minor violations of improvised laws. On a few occasions deputies beat the demonstrators and fired point-blank into automobiles. Things were getting out of hand.

Square Mormon

The first time I ever got arrested was for walkin on the grass of the courthouse. We were marchin because the Hobson girls was beated by the Pulliams. The man what done the beatin hadn't even been arrested, was still walkin around. If the man had been put in jail, as he had committed a crime, probably there wouldn't have been no protests. But the man had beaten up on this family and we knowed if this had been a Negro had beaten up on a white woman, he probably wouldn't have had a chance to have a trial. They probably would have killed him even before he could even have a fair trial. He may have been tooken outa jail. It was clear we didn't have no law—we just livin in the county.

At that time we were havin mass meetins on the courthouse lawn every Sunday. There was so many whites standin around. They hadn't had the facts, the truth, you know. The league was bringin out so many things that would make em feel ashamed, I mean bout what kinda county this is and what caused all these things. It made so much sense that, the way I felt, they was ashamed for their young to hear all this kinda stuff. So they wanted to get us out from that lawn and get us out where wouldn't nobody hear any speeches but us. The young white wouldn't be able to hear. Some kinda way they found somethin that say it wasn't right for us to come on the lawn and we didn't believe it. We believed that it was the courthouse and belonged to the peoples in the county and that we had a right to go there to sing and to pray. So we decided we would go up and test that. So we did. We went up.

When we got down to the courthouse, Mr. Sheriff Bolton came out. He sticks his hand out. "Don't you all come on the lawn, cause if you do I'm goin to arrest you."

So I says to Mr. Boll, "Don't stretch your hand out cause you gonna say we resist you. We not gonna resist you. We feel we have a right to come here. And if we're violatin you have a right to arrest us and we will be arrested. But you don't mean to tell me you goin to deprive us of our rights."

Mr. Boll just dropped his hand and we walked right on the grass. Viola stood right behind me and by that time many more children were comin in a crowd.

So he said, "Well all of you that walked on the courthouse grass, just walk on to your right. Consider yourself arrested." It was a large number of us got arrested that Sunday.

When we were protestin the Pulliams beatin the Hobsons, the students at the school, they made their own suggestion to go down to integrate the white school. That mornin I was on my way back to Somerville and when I got to John McFerren's I saw all those children comin out and goin down the road singin. I said, "Lookee here, what's goin on here?" By bein supervisor I just jumped right on down with em. I didn't ask any questions because I felt like the movement was goin on and their movement was mine too and ours was theirs. So I went on down with em to supervise em and keep em on the right side and note the cars and see if anybody run over em.

So we marched around the courthouse and we come back on the north side of the courthouse and one of the boys made his speech. We left from there and come back to the school. So the police come up and start to beatin. We run out there and three deputies come up to our car and says, "What's you all doin sittin here in this land?" We say, "Oh we come down to get the children back to the school." By that time about two or three come through the window and jab me right in my side. Don't you know my rib still hurts me from that. Sometime I can't raise my arm up.

I didn't hear the shot. There was a lotta hollerin at the time—beatin, hollerin, the motor was goin. So we backed around and come up the road and Velma Coach's head was bleedin, you know. Just as we backed out in the highway one of those guys draw back and rapped at my head. Like he was battin a ball the way he hit that car—boom! But I looked thataway and by the car bein movin the top of the car caught that lick. If that had hit on my head that time, I would've been in serious trouble.

What was so pitiful, Jim Bolton was a sheriff that I help elected. And he was sittin up on a car with his legs crossed lookin down at the deputies and he didn't say one word. He had told me that mornin, he had told me, "Square, keep em on the left side of the road so cars can pass." He knowed that I would not ever leave the nonviolent movement and would keep down any violence. The next day I come back to Somerville and went in the courthouse and I told Jim Bolton, "Well you sure did treat me nice. You set up on your car and let your deputies beat on me and you didn't say a word. That's the thanks you give me for helpin elect you sheriff."

Some of em had said, this is just hearsay now, "If you beat the hell outa Square and get him off the street, the other boys'll go home." And so they did beat the hell outa old Square, but Square went back the next day and walked the streets. I told some of the boys, "Look, I want you all just to stand out here and watch me. I'm gonna walk the street about thirty minutes by myself and I'm gonna really let em know this beatin don't worry me at all." At that time I had two signs. I just throwed the signs back on my shoulder and walked out of the courthouse back on the street. The boys stood around and I went from one end of the street to the other. Nobody with me, up and down the street. So after about twenty or twenty-five minutes the rest of em joined me on the street. I wanted to let em know we wasn't there to be run off the street because we got beaten there. As long as the people wanted to do a job I was there with em.

Velma Coach

My name's Velma Coach. My age is twenty-seven. Born 1943 in Fayette County. My first civil rights march I went to Memphis right after Dr. King got killed. Really, he just seemed like one of the family got killed. I wasn't angry, just kinda sad. Then I was on the Poor People's March in '68—we went on into Mississippi and went on into Washington.

In '69 I started marchin in Fayette County. We marched from McFerren's store downtown and went to jail. They had said if we walked on the courthouse grass we'd all be arrested. So we all went on the grass and we were all arrested. The first time I ever been in jail. I wasn't afraid but the two or three days I was there it seemed like it was about a month. It's not no good feelin. Cell door locked.

The day that I got shot I'd been marchin that day. Mrs. Wright, she came up and said the police had baseball bats and shotguns and things. We thought we would go down and tell the children to come back up here to the school. By the time I got there they said, "Any damn niggers here?" and by the time I looked around they was jabbin sticks in the car. Didn't want one of em to hit me. By the time I looked around to see what was goin on, why that's when Brother Doyle shot me. He was right there at the car with a pistol. Musta been a bad shot not to kill me. Shot me in the head. Then they wouldn't let the ambulance come by.

Later some FBI from Memphis, they came up to talk with me. He told me to leave everything up to them and he would do the rest. He hasn't talked to me since. That's about all I can do about that. After what he said I lost confidence. I feel kinda shaky when I go through town.

Harpman Jameson

I have felt violent several times. In dealin close with the organization we always call our marches nonviolent. And we made up our will and free mind for nonviolence and we marched. But I often had the feelin that just a little bit of shovin, they'd've had good exercise if I'd've had a few licks. I saw that point. I woulda liked to done that a lot. But goin along with the organization I went nonviolent. It was hard to keep that violence down. It really was. I had to work with myself close to make the movement nonviolent like I did because I did spend some time overseas and I did know a little violence and it was hard for me to stay away from it. Just shovin—there wouldn't've been much to it. But that mighta brought on a gunfight and triggered the thing off, so I'm glad that it stayed nonviolent as far as it did.

I have a jail record now. I got to be forty-seven years old in this mean county and hadn't had a jail record. We was marchin, a nonviolent march for the Hobson women, and we had had several nonviolent marches before. We always marched from McFerren's store downtown and we would have our speakin rally on the courthouse steps. So this particular time we marched down and the sheriff said we couldn't have it on the steps. To keep the steps clear he said we couldn't step on the grass—if anybody stepped on the grass he could consider hisself arrested. I thought I payed as much tax at this particular courthouse as the sheriff did and I just wanted to feel that grass. But if I stepped on my tax-paid grass I would be arrested. So I was the one stepped on the grass—there was about three hundred of us stepped on the grass. But I was one of the first that stepped over on this grass. So I was arrested.

They didn't put us in jail that day—this was on a Sunday. So they told us to come back Monday morning, nine o'clock. We went and they couldn't get the deal cooked up, what they were gonna put us in jail on. They got some lawyers outa Memphis and whatnot to work em outa the sweat box. So they told us to come back Tuesday. We went back up there Tuesday. Anyway they got some kinda cooked-up case on us. So all that couldn't give a $350 bond had to go to jail. So I was one of the ones that couldn't give it, or didn't try to give it, and I went to jail along with about forty or fifty more.

One cell would accommodate eight people. They had eight bunks in there and four mattresses. And they had twenty-eight of us in this cell. There was a little window on the east side and two on the south side. The two on the south side of this cell—they was nailed down. You didn't get no air outa these particular windows. So there these twenty-eight men was—in this small cell. To get to the commode when they was layin down on the floor at night you had to pick a place, step maybe between a man's arm or down by his neck. We had the whole floor covered. I laid on the table—one of these picnic tables like—and another fellow was layin on the bench parta the table and there was two under the table. So we took up all the room that was in this particular cell.

It gives your mind a long wonder back. Especially, you been in service. You go back and think about the hard days you had in service—in your mind bein fightin for your country—and you come home and be treated like this. It gives you a no-good mind towards the power structure. I knew I hadn't done nothin. And then too, I guess why it went so hard with me bein in jail, I hadn't never been in jail, and old as I was it was a completely new experience to me all around—to see the sheriff lock the door.

And let me tell you another thing. I saw the damnedest thing in jail ever I saw in my life. There was a damned white prisoner sittin up there playin cards—this is what got me—and he was key-turner to the jail. He was a white trustee. Playin cards. Sittin on the counter playin cards. And he had this whole big ball of keys on his side. I come to find out he was cuttin time for stealin somethin. And I'm locked up and he had keys on his side. He had committed a real crime and I hadn't done nothin but stepped on the grass. I always thought a deputy sheriff or someone kept the keys.

Later on they moved me upstairs and I looked out one mornin and what did I see—they had two Negro deputy sheriffs on the force at this time, wearin uniforms and a big .38 set up on their side. These Negroes was walkin around down there pickin up paper offn the jail campus with a stick and then this white trustee walkin around down there totin the key. I thought, that's the damnedest thing ever I saw. They were used as janitors. Pickin up paper around the jail. And I didn't know they could put a man so low with a .38 on his side. And I didn't know a man stealin somethin could have so much honor to tote the keys to the whole county jail.

So I got quite a experience down there. Before I got out I guess they thought there was gonna be some inspection of the jail. They moved all of us outa that jail to other jails—about five of em. They were gonna have a clean jail for the day inspection come.

The day I was gettin out my wife went with bond. The meantime the sheriff was in charge. We'd been knowin each other all our days from six years old on up. And he knowed where I lived. He used to be my insurance man. And he knowed my whole family and I knowed his. Meantime my wife was up there makin my bond. And well as he knowed me he could not call down to the jail and tell the key-turner to let me out and let me come on up to the courthouse to sign the bond. Here he comes sendin two big deputies down there to march me from the jail uptown to the courthouse—like I had probably broke in a bank and stole thirty thousand dollars or somethin. And the hell parta it—I was makin my own bond and my wife had signed it—now what was I gonna run for? And then these two big deputies—one of em was a farmer in this district. Anyway, I passed a few words with him and he said, "Remember, you're still a prisoner."

I said, "Yeah, I know that. The county said it but I don't feel like I'm one."

So it was a great experience bein down there in the jail. I've often heard of people sufferin in jail. I've often heard of people killed in jail, beat up in jail. With a trustee totin keys any damn thing can happen to you in jail.

Linnell Settles

Linnell Settles was one of the leaders of the boycott and demonstrations. His memories of violence and southern justice show why the Hobson incident aroused his passionate commitment.

My name is Linnell Settles. I'm thirty-two years old and I was born in Fayette County. What really got me into the movement was the experience I had with the police. I was speedin goin through Germantown and a roadblock was set up and I was headed off by the city policemen of Memphis. I turned on a dark street where they surrounded my car. I was told to get out and put my hands up on top of the car, which I did. And they went to searchin me and searchin the car. I was hit back of the head with somethin and I was knocked down. I was picked up by two officers and they held me up and two officers beat me in my stomach and lower, in my pride. After they beat me, when they turned me loose, I fell on my face. They started stompin and kickin me then. I was kicked and stomped in the back of the head, all in the side, and after they got done kickin me they raised the hood of the car to search the trunk and I just lay there on my face. They came back and started kickin me again, told me to get up. And I told em I couldn't get up, my back was hurtin. So they kept kickin me. Then this one officer pulled a gun and threatened to shoot me. Another one went to the car and I figured that they were gonna run over me or do somethin cause I heard em talkin. I told em to give me a chance to get up. I crawled up to the car and tried to pull up by the trunk. They started beatin and kickin me and it took a long time to get up. I know it was a good while because I fell back down sometimes. Then they put me in the police car and on the way to jail they beat me. I was unable to sit down on the seat because my back hurt so bad so I had to lean to one side. And they would shove me. One would shove me to the other one. And they kept hittin me. One would hit me, then shove me. They did that all the way to the police station.

They took me to the hospital after they wrote me up a ticket. I was hand-cuffed to the bed. I was told to give a urine specimen which I was unable to do—my pride was swollen so, I was unable to make water. The doctor came and looked at me. They went out. Really they didn't do anything. I just lay with the handcuffs on. I complained that the handcuffs was hurtin my hands but they wouldn't do anything. So I just laid there that night. Next mornin they came and told me I could make one phone call. They took the handcuffs off and my wrists was sore. The blood circulation was cut off. I was unable to dial the phone. A lady dialed the phone for me and I called my uncle and he came to jail for me and I was bailed out.

I got a lawyer and went to trial. I was fined for runnin several red lights. Some I didn't run. I only remember runnin about three red lights—two or three. I was charged with about six I guess. After I got outa jail I went back to the hospital because I wasn't able to straighten up—I could hardly walk. I had to hold on to somebody to get around. I stayed in the hospital for about a month before I was able to walk. They put me in a sling and put some weights on my leg and I had to have my bed elevated a certain way. And they kept heat lamps to my back for a long time. When I did get out I couldn't straighten up.

About a week later I went back to work and they told me I had to wait for the security man to check it out before I could go back to work.

The thing that hurt me most in this first case was after I went to this lawyer he told me, "I have to have three hundred dollars to even take the case." I later went back to him with the three hundred dollars. I had to quit my job in order to get it. I had the money up there in credit union but they wouldn't let me have it till I quit. So I drawed all my money down from Sears and I went back to him. He looked at me, he told me, he said, "Seem like you been hurt bad enough. I'm gonna tell you, I'm gonna be frank with you, you don't have a third of a chance of winnin." He said, "I'm not gonna hurt you more. I'd rather not hurt you more, I don't want to take your money because I've had too many cases like this and there's nothin you can do about it." I still didn't stop there. I went to several other people. I filed a complaint to the Ad Hoc Committee and I talked with some preachers and I talked with some federal men over in the federal buildin. But it all led to nothin. It was just disgustin.

After that I had the same thing happen. I was beaten again. My cousin was arrested and I happened to be at the place he was arrested. I was fixin to take him home. I didn't know the lady had called the police. I was carryin him out the door and the officer came in and they stopped me. I told him, I said, "I was fixin to carry him home up the street."

He said, "We got a disturbance call or somethin."

I said, "Well, he's been in the hospital and he's been under some treatment. If you'll let me I'll take him on home. He stay right up the street."

By that time another squad car came up and he jumped from the car, the policeman did. He said, "You wanna go with him?"

I said, "No. Forget it." And I turned away to walk on off.

He said, "Wait a minute. You wanna be smart." And I kept on walkin. He grabbed me by the seat of my pants and brought me back to the car and said, "C'mon, you can go with him." When he brought me back to the car I believe my cousin kicked the door open. The door came open and it shoved me back against the police officer and then he hit me and there was a few licks passed. Later, a friend walked up to em and said, "Go ahead on to jail. Don't you all beat him. Take him on to jail if he did somethin wrong." And so I agreed to go on to jail. I wasn't hurt at the time. Everybody seen that I wasn't hurt.

When I got to jail there was about four or five officers there in the back waitin on me. There may've been more than that, I don't know how many more. Some of em was with us and some at the station was waitin I guess. As we walked around in the hall there they told us to get against the wall. Then this colored officer pulled his pistol off and asked if anybody wanted to fight now. Ain't nobody said anything. I was watchin him. I thought he was gonna be the one that hit me, but somebody come outa the other end of the hall—a white policeman—and he hit me. I don't know what he hit me with, some knuckles or somethin, cause I was lookin the opposite direction. When he hit me blood flew from my face and I caught my face with my hand, and at that time they all just started beatin and swingin on us. They beat us all for a while and then they started beatin just me. After I had fell on my face I was layin there bleedin and they stomped me. I bled quite a bit. There was a large puddle of blood—I guess as wide as I am tall. Blood was all around. Just layin in the blood. And they stayed there stompin. Colored officer, he quit after I had fell. I was stomped severely on the concrete and I had my teeth broken. My teeth were broken in little pieces in my mouth. And I was cut up over the eye real bad. One just took his shoe and just kicked down on my ear till he tore it loose. My ear was tore loose plus my eardrum was busted. After that I just lay there in the blood.

They thought I was dead, my cousin and them, they thought I was dead. Later they came back. Seems like both times they just stomp you till you get up. I don't know what kept me alive really. I got up with a little help and they carried me on back to the paddy wagon and they carried me from there to the hospital. I was so bloody. They sewed me up and one doctor came back later. He hadn't even noticed my ear was tored loose. I was so bloody, he was wipin blood. He sewed my eye up and after he got through wipin blood he said, "Oh, your ear's tored loose!" And he sewed my ear up. Of course, my eardrum was busted too, but they didn't detect it at the time. I was later carried on to jail. I was bailed out the next day. Again my back was hurtin me. I couldn't straighten up. I could not walk. I went to this friend's house because I didn't want to go home by myself and they cared for me a little while. I didn't want my parents to be involved. I really didn't want my mother to know about it.

I lost all respect for law and order. I lost faith in people because I filed all kinda complaints and there was nothin bein done about it. And this last time they threw it out. I never even been to trial for it because they didn't want to hear it. I had so many witnesses that I wasn't hurt when I left the corner. They denied beatin me in jail. What happened was—somehow I just kept hopin that someday somebody, you know, people would wake up to what really happened. It was hard for me to believe at first that that could be done to a person and nothin would be did about it. I didn't give up. I kept on. But it was still nothin did.

I guess that was why I got into the situation in Somerville. I heard about the beatin of the Hobson women and I knew the law enforcement wasn't goin to do anything about it. And the people seemed to be gettin together about doin somethin. I was behind it all the way because I knew what it meant to be beat by people—by a lotta em. I knew what it was to try to get justice. I thought somethin shoulda been did about it. I was willin to help in any way I could. I knew how it was with me. I couldn't get any help myself. I went out all the way and I boycotted the town. I helped with the McFerrens and so forth. At one time we was doin good, havin nice marches and the people was really willin to do somethin about it. They wanted to know what to do. And then here came a split in the movement. I think some of the guys was bought out.

We marched on the courthouse lawn and a lotta us was jailed. We couldn't meet on the courthouse lawn. We had to go to Memphis to get southern justice. Really, we couldn't get any out here. We had to get a permit to march and we had to wear a armband or somethin like that.

One Saturday we was beaten by the people of the town. Some of em wasn't even from the town because I saw some from the city. There was a whole lotta whites with baseball bats and so forth. We was tryin to boycott the town non-violently because we know we didn't have no help from the police department and all we could do was try to stay together. After they started swingin baseball bats I noticed this lady bein hit and she had fell. I ran over to protect her as best I could. There were eight or ten men over her with baseball bats and I was hit once or twice. I pulled her back and a lotta these people became frightened and they ran at this point. They ran back under cover. Some of the marchers tried throwin bottles back at the people who had attacked em with baseball bats. After that I got mosta the people offa the street. Later I was arrested with some more fellows. Wasn't none of the people with baseball bats arrested. They all went their way I guess. They carried me to jail. I stayed in jail quite a while. I stayed about three days. In jail they beat one fella. He had a camera; he was takin pictures. They beat him real bad. In fact I think, I know he had to go to the doctor. They didn't beat me, but they beat him really, really bad. It was real crowded. They put me in a cell with more prisoners and a few more guys. It was unsanitary all the way. Just filthy.

The boycott was finally broken when white leaders managed to pay off some Blacks and intimidate others. This discouraging turn of events was made possible after league leaders agreed to permit a handful of young Black organizers from outside the county to assist them in coordinating protest activities for the Hobson incident. White money eventually turned these young organizers against the league and the Black people of the county. They turned their energy to creating confusion and division among the people. Picketers marching in support of the boycott found themselves challenged by picketers declaring the boycott was over. Rumors were circulated to add further confusion. The league reasserted its authority and the discredited organizers left the county, but the damage was already done. Blacks began to trickle back into the white shops. Many league members will still not buy so much as a candy bar in Somerville, but, from the storeowners' point of view, the Black stranglehold has been broken. All this left loyal boycott leaders like Linnell Settles angry and frustrated.

In some ways the boycott worked. At one point they were ready to give in to our grievances. We'd asked for better police protection. There were several things we asked for and they was willin to meet us at every point at one time. And that's when this split came in the movement. We stayed on the streets and a lotta people said, "Pull outa the movement. Pull out and pull back." They tried to get me to pull back, but I knew it was a sellout. I tried harder to keep the boycott effective. But there was different rumors; they'd tell different stories on me to different people. Some of the leaders had sold out and then they tried to brainwash the people into believin it. And while I was walkin the street boycottin the town, they was ridin around misleadin the community, you might say. That's what tore the boycott down. Later they had some Black people come on the streets sayin, "Shop, shop, shop." I understand they were paid to do that, to walk the streets sayin, "Shop, shop, shop." We were picketin sayin "Don't shop" and they were sayin "Shop." I had to go to Memphis to go to court one day and that was the day they came on the street to fight the picketers. They was paid to do this. And all the time they spread rumors that I was workin with the McFerrens and that the McFerrens had sold out. I knew it was wrong because the McFerrens would carry me and bring me to picket the streets and they got me out every time I was arrested. The people who were out to break us would have little boys doin things, little children doin things. They'd throw cans at us and so forth. One day I was marchin and they said that I walked into a little child and I was arrested for it. I was carried to jail and I was fined. And each time I was arrested John got me out. John McFerren. He put up the money.

Mosta the Negroes, the majority of em, really didn't know and understand. They knew only what they were bein told by certain leaders. After the split in the movement they was confused—they didn't know what was right and what was wrong, really. By me stayin and boycottin the street every day I was unable to communicate with em because mosta em was afraid to go out on the street. A lotta em lived on white peoples' places. Some had been threatened. I think a lotta em was a victim of Tent City too—they knew what it was like. They had got pushed till they were afraid to come out really. They didn't know what step to take, a lotta em. They told em we had sold out and this and that and so I said, "Only thing I can do is demonstrate and prove to em that we haven't. I'll do the best I can." But a lotta em became frightened. They even told me that "you're gonna be killed, so you better come off the streets." Certain people goin around tellin people this and that, sayin, "You gonna have your own people fightin you." I understand that some of em was paid to go against us. Some of em were given guns. They were told, "If you shoot a man there'll be nothin done about it." There was a lotta loose guns. I know because I had the opportunity to buy one if I wanted one. They had just put guns in the hands of people to go against us.

The split came with this young organizer we brought in from the outside. At one point I think he was doing real good. In fact, I think he's a great organizer myself. But I have seen this happen to lotsa people—they'll reach a point and seems like they'll sell out. That's what I know happened. He sold out to the power structure. I couldn't name em, but the result was that people started tellin me to come off the street, that somethin was gonna happen if I didn't. I refused to come off the street because I knew what they had did. But by me stayin out there I missed out on a lot that was goin on in the neighborhood—I didn't know that they was passin out different pamphlets sayin things contrary to what we were tryin to do. They had people so confused they didn't know what step to take. That's why we were unable to get a march together. While I was boycottin the street they was ridin around gettin the people confused and flustered.

Several times I was approached by people with guns and so forth. Like a man walked up to me once with a gun. I could see it in his pocket, his hand in his pocket. And he told me I'd cursed his sister. He was a white fellow. And all I would do was keep watchin him and turn my back to him. I thought "Maybe he wants to shoot me in the back. At least I'm gonna give him the opportunity." I knew he wanted me to fly off the handle and argue with him, but I never would stop and talk to him. I said, "No it wasn't me. In fact, I'm not supposed to talk with people on the street. I'm just marchin."

I've tried to get work, but it's hard to get on any decent job since the boycott. I've worked several places, but they wasn't payin anything. Anytime you go try to get a decent job they gonna ask you this and that and they check your record. And I think that boycott affected me gettin a good job. In fact, I'm sure of it. I just feel like the way it is outside I'll just have to learn somethin on my own. I used to hate bricklayin but I tried that. I said, "I'll go into that. My father was real good at it." I made myself do it. I said, "I'll just have to do my own thing." I've got to where I can lay pretty good, but my back—I just can't stand to bend since that beatin. I find if I work a day, at night if I don't get in a tub of hot water or do somethin my back is gonna bother me all night.

I wouldn't say things is as rough as ever, but I wouldn't say it's too good. Mosta the Negroes hoped there would be a change, but there was the split in the boycott and confusion and mosta em still depends on the white merchant to get his credit and so forth. It's not better. You still have a majority of em dependin on the white man. As for me, I'm not really afraid of the police and the power structure—I just know em, I know what they can do. They won't beat you in public too fast—they'll try to be nice—but if they catch you on a dark street and a lotta em get together they'll beat you. That's why I knew what happened when I read about that Hayes boy in Memphis a few months ago. He started speedin in the city and they caught him and beat him to death and they turned in a report that he was thrown from a truck. But they beat all three of the boys—there was two others with him—and they told that they hear him hollerin. He was beaten. Then he stopped hollerin. I guess they killed him at this point. I've been in a nervous shock since then because I knew how they did me. I just said, "They killed him." Later, an investigation proved that he was beat to death. There was about thirty policemen suspended after that. To tell the truth, I haven't had too many good nights' rest since then. It's a horrible thing, you know. It's horrible. People are just—just to see a person beat another person when he's helpless. Cause I know the way they did me. I begged em to let me try to pull up. I couldn't even get up. And every time I'd get up on my legs they'd stomp me right back down. And I did that for so long I decided to lay there. Then I was threatened. If I hadn't gotten up they would've killed me too. I hate to think about it really.

Viola McFerren addressing a rally demanding justice for the Hobson women

Boycott march supporting the Hobson women

Justice for the Hobson women! Women take the lead.

Somerville police subdue protestors.

"Black man don't get no justice here. I'm tellin the truth. Black man do not get no justice here. Not here in Fayette County. They just do what they want and nothin to fear, nothin to say."
—Mrs. Raymond Hobson

"I don't know of anything that I have done that I would not redo. For example, spending too much time away from home or from the children or not having very much of a family life when it comes to my husband. I know that we're short on these things. But at the same time I feel that the things that we're doing are worthwhile. I don't regret it. I don't think I can stop yet."
—Viola McFerren

"I had my half-brother come sit down with me and talk hours at a time tellin me, 'You oughta drop this kinda stuff because, man, you got a big family before you.' And I told him, 'I think about what Martin Luther King said—'A person that haven't seen nothin worth dying for, he's not fit to live anyhow.'"
—Square Mormon

"When I was young and never been nowhere I was livin in dreams. That's what started me goin. I'd dream about all the places everywhere and decided I'd see if I could find em. I found em. Yeah, I found the things I dreamed about. I don't feel sad now. I've traveled."
—Gyp Walker

Minnie and Harpman Jameson

"I was married in 1948. I guess I thought I had saw the world and done some of everything and figured the next thing was marryin. . . . We'd known each other about seven years before we married. We was walkin, comin from a neighbor's house of hers across the woods there on Sunday evening, and I asked her to marry me, and she didn't say much, she didn't want to talk too much. I hadn't prepared no speeches. Just somethin she said made me—and I asked the question. And so she looked at me and she didn't say nothin. I said, 'I know what the answer's gonna be.' And she said, 'You do, huh?'"
—Harpman Jameson

John and Viola McFerren lead a march to honor civil rights activists killed in Selma, March 1965

PART VII

"DOIN SOMETHIN YOU KNEW WAS RIGHT"

Trouble in the Schools: 1969–1970

Tension from the Hobson incident remained when school reconvened in September. The blatant injustice of the Hobson beating stimulated Black high school students to protest the injustice that affected their own lives most directly. Since Edward Gray entered Fayette High in 1966 there had been some integration in the schools, but not very much. The high schools remained segregated by any reasonable definition of the word. W. P. Ware High School remained entirely Black whereas Fayette County High School was predominantly white. In addition, the facilities of W. P. Ware High School were far worse than those in the white school. The Board of Education could not even honestly claim that schools in the county were separate but equal. Students at W. P. Ware decided to dramatize this situation by leaving their classrooms and marching into the white school to register. There is no reason to deny that this action was provocative. But surely a county Board of Education that ignores the law of the land for fifteen years is being far more provocative. The band of demonstrators arrived at Fayette High and the sheriff and his deputized mob rushed to meet them. Ophelia Gray describes what happened and David Niles recounts the tense aftermath to the confrontation.

Ophelia Gray

When I was workin at Fayette High, the previously all-white school, the students marched from the Negro school to the white school. I was at the white school.

When the students got there—somehow, I guess the principal had called the other principal and told em that they were comin—the principal at the white school had all the doors locked, told everybody to lock the doors and don't let anybody in. However, one of the doors wasn't locked so the students came in. They said they wanted to register.

I guess the principal must've called the police. When the police came, I'm standin there lookin about to die cause of what's happenin. They came in. They didn't ask any questions. They had, you know, these long blackjacks; they didn't have these small short ones, nightsticks I guess you call em. They just started beatin heads, you know, beatin and runnin, beatin and runnin. They didn't ask any questions. They just started beatin, beatin, beatin. Well the kids they got hysterical. It was about six hundred of em. If everyone's crowded in the hall, well there you are. They beat everybody out. Kids lost shoes, pocketbooks; they were bloody and everything else. I'm standin there watchin and here comes this policeman. I guess he thought I was a student and one of the white teachers say, "Hey, that's a teacher." I guess he was gonna start beatin me too. So I just stood there. I just shook my head. They beat everybody out there and run em all the way back to the other school just beatin. After that we had several more marches on Saturdays, but there wasn't too many more teachers. Then we formed a union.

David Niles Jr.

I really believed in Martin Luther King. I appreciated what he done all over the nation for colored people. When I heard that he died in Memphis it sorta shook me up a little. I felt that the things he said and done, they didn't bring harm to no one. He was only tryin to do God's work. He was only tryin to bring love and peace to white and colored. But the whites just wouldn't accept it.

I got sorta involved in the Hobson protest because they related to all my people. I had to get involved in that because I felt that it brought some shame to the colored people that hadn't done nothin about it.

We young people got along pretty good with people like the McFerrens and Jamesons and Square. The way that they were explainin things to the younger people and also the older people made sense. It wasn't complicated or nothin. So the young people they went along with the boycott. They appreciated it. They had lotsa love for the McFerrens and Square.

We would meet either up at the community center or McFerren's grocery. We'd congregate together and then we'd march downtown to Somerville. Then we'd start our protest. And all of us agreed no kinda violence and stuff like that. In a way it sorta upset you. It'd bring different ambitions. Inside of you you feel like that you want every white person you see—you want to kill em and stuff like that. But still, like I said, we was nonviolent. We was tryin to fight against all the confusion and stuff. We just ignored all the yellin and stuff like that.

Then there was one mornin we marched from W. P. Ware down to Fayette Academy. On that particular day a couple of friends of mine and I, we joined the protesters in town. When we got there we met Baxton Bryant, the representative from the Tennessee Human Rights Commission. All of a sudden these two men, the McQueen brothers, they ran across the street with a shovel. They was plannin on killin that day. So Baxton got up—hurried over to the sheriff's office to report it. The sheriff ignored Baxton. So Baxton went back across the street. He told us, "The sheriff don't give a damn about nothin." So anyway, we was goin out to the cafe to decide on somethin about the boycott. As we was on our way down there the McQueen brothers ran over again and made threats to Baxton, but I stood in front of him and a couple more of my friends was on the side and behind. Anyway we shoved the McQueen brothers outa the way and we told em we didn't want no trouble. It broke down in confusion and we had a little fight. All of a sudden the sheriff ran out and told em to lay off him. I guess they hated to see a Negro savin a white man's life.

That same day Julian Pulliam pulled a knife on Baxton. It looked like every white in town, they wanted to get next to him, they wanted to kill him. I guess the good Lord was with all of us—there's no tellin what they would've done to us that day. We just stuck with it. Pulliam's a big man. It sorta shook us up when he pulled a knife. I was sure of myself defendin myself cause I'm like this—I'm not afraida nothin. I think that I was well protected with my friends. It puts your mind on a gangster picture or somethin. It sorta made me feel like a hero that day. Some of the whites and colored felt proud of what we did that day—savin a person's life. Baxton was pretty cool, but he was shook up also, sorta shook up about the whole deal.

There was quite a few white and colored standin around watchin. The colored, I don't know, it looked like to me that they was scared to come on around and give us a helpin hand. I guess because they lived on the white people's places. They was afraid they would lose their homes and stuff like that and be put out.

Later on that evenin the sheriff had a warrant out for all of us. We went to Memphis to the federal buildin to discuss some different things with our lawyers. On our way back we stopped at McFerren's grocery. All of us were in the back talkin. All of a sudden here come thirty-five or forty cops grabbin Velma Coach, Pepper Jenkins, and also I. Anyway they throwed us in the cell and they kicked us and went out. We stayed in there two days. We got out on bond and when court come up they had me charged for throwin a missile. They made this up—they said they saw me throwin a missile at a motor vehicle. They had Velma Coach charged with obstructin justice. They had Pepper Jenkins also charged for throwin a missile. They charged me a sixty-five-dollar fine. They charged Pepper Jenkins the same thing and three months in jail.

TWO TEACHERS

Myles Wilson was the person most responsible for forming the teachers' union mentioned by Ophelia Gray. For years Black public school teachers had been either cajoled or intimidated into remaining clear of local political issues. Some teachers might privately acknowledge their support of the league's activities, but few of these teachers ever demonstrated this support with meaningful public action. Myles Wilson and Leroy Shaw represent a new breed of teachers who take an active part in community action. The Board of Education's response to these people was to fire thirteen young Black teachers who took an active role in forming a union. The threat of countervailing power had to be crushed. A year later the United States District Court in Memphis ruled that the teachers be reinstated. But a year is a long time and court proceedings are expensive and exhausting. Even when the white community loses a case like this, it manages to make life hard for the defendants.

Myles Wilson

I'm Myles Wilson. I'm twenty-five. I was born in 1945. I was born in Oakland, Tennessee, in Fayette County—a small community. We always lived with white people. When I say lived with em I mean we rented and sharecropped on their farms. When I was about in fourth grade, we had to walk a long ways to school and white kids would always have a bus. We would pass their school goin to our school. They had a brick school and from way back, just as long as I can remember, they always had gas heat and everything. Many times in the winter my little sisters would be cryin and all. Their hands were gettin cold and feet were gettin cold. Mine would be cold too, but I would never cry, you know. I'd try to hold out and set an example. But anyway, even a child at that age could see that there was certainly something wrong with the system, that Black kids shouldn't have to walk that far to school. And you're passin a school just to get to the Black school, when our school was much worse off than the white school. We had a little two-room school—a wooden buildin with two teachers and eight grades. We were supposed to've been takin five subjects each a day and many times we just got left out. So it hindered me as far as my education was concerned and all the other kids also, because it was impossible for two teachers to have eight grades and offer the kids the kinda education they needed and were supposed to have.

I never had any contact with white kids at all. I just remember sometime we would be goin home—they would pass ridin horses, some of the kids round the neighborhood. We used to get in arguments with em all the time. They would call us niggers or throw at us or somethin like that. About the only contact I had with white people was with the white man that owned our place and also a white man owned a little corner-grocery store where mosta the Black people went and got their groceries on credit and stuff. He charged em high interest and stuff. I didn't realize it then, but since I've been grown I found out some of the things that were really goin on back there then as far as white people usin Black people to do their labor almost free. Back when I was young, in elementary school, a lotta white people around in the community—a lotta Negroes thought they was real good people because they let em have groceries and stuff like that. But they didn't really look, or wasn't able to understand that they was just doin this because they wanted em to do their farms free.

One thing that I really look back at is the fact that in 1950–1955 people in my neighborhood were workin for white people for two dollars a day. And I'm not talkin about a eight-hour day—I'm talkin about ten hours. They would go to the fields at six o'clock in the mornin and get an hour off, sometime thirty minutes, for lunch, and stay until six or seven in the evenins. Two dollars a day. It finally went up to two-fifty a day and when I left it was three dollars a day. Three dollars a day and you work five days a week—that's fifteen dollars. My family was a small family. We had four kids and my mother and my father—that's six. You can imagine a family of eight or nine or ten tryin to live off fifteen dollars a week. You couldn't do it. So what they would do, when they got the fifteen dollars—and maybe if your mother worked or somethin you got twenty-five or thirty dollars—you could never buy anything, you'd just go and pay the white fellow fifteen dollars and take up some more stuff. Next time you take up some more. And they were gettin rich—gettin the labor done free, you might say. The man that we stayed with then, Mr. McLennon, he has retired, sold hundreds of acres of land. He has a house now, sittin way up on the hill, about thirty-five or forty rooms. You can see him out playin golf and I just think back—how he used Black people way back there to get rich and they are still poor. They really made his money and built the whole community as far as I'm concerned. It's kinda bad to look back on, but it's history now. It's terrible. And sometime you build up a certain amount of hatred in you for that, but I guess it's somethin we have to cope with and try to use our best judgment.

When I had got to high school I had only been to the movies one time—to see Elvis Presley in *Jailhouse Rock*. My mother carried me to see that movie. We sat upstairs in the balcony. Whites were downstairs—that's where we had to go then. But anyway, it's kinda amazin, you look back and say, "I was in high school and only been to a movie one time in my life."

I had some friends that planned to go to college and I guess about my junior year we all—there was about six of us—we decided to go to college. I figured if I went on to college to further my education I might be able to come back to Fayette County and help some kids that were there. I thought I understood the problems fairly well. I didn't have any money but when I first went to college that spring my father managed to raise four hundred dollars to start anyway. They borrowed money from kin and tried to pay it back.

One thing in high school we always wanted to do was to change the name of the school from Fayette County Trainin School to some other name. We always resented the school bein named a trainin school. The "trainin" part seemed like you were in some kind of institution. I remember how when I went off to college—I attended Lane College, a small private college in Jackson, Tennessee—I remember we had a freshman-orientation program the first week and we had to stand up and tell our names and where we were from and the name of the school. And so another fellow and I gave our names and our address and said that we were from Fayette County Trainin School and everybody started laughin. It really got me. I was very pleased about my junior year in college when they got the name changed from 'Trainin School' to 'Ware.' After the first court suit the county Board of Education started going along with Black schools as far as doin things. See they wanted to keep em separate, so what they would do was to try to please you as much as possible to keep you from wantin to go to the white school. So if this meant kinda quietin Black people down, then they would go on and change the name. I think they would rather you have almost anything in the Black school than to mix with them.

After I finished school I came back to Somerville to try and help and straighten out some of the problems there. I feel that we have done some of the things I set out to do, but we still have a long way to go. It's kinda hard workin with the people there. They don't want it. Anytime you have people in charge of an establishment against somethin and your forces are at a minimum you have a hard time getting somethin done. Even though we are in the seventies with Black people in good positions throughout the country, in Fayette County you still have white people dictatin to Black people. Black people have had it so hard till now, they fight each other for position, you might say. A Black person in the school system won't hesitate to hurt a Black person or to try to gain somethin for himself. We were kinda faced with that at the time. I don't call any of the people Uncle Toms and all, I just say that some of the people—I try to understand some of the things that they went through that caused em.

When I first got there I worked in a Black school—all-Black administration. The people in the top positions wouldn't go and help fight. In other words, they would just say, "Well, they're not goin to do it. Don't worry about that." So I had to find out what I could do next. I had to try to bypass them in order to get somebody else who could do somethin about it. It was very hard to do that. We worked on some things and drew up a proposal and submitted it to the board—to make the learnin situation conducive. Gettin hot water in the showers. You just couldn't get it until we had some demonstrations. After that we finally got some of the things, but we still don't have many of em. As far as attackin the problems, not only then but now, I'm still runnin into complications gettin some of those solved.

In September 1969 school started and I was the student-council advisor. When I was in high school I never played football. Always liked football. Matter of fact, it's my favorite sport now. But I never had an opportunity to play because we didn't have a football team. They had a football team right down the street there at the white school. So we tried to work on getting a football team started, gettin our baseball field lighted, gettin some hot water in the showers. Anybody, any fool, can see that if a school right down the street, supported by the same tax money that our school is supported with, that if they have a lighted baseball field we oughta have one; that if they have football we oughta have it. The reason I worked on football and sports so hard is that we have a large student enrollment, a lotta boys, and they had good talent. Sports have provided great careers for many Black people and I felt that a lotta kids could go to college on athletic scholarships and receive a college education and could come back and help their parents and community. But the community missed out on that because the Fayette County Board of Education failed to provide these things for the Blacks.

We also wanted some more courses added to the curriculum to expose the kids to the things that they would need in order to go on to college. I don't think a kid goin on to college, especially a major university, would be able to make it with the limited amount of knowledge they were providin the kids at that time. The administration didn't want to deal with the proposals. They were saying we teachers were tellin em what to do and we didn't have a right to tell em. They saw fit that if the school needed somethin then they would do it. We had some marches at school. The kids walked out one day and marched downtown to the other school. I think this was a brave effort, a courageous effort on the parta the students—for young kids fourteen and fifteen and sixteen years old to stand up and say, "This is wrong."

When I was student-council advisor, the student council drew up a proposal. The president of the student council signed it as president, the secretary signed it as secretary, and I signed it as advisor. And later on, the superintendent tried to make an issue of me signin it, sayin I was instigatin this. Matter of fact, we went to court later on. I was fired from the school system. It was because of these things and my opinions. They never gave any reason in federal court as to why they fired us. I've concluded it was because of these things. In federal court he once mentioned that it seems like these teachers didn't do what they could have done to try to stop the kids from doin some of the things. And once he mentioned the fact that my name was signed at the bottom. But kids now—they have the ability to think and they understand things and I'm not afraid to say that I will try to help em, or did help em, to change things that need to be changed, as long as I stay within the framework of the law. I understand the process pretty good and I try to stay within the framework of the law, but not necessarily the regulations that they have—I don't consider all the rules and regulations that they have to be within the framework of the law. You have the right under the Constitution of the United States to protest your grievances anytime you want to in a manner that is not disturbin to other people and as long as you're nonviolent. You have a right to do this. As long as they're within the framework of the law I wouldn't hesitate to help the kids do anything.

The first two years I was teachin, my messages and my efforts didn't really get to the people in charge. They didn't pay em any mind. But then the third year we formed a teachers' union associated with the AFL-CIO. They found out about this. We didn't try to keep it a secret. We opened up a bank account in one of the local banks and rented a mailbox at the post office. Some of the teachers, they were willin to join—they wanted to change things, they wanted a pay raise, and they wanted workin benefits better—but mosta em were afraid to sign their name for membership. We did get enough members to get out a charter. Even when we started payin dues, many Black teachers who were afraida the administration wanted to pay in cash rather than to pay by check so the check wouldn't go through the bank. That was durin the same year as the demonstrations, the same year I was advisor to the student council, and the same year that we got some of the things done that we wanted to get done.

So at the end of that year I received a letter along with all the younger Black teachers in the high school. Younger fellows, under twenty-five. Some of em were the most competent teachers in the school. We received a letter. It didn't say anything specific. It just said that you wouldn't be rehired. I kinda felt that this would happen because we had heard rumors. One thing I have to say about Fayette County—if you hear rumors, they're just about true here. The thirteen of us received our letters and all. We filed a suit in federal court contestin this because we felt it was wrong. We hired a Black lawyer from Nashville—Attorney Avon Williams—one of the most competent lawyers in Tennessee, I feel. We went right into court that October.

When we got into court they had different reasons on different people. Some of the teachers, they said outright that they were incompetent. They had arguments, or didn't pay debts, or things of this nature. The judge really came down on em about that one Black teacher, Mrs. Johnson. The superintendent got up there in court and said that the tennis teacher recommended that she wouldn't be rehired. The tennis teacher didn't have any official capacity as far as recommending teachers be hired or fired. Mrs. Johnson was a teacher with twenty-five or thirty years of service. Back when they had the small, Black, one-room schools, one like I spoke of attendin, her school was way back there in the field—dirt roads, muddy and all. The milk trucks didn't go back up to the Black schools. We didn't get milk for a long time, but when we finally started gettin it they would put it out way up at the highway somewhere and left it up to you to get it there. So she had been carryin the milk up herself, carryin it on her back, and one day she didn't take it. She just didn't feel like it. The tennis teacher said that she had to take it. He said because of this he didn't really think that she was a dedicated teacher. This was the tennis teacher speakin. That's what they fired her about. That's the only reason they gave for firin her. They got up in federal court and said that. The judge said that was the most ridiculous thing he had ever heard of.

I think this is what made our case so strong in court. They really didn't have a case. They wanted to fire all the younger people because we had started a movement, so to speak, somethin that would help the Black people, and they found out that we would stand up for just what was right. You know, the same way all people should. They had decided to get rid of us. I will always believe that the other ladies that were fired with us, that they called incompetent and all—they just wanted to put some more people in so it wouldn't look like they just fired all of us. I felt kinda sorry for em. The reason I worked so hard to get all those people reinstated was because I felt they had been hurt because of us. I don't think they would have been fired if it hadn't have been for us. That summer after we were fired I went to Nashville, which is two hundred miles from here, eight or ten times. And I worked all summer and all fall tryin to get the case in court and workin and supplyin the attorney with information.

I think it really showed some of the older teachers—they have joined the union since then—that these things are possible. It's just not a lotta rhetoric—you know, somebody runnin around talkin and wantin to be seen and all. These things are possible as evidenced by the thirteen teachers bein reinstated. We need these things. We might as well get together and try to work to get em. I think it really helped em in that respect.

Leroy Shaw Jr.

I'm Leroy Shaw Jr. I was born in Fayette County, Tennessee, 1942. I was raised on my father's farm and I didn't have to go through a lotta things a lotta Black people had to go through—sharecroppin and things like that. But soon as you entered school, even at a small age, you could tell the disadvantage of the thing you had to go through. One teacher in a one-room school for the first eight years. And you always wondered why you always got the old books, the old chairs, and everything like that. And when you got in the high school it was still the same problem there. The old desks, not many books in the library, and teachers that were unqualified to teach the subjects they were forced to teach. You might have a math teacher teachin English or an English teacher teachin math and so on like that.

Durin the early parta the summer of '65 there was a program sponsored by the government. It was the Head Start Program. Mrs. McFerren got me a job in the teacher-trainin program at Memphis State University where we worked to prepare to teach Head Start students. The job I got was outa my field, but I got a temporary certificate which lasted two years. Durin the first year of teachin there, you became aware of a lotta things that you never thought about while you was in school. You could see the problems of the children there—they was undernourished, they didn't even bring lunch to school, they didn't have a cafeteria at the school. I don't even think we had the free-milk program there at the time. There was over-crowdin of students there. I had about thirty-nine pupils in my class and there was two grades. I had to teach sixth and seventh grades and about six subjects. That was twelve subjects I had to get over and you can imagine how that was. You only had so much time and you had to split the time up, but this would deprive the children of their learnin.

Around '69 integration was becomin a factor. The schools had the Freedom of Choice plan where you could go to the school you wanted to, but just a small amount did it because it still went back to the problem where you had sharecroppers. If you stayin on the white man's place and he told you not to go to that school, you went to the school he wanted you to go to because you had to think about yourself—eatin and things like that. But durin the last parta that school year it was getting pretty much aware to the white people that integration was comin anyway and they were gonna have to think of some other way to stop progress. Durin that period in '69 I got a letter sayin I wouldn't be rehired. Well I went back to the board and tried to find the reason out. They tried to say it was somethin about my trainin, but yet altogether they was hirin young white mens with less educational experience than I had. I had gone back to school and prepared myself—like I told you, I had a two-year teachin certificate. I had gone to Memphis State University and had met my requirements for another two years. I only lacked about six more hours to be certified in elementary education. I was discriminated against for bein Black and for my sex. Sex, because female Black people then weren't affected—if I had been a female then I woulda still been workin. They were tryin to get rid of mosta the single males because I'd probably have been teachin white students if I'd stayed in the school system. The year afterwards the school I was teachin in was no longer in use and all the students there went to a white school which was about half a mile away.

I had an attorney, Attorney Avon Williams of Nashville, to take up the case. I wasn't really goin into that case tryin to win. I really wanted to protest. I woulda just put up all the money I had just to protest because that's the way they did to hold up things. There wasn't a mass of teachers bein fired like in Myles Wilson's case, there was just my one. I knew that I was right. I knew that they had no business firin me and not rehirin me on the basis that they did. I knew they didn't have a case against me. I had heard a lotta things the principal had said, but not any of those things was true. After goin to the board several times and talkin to the superintendent, he kept pushin me off and tellin me the board just didn't see fit. And I think all the time that he was the one that was head of it all. I could see I wasn't gettin anywhere, so like I said I went to Attorney Williams. It came up in the fall of '70 and it took place at the same time as all these other teachers with Myles Wilson. So we had this altogether at one hearin. It was just amazin. Durin the hearin the Board of Education, they kept turnin things over and over. Everybody they brought to testify against me really proved to be the other way. The principal who they said earlier had caused the firin of me really spoke in behalf of me. I was kinda surprised of that. He didn't say what they wanted him to say. After all of that Judge MacCrae come out at the end of the trial and said there wasn't enough evidence to prove they were discriminatin against me, even though he knew everything they said was really a frame-up, but yet that wasn't enough information. I was dismayed after I lost the case, but I still got an appeal on the case.

I really was surprised to even get hired in the county in the first place because I was involved in the first demonstrations and marches they had in Fayette County. I was leadin the first march and got arrested there. So I had been in jail the summer before the thing started. And I had been involved back in the early sixties, early '61, when everything was breakin loose all over the South. You became aware of things—when you had to go to a movie and go up to the balcony, or go to a lunch counter and you had to stand up there and get your sandwich and leave. You paid the same amount of money as everybody else was payin. We would always march up to the movies and go in. And it was the strangest thing how people just hate you in this country. There was a Black man and a Black woman from another country; I don't know what country they was from. You could tell they was foreigners. And we was all in line and they went right up and got their tickets and went right on inside the movie and nobody really said nothin. We worked for this country and brought it up what it is, yet they hate us. A foreigner can come in this country, people they fought against in World War I and World War II—they have more advantages than we have.

Durin those sit-ins we really stuck to it. We stayed there day and night. I went to jail in Nashville. We got out—we might be right back in there the next day, but we fought it out. We kept puttin so much pressure on the people that they was losin business. The white people didn't want to come because the hecklers on the other side were throwin bricks, bottles, and rocks and they were as likely to get hit as we were. There was a lotta brutality there and mostly from the white hecklers. The police, they were standin back there and lettin em do it. So the movement finally opened up the lunch counters. I think everything we did throughout the country helped influence the Civil Rights Bill that really opened all those things up.

The first march we had in Fayette County, I was leadin the march at the time. There's one little lunch counter, a Rexall Drugstore, in Somerville. They'd let you go in and buy a cream or soda, but you couldn't sit down and eat. So this particular time we—I forget, it was maybe like five men and twenty-five or thirty people there—we went inside and took us a seat. They asked us to leave. And we said, "I came here to get a soda and I'm not going to leave until I get one. I'm gonna pay for it and eat it right here." I'd say it was about three or four o'clock p.m. The store was gettin ready to close up. It normally closed about eight on a Saturday. So he wanted to get the sheriff then. He was gonna swear the warrant. And we said, "We're not gonna leave because this place is not closin up. He's only closin up to keep us outa here. We know the time you close normally." They didn't want to arrest us, but we still didn't want to leave. The man who owned the store swore out a warrant so they arrested us that time. They arrested everybody in that group—a lotta teen-agers and a lotta us also. Mosta the teen-agers were let outa jail that time in custody. But several of us stayed there three or four weeks. I know I stayed there three weeks myself and some stayed longer than I did. I don't know how other people felt about it, but I felt I was doin somethin worthwhile so I'd stay in jail there a year if I thought I could get somethin accomplished.

Later on that year I organized a second march, at the only movie in town, which is the Felt Theater. Kids was jumped on and beat up on that night.

Durin that time we couldn't really see where we were accomplishin too much. We did do one thing, we made Rexall Drugstore take all their lunch counters out—whites couldn't sit down or the Blacks. The peoples weren't as violent then as they are now. The peoples in Fayette County now are worse than the peoples in Mississippi or anywhere else. I never doubted myself. My parents were churchgoin people and I was too. I was really filled with pride. What I was doin, I thought was right. Whatever happened to me, it didn't matter because I was doin somethin I knew was right. And I felt that it was right. It didn't bother me if I got killed there, if I got cut, or beat up or got hurt, because I was doin what I thought was right and I was gonna do it, I don't care what. That's the way I felt every time I went into one. I was never scared. I mean you could be nervous or tense when you got bottles and bricks maybe flyin around your head, but the good thing about it was that you were doin somethin you knew was right. So there wasn't no fear involved for me.

Viola McFerren

The McFerrens had been active in bringing league support to the thirteen teachers who were fired. Once again the white power structure applied vicious pressure.

In October of 1970 we went to federal court with the Black teachers who were fired by the Fayette County Board of Education. We intervened in that case because of being the original plaintiffs in our local school-desegregation case. We'd been in court so many times, I guess it was just like going out on the job again. We got out of court quite late that day. It was about seven o'clock when I got home and I was greeted at the door by John Jr., who's twelve years old and is a very sensitive child. I've had some problems with John. I've never been satisfied with John's ability to read and some other things I've been concerned about.

Anyway, he said, "Mommy, do you know I was going into my classroom and Mrs. Fowler was standing inside of the doorjamb and another girl bumped into me and it made me bump into Mrs. Fowler. Mrs. Fowler caught me by my arm and slammed me against the wall. And then she slammed me against the door and threw me in the room into a chair and said, 'Write five hundred times—I will not hit my teacher.'"

I said, "Son, why didn't you tell her to excuse you and tell her that you were sorry you bumped into her?"

"Mommy, I tried to, but she wouldn't give me time. She just kept slinging me around."

Well, at the very beginning of that school year John and Claudia would come home every day complaining about this lady's attitude towards Black children and towards them especially. We didn't go running cause we realized that children don't always agree with their teachers. And we tried to have our children understand that we want them to respect and obey their teachers. We try to cooperate as much as we can. But we had paid attention to what they had said all along about the attitude of this lady. And John came home for a number of days altogether saying, "Mommy, Mrs. Fowler put me into a hallway." And when the principal, Mr. Glass, catches you in the hall, he'll paddle you and then send you back to your classroom. I asked him why was he coming home, day after day, having been paddled so much? What was he doing that he should not have been doing so much of the time? Cause it bothered me, the fact that if he was just constantly doing things he shouldn't do that caused him to be paddled, then I figured that we needed to check up on this to try to help him overcome what he was doing. But on the other hand, I didn't understand how the principal, even though I knew that they must have policies around the school, I don't see how a principal can just walk up on a child put out in the hall and jump on him and paddle him without knowing anything. It seemed to me he would need to do some investigating because, in my opinion, if you use paddling for punishment, there are some children that don't have to be paddled as much as others. Sometimes, just being placed out there in the hallway—and having your classmates see you leave the classroom and other people see you out there—sometimes that within itself is punishment enough. But I couldn't figure out why he would come home almost every afternoon and he had been paddled.

So John and I talked with little John and we tried to counsel with him—to show him that if he was wrong he would have to refrain from it. And we really had gotten so tough on him he wouldn't tell us anymore if he had been placed out in the hall.

But Claudia, being his classmate, would come home and she would tell me, "Mommy, Mrs. Fowler sent John in the hallway again and Mr. Glass paddled him."

I asked Claudia, "Claudia, do you see John when he's doing things that Mrs. Fowler says he's doing many times?"

And she would say, "Mommy, he wasn't doing anything. Everybody in the room was talking, Mommy, and she didn't send the other children out. She sent him out though."

Or John would say, "Mommy, some other boy was throwing a paper and Mrs. Fowler said I threw it. I told her I didn't throw it and she told me to go out in the hall and stop talking back to her. And I had to go to the hall, Mommy. She told me I had to go. And when Mr. Glass come down the hallway and paddled me, then you'd see her with a smile on her face. She'd be grinning after Mr. Glass paddled me."

So this went on and on until finally Daphne said, "Mommy, why don't you and daddy go up and see about little John before he gets suspended from school."

And I said, "Daphne, it does seem to be a problem."

Finally this thing happened again. John and I went up to talk with the principal. And we told him that John had come home after being paddled so many times that we felt that we needed to come up and have a conference with him and the teacher that had placed John out in the hallway, to see if he was actually creating a problem and to see how we could work together to prevent this thing from continuing. The principal was very nice to talk with on that day, and he said that all of John's teachers admired him and that he was not a problem at all. He had his little file card down on the desk and he said, "Look, I'll show you now all of my problem students. I keep a file on them. And any student that's sent to this office three times—when he comes back the fourth time, then I send him home. And John's name does not appear on this file at all. And John, John is all right. He's a fine boy." And John told him, John Sr., that he had been a boy once. He just wanted to know what was going on and wanted him to feel free to call upon us if they felt that there was something that we needed to know.

I had talked to Mr. Glass earlier about Mrs. Fowler's attitude and I told him, "If you remember, I told you that she even refused to speak to me, Mr. Glass, and I have been here many times in regards to my children and I know she knows who I am because I have been in her classroom with Claudia. And she didn't speak that time. And it's nothing strange at all to meet her in the corridor and she will look the other way." I reminded him that we had even requested that John be transferred from her classroom to another classroom. School had not been in session for more than about two weeks before we made that request. And they did not honor that request. We even talked to the superintendent about it and he seemed to have been afraid. I think he knowed this lady, you know. But he seemed to have been afraid. He didn't say he was, but I could tell from his conversation that he was not free to be a superintendent. Anyway, Mr. Glass never took any action or didn't investigate, it appears, anything we had said about the way this lady had deliberately been harassing Black children and Johnny most especially.

When we went into court with the teacher case—when the motion was filed, the motion also included a number of things such as requesting that all white teachers sending their children to the segregated private schools be dismissed from the public school system as teachers. And I think this really got them uptight. It appeared that she couldn't think of anything better than to do everything she could to try to hurt us or hurt John. So to hurt us she decided to work on the children.

And on this Friday night when I returned and John was telling the story of what happened, I listened and then I went over to the telephone to call the principal. And I asked him if he knew of this incident. Oh he was really ugly and rude on the telephone. He talked to me so ugly and he said, "All of John's teachers are having problems with him." I knew this wasn't true because I know most of John's teachers and I see them passing almost daily, and I think they know me well enough too to stop by and talk to us if they were having this kind of a problem with any of our children.

I then asked him, "Mr. Glass, will you give me the names of these teachers? Who are these teachers?"

And he called the names, "Mrs. Jefferson, Mr. Ewell, Mrs. Knight, Mrs. Smith."

And I contacted them as soon as he hung up. I contacted them and asked them—have they reported problems to him about little John. And they said, no, they had never had to report any problem because they been able to master their classroom with all their students in it. But they didn't know, you know, that this thing was developing, and I didn't tell them that it was because I was trying to build a case if we had to go to court. Then I asked them if they would send me a letter in writing of John's conduct in that classroom and they all did this. After getting these letters I sent copies of them to our lawyer—I sent it to Avon Williams in Nashville, Tennessee.

But in the meantime I talked to our superintendent again about this punishment John was given by the teacher—to write "I will not hit my teacher" five hundred times. And I told the superintendent that we had not had any cooperation from the principal or this teacher and we had tried to communicate with them from the beginning of the school year. We felt that this was pure harassment. John is an energetic child, but we were not impressed that John would attack this teacher or any other big person. I don't feel that way, I really don't. I know children would do something in your absence that they won't do in your presence, but I'm not convinced yet that any of them would strike an adult person at this time. Maybe I'm wrong but I don't feel that way yet.

On this Friday night I asked the principal if he could arrange a conference for us with this teacher. And I asked him if he would invite all of the other teachers that had complained about John to this conference. I called the superintendent and I related to him my call to the principal, Mr. Glass, and what was said in the conversation. I said, "Mr. Bagwell, I don't mean that my children won't do things that they shouldn't, but I don't feel he struck this lady. It seems to me the punishment is wrong. If she wants to punish him because he bumped into her through a mistake I think she should have worded that punishment, 'I will try not to bump into my teacher.' This sounds better than 'I will not hit my teacher.' It seems to me that she's saying he deliberately went up to her and struck her.

And this is what bothers me. If she wants to punish him for being pushed into her through a mistake then spell it out—that this is how she feels. But what actually is going to happen, Mr. Bagwell, they are after us in every way that they can be. She has children over here in the segregated private school and so does the principal, and this will go on John's record. If John writes 'I will not hit my teacher' then he has pleaded guilty to something that he's innocent of. And with us having all the problems we've had, we are not willing for him to write it."

He said, "Oh, Mrs. McFerren, I understand. I suggest you take him to school Monday morning and explain to them why he does not have that punishment written."

So I carried him to school Monday morning. We went past her classroom. She was not in her classroom. Then we proceeded to the principal's office. She was there in a conference with him. They finished their conference and he excused her. She went back to her classroom and he called me in. I left little John out in the waiting room. I told him just exactly what I had told the superintendent. The reason we wouldn't let him write it was we knew this was something she was deliberately trying to do to hurt him and that her attitude had been bad towards us.

And Mr. Glass said, "Well you think she doesn't speak to you, but she has a very bad hearing problem."

And I told him that if her hearing was so bad that she couldn't hear me speak to her as many times as I've spoken, that I didn't believe she could hear those children in her classroom well enough to teach them cause they talk much softer than an adult for most of the time.

Well, he didn't comment. Then he said, "Well, I'll tell you. Everything is all right. We'll just drop that punishment. We'll just drop it."

So I told him we certainly didn't mean our children to be disobedient and we wanted them to respect the school rules and officials and etcetera, but we did want them to talk with us about problems if they felt that the problem was that great. And I asked him if he would just sit in on her classroom sometime. I asked, "Have you ever done it?"

He said, "Well no, I've walked to the door for a few minutes."

I said, "Well would you just sit in on her classroom and see her methods and see how she conducts a classroom? My children come home all the time talking about the funny things she does. If they're telling the truth she does some funny things, You really need to observe this and then you can determine whether or not you can paddle a child every time she puts him out in the hallway."

He didn't talk too much on that. He didn't seem to want to listen to that from me. Anyway he said, "Now Mrs. McFerren would you like for me to call her back in? I'll just tell you the truth—Mrs. Fowler is afraid of you."

"Afraid of me? And she doesn't even speak if she meets me in the hallway. I don't think she even cares about Black people. She doesn't look afraid to me."

"Well she can't hear. She has a hearing problem."

I said, "Well she can see. Each time that I've met her, at one time or another, she looked at me. And I tried to put a smile on my face to say hello and she wouldn't even accept that. She acted as if I was dirt. She's deliberately trying to do this."

He said, "I'll call her back in if you want to talk to her."

I said, "Well Mr. Glass, since you have said that everything is all right and that he will not have to write this punishment—I'm late for federal court. We were to have been there at nine-thirty and it's a quarter until nine now. Could I go and we will contact you as soon as we are out of court and we can arrange a conference at that time and perhaps Mrs. Fowler and I can get to know each other better?"

And he said, "All right."

And I got up and extended my hand and we had a good handshake. I thanked him and I left knowing that everything was all right as he said.

Then on the Thursday of the same week John told us, "Mommy," Mr. Glass told me I've got to write that five hundred sentences 'I will not hit my teacher,' but he told me too change the 'hit' to 'push' and say 'I will not push my teacher.' "

I talked to his father about it. I said, "John, I have tried to communicate with those people. And I thought this thing was all straightened. Would you try to talk with Mr. Glass? Maybe you can talk to him.

Well this was on Friday morning. The children were all going to school. John called up the principal and I heard John say, "Mr. Glass, my little boy said that you told him he's got to write the five hundred sentences, and my wife told me that you and she talked this thing out and that you told her that everything was all right and that it was all dropped. What happened?"

And Mr. Glass told him, "I must uphold my teachers regardless of whether they are right or wrong."

And I heard John say at that time, "Well I'm not going to have you beating him every day."

And then I could see that John was getting angry. I said, "John, don't get in an argument."

So John hung the phone up. Well I turned then to call the superintendent and I couldn't get him. I assumed Glass was on the phone talking to him. After thirty minutes I did get him. I attempted to tell him what had taken place and he sounded so nervous and afraid.

"Well, Mrs. McFerren, you'll get a letter today. Mr. Glass said your son's suspended as of today. He'll get a letter. He'll bring a letter home for you."

So I said, "OK. When we get this letter then we'll contact our lawyer." And I hung the phone up.

We called Attorney Williams that night. They had the hearing set for the Thursday night of the following week. This letter said we could appear before the Board of Education. Attorney Williams said, "I don't want you to go there without me and I am tied up for that day, but I will give you two other dates that I am available, and will you write them a letter and ask them for a continuance of this hearing until such time as your lawyer can be with you." But they went on with that hearing.

We received a letter from the Board of Education saying that, "The Board of Education upheld the suspension of your son John. The principal and teacher were here and we heard from them. And the board feels that this is a reasonable punishment and he should remain suspended until he has complied with the wishes of the principal and teacher." We sent a copy of this letter to Attorney Williams and then he sent them another letter demanding a hearing. And finally they set this hearing for the tenth of December. Well John was out of school from I think about the thirtieth of October until the thirteenth of December. We just couldn't permit him to write that punishment and go back there for them to do something even worse to him.

The first night the hearing was downtown here at the bus garage. The school board has some very cruel-acting members on it, but some of them acted like they were concerned. But their lawyer, he's out of Memphis, he seems to have encouraged the board to just go wild and just be ugly as they could be. The lawyer wrote notes to them and they would read the notes and they would look at each other and they would giggle out loud. And when we were testifying along with the children they would even sniggle at us and—oh, it was just a horrible sight. So, we could see we were not accomplishing anything, but that was the process that we felt we should complete. The thing went on for five different times before it was ended. After they heard our side, then they went out to try to get proof that they were justified in doing what they had done. And after they would run out of ammunition they would recess this thing for two or three days and set it for three days after that time and we'd go back into this thing. I don't know—the children, there were fourteen children that testified and they were simply beautiful. They were students of this lady and they all talked about her—the way she treated Black children. And none of this meant anything to them at all. So the hearings were finally closed and they waited for about a month before they sent us their decision. Their decision was, "We do not find Paul Glass and Mrs. Fowler to be guilty of a wrongful punishment and your son has three days, after the day you receive this letter, to comply. And if he doesn't his suspension will be continued."

We filed in federal court. I don't know what date it was filed, but seemingly in a period of two weeks the judge had arranged for a hearing. We went into the federal court with the same proof we presented out here—the same children. And the school board didn't even have all of the proof that they presented out here, because they had prepared some Black children that testified that John was very bad in class and that he would run around in class and hit other children on the head and this is why she put him out in the hallway. But she never even said that he did those things.

When our lawyer would ask them, "Now little Johnny, did you see this? Did you see little John do this?"

"No sir."

"Well who told you to say this?"

"Mr. Bagwell, that man right over there at that table." That's the superintendent.

"He told you to say this?"

"Yes sir."

You know this is the kind of testimony they had. They didn't even carry all of this stuff to federal court.

The judge was just very upset all through the case. He bawled them out all the way. He told them, "I'm sure the Black community, along with the court, is wondering, 'When does justice prevail?' Now here you are. You had a hearing. You received a letter asking these parents for a continuance of the hearing because their lawyer could not be there at that time. They did not have due process of law granted them. You carried this white principal and this white teacher in before you, a white board, and you made a decision on a Black child. I'm sure the Black community wants to know what kind of school board this is. And I want to know too. Here you have the parent who tried to communicate with the principal and the teacher about this thing and you didn't listen to any of this. If this is the way, if this is what you based your judgment on, I'm ready to rule right now in the interest of the plaintiff in this case."

I don't see any favoritism in him at all. But I honestly do see him as a judge who's interested in fairness. I really do. This is something else he said that I thought was great. He said he really would like to see the child back in school instead of coming down to court every day. We were in court about eight days. And he said, "If you're using him as window dressing"—he was speaking to us and our lawyer—"If you're using him as window dressing, I'd like to let you know I'd like to see him back in school. Now this does not mean that I've given my ruling. He may have to do the punishment or he may not have to do it, I don't know yet, but I'm interested in him getting back in school. I feel sorry for him. He's been behaved here in the courtroom."

Then the school board lawyer said, "Well judge, your honor, you wouldn't be disappointed if you didn't see him back in school before the ruling, would you?"

So we didn't even try to send him back because we could see that they were going to reject him until the ruling came. Well little John wanted to go back every day so we carried him back to court every day. And finally when the judge gave his ruling he said that this was the worst predicament he'd been placed in since he was a judge on the bench. He said that Fayette County was dripping with prejudice and that the people of Fayette County were just going to have to get together and try to work together as some people are doing in other parts of the country. He said, "I can't solve the prejudice in this court." And he said, "You have no Black representation on the school board. You have a vacancy on the school board. I don't mean you should go out and handpick some Black person either, but there should be representation on this board from Black people." And he suggested that the parents get together with the superintendent and work out something whereby John and Claudia would not have to have that teacher anymore. He also ruled that John be compensated for the educational loss of being out of school all this time. And he ruled that the school board pay our lawyer twenty-five hundred dollars to help take of his fee. And he said, "Mr. Williams, I have a heart to rule that they pay you more so you'd end up owning the school system. They don't have any money out there."

I was very well pleased. We had asked that she and Paul Glass be fired and all, but I'm certainly well pleased with the way it worked out. I really was. And well, the superintendent come over to us before we left the courtroom that day. He wanted to know if we would have a conference with him the next afternoon. And we told him we would. So John and I went to the Central Elementary School and we had this conference with the superintendent and the principal. And we requested that none of the children that testified should have to have classes under this lady. And they arranged it—they gave her a remedial group unfortunately—and they placed another teacher as the English Arts instructress. So she was taken completely away from these children. And I asked the principal, "What if in future years some of the parents that had children participate in the hearings had other children coming along in this lady's class?" We didn't feel she should teach any of them at any time. And Mr. Glass commented that Mrs. Fowler had not applied for a teaching job for the new school year. I don't know what this was supposed to mean. This is what he said. And I think it will be good for all Black students and whites too. I don't think she would make a classroom teacher for any color child.

In ruling against the Board of Education, the school principal and Mrs. Fowler, Judge McRae described the situation in Fayette County as the "worst predicament I've been put in since I was a judge," and he said the county was dripping with prejudice. He told the courtroom about the mail he received from indignant whites:

People think I am promoting such things as Black people carrying knives in schools. This is a hard thing on a judge.

A Vietnam widow said if I let John McFerren back in school her husband died in vain. This is hard on a judge but these are examples of how ridiculous things can get.

Today the schools continue to be beset by the same pressures that divide the community itself. Racial tension runs high and violence is always close to the surface.

Kathy Westbrook

My name is Kathy Westbrook. My age is twenty-three. I was thirteen years old when we moved to Fayette County from Memphis. It really became quite an interestin place. There was a girl named Felissa. Felissa used to get into it with the teachers a lot because it was somethin involvin her parents that they didn't like so very well. She participated in some kinda civil rights movement. Her teacher had a right smart of trouble with her. They always would ask her silly questions that wasn't necessary. Sometimes she'd get put outa class or expelled from school for a little of nothin, just minor problems. And nobody really paid much attention; nobody tried to do anything. Not then. Not very much. Kids used to get kicked outa school for little-bitty things. I have a friend stay up the street here—he got kicked outa school a couple of years ago. The bus driver, Mr. Williams, he was drivin to school and he run the bus off in the side ditch and he got outa the bus and went to get help in gettin the bus outa the ditch. He left all the children in the bus and the keys was in the ignition. While he sent for help, this young man, he drove the bus outa the ditch and got it back on the road. When he came back he got very angry about it. He had him expelled from school—he haven't been back to school yet.

This bus driver gets involved quite often with students. He would always make you stay at home two or three days. He'd set dates he didn't want you to ride his bus and you didn't get to ride. Or like one accident happened on the bus once with us. Students on the bus were talkin and he told us to be quiet. So somebody said, "We have to be quiet enough in the classroom. When we get on the bus, it looks like we would have a little pleasure to talk. We're not harmin anything."

And he got mad. He said, "Who's that tryin to sass me back there?"

She said, "A fairy said it."

And he got real angry and we began to laugh at him. And now we was comin up to an overhead bridge and there was one of these Mustang cars, and him and this car had this collision. The little car went under the bus, and he got so nervous he run into the bridge and he faulted all of us for it. He wanted to make us stay at home and him and two of my cousins got into it about it. He told em, "Sit down and shut your mouth up!" Just like that, you know. And we were laughin. It was funny to us after he didn't hurt us. He got mad at us cause we hollered. We thought he was goin over the bridge at first. But afterwards it was funny to us because he was so nervous. So he told em, he said, "Well you all won't get to ride this bus no more this week. You gonna stay at home." He was blamin em for what he did. So he didn't let em ride the bus for a few days. One day they had to go to school to take a very important test. They came out to the bus and he refused to let em ride. They said, "Well we haven't done wrong, and we haven't been expelled from school or anything, we got to go to school today. If we miss this test we might fail." He wouldn't let em go, and they had quite a few words. And he turned em in, and the principal didn't seem to think anything of it. There are limitations to the number of days you can stay outa school and we've had this problem with him for a long time and he's still on the bus.

Every year we have the same problem over and over again. We had a problem with him this year. My little girl was goin to school. They had a little transistor radio playin on the back of the bus and he wanted em to turn the radio off. So they turned the radio off and he wanted em to bring the radio to the front of the bus and they refused to do so. So he wanted to take possession of their radio and they wouldn't come there and give the radio up. So he got to Rossville and called the police to come search the bus for the radio. The kids were hysterical at him. He got real furious with em. He made Mrs. Hays's whole family of children stay at home because of that radio. One of her daughters had the radio and he made all of em stay at home.

This happened this year too. Two boys got to fightin. The children was laughin and hollerin and goin on in the bus. And he wanted to know who was keepin up all the noise. And everybody started sittin in silence. Nobody said anything. "Who started the fight?" Nobody was tellin. He got mad at everybody cause nobody was tellin and he made about every child on the bus stay at home. They were just laughin at the fight, that's all. They weren't tryin to make him nervous. He kicked a whole bunch of children off for nothin. These were little six-year-olds and they was just startin the school.

My little girl told me one day, she said, "Mamma, the bus driver told me I might have to stay at home."

I said, "Why?"

"Cause some girls got to fussin on the bus, they almost got to fightin. He wanted to know who it was. I didn't know."

I said, "You didn't know? Why's he gonna make you stay at home?"

She said, "I don't know. But he said I gotta stay at home."

So the next day he stopped and I came to the door with her cause he wasn't gonna let her get on the bus. And he looked at her and opened the door and let her get on. She's such a little girl. That guy would be really pitiful to make that little girl stay at home.

On the school board we don't have very many colored people I can go up to and complain about it. A lotta the parents went up to see the bus driver and he gave em a lotta talk. The people around here can complain about somethin, but they're not used to seein anything get done with satisfaction. They'd think it'd be useless to complain, cause they're not gonna do anything about it anyway.

Maggie Mae Horton

They beat my son up in this white school in Somerville. Even the schoolteachers stood by and looked at this happen. They splintered his backbone. They even took X rays the doctor did, and seed that this had happened. When I carried the boy into the doctor, I said, "He can't stand up good. Sometimes he goes blind and can't stand."

So he examined him and he say, "I better take a X ray." He took a X ray and told me his backbone was splintered. It wasn't broken but it was a crack in it. He pointed out to me on the X ray. Then after he done all that he told me he should be in the hospital. He said, "Where did he get hurt at?"

I said, "School."

"What school?"

"Somerville school."

"That's the name of it?"

"Fayette High."

Soon as I said Fayette High everything dropped. I haven't got one word outa the doctor since. Don't know where the X ray's at or nothin else. We put him in a hospital and they verified this. I talked to the FBI so much that I almost dream about it. And soon as my son's back got so he could travel he hightailed it off to New York and he's been gone ever since. He feels there's no hope. And there's plenty of Negroes like that. You take me—I'm goin to the end with it and see what's at the end. I believe that someday we will overcome. We just gotta outwit em. Now I know somebody else will die. Maybe me. That doesn't matter. The thing I wanta see is things like that be stopped.

If that had been a white boy that this had happened to—hell, they would have strung up me and everybody else. But that was Maggie Horton's son. Hadn't been one thing done. Hadn't been one boy been expelled from school; hadn't been one boy had to stay outa school one day with all this happenin.

I went into the school the next mornin to see what happened. The principal, Jack Morton, said, "I wasn't there, I don't know what happened, or what they told me. I don't know who was in it."

I told him, "Don't tell me that cause you see all those damn black eyes out there and you know somethin happened. Why don't you ask em what happened?" I counted seven couldn't open their eyes, so I knowed all seven was fightin my boy. And nobody helped him fight those white boys. It was more than seven was on him. He just fought em till he passed out. They just got the best of him while the rest stood by and looked. So when the white man gets ready to beat the hell outa you—oh yes, he can do it, very easy, very legal, so nothin can be done about it.

Magnolia Horton

When we first got back to school in 1971 they didn't have a study hall, they didn't have nothin. They started a new system. It was altogether different from what we were doin last year. Schools are still divided. One south campus and one north campus, but on our campus the juniors and seniors—we didn't even have an auditorium or nothin. They had to put classrooms in there and build partitions and put two new classrooms in. We didn't have no free time or nothin. We had an hour and fifteen minutes in every class. So Charles Sain and more boys, a whole group of kids got together.

The Black students made up a grouch list. On the grouch list, the first thing we demanded on there was an hour and a half for free time—for activities and things like that. And if we didn't get it we were goin to boycott the school—we weren't goin back to class. So the Board of Education sent a message down by the principal that if we did they would close the whole school down and we wouldn't even go back—that the grievances, the grouch list, we had given didn't make no sense and they weren't goin to do it. So we boycotted classes again.

They didn't close down the school. They got a committee of teachers and parents to work together and try to get some of the things we asked for. So the first thing that they did, next Monday, when we went back to school, we had an hour and a half free to do anything we want. And they had the kids to write up a list of clubs and anything they'd like to do durin this hour and a half. But now they want to cut it out. You know, anything just to get rid of that hour and a half. They said there was too much courtin.

Another demand was that they move all the police off campus. They had police standin on our side of the campus, five or six patrol cars there, and it looked like a real prison. They removed all the police and we had a Halloween dance. This boy, Willie Harvey, came down from the other campus. He was supposed to be on this campus, but he had one class on the other campus so he drove his car down. And he was sittin on his car. The policeman had followed him all the way up from the other campus and he was sittin out in the parkin lot right across from the football field where we were havin the dance.

The police walked out and asked him where he had been and he said he just came from the other campus. So they told him, "Pull up"—and this is the funniest thing I ever saw in my life—they told him to pull up to Mister Jack's car. *Mister* Jack. He was the principal of both schools.

And he said, "Oh, over there by Jack Morton's car?"

They said, "Boy, don't you know better than to call Mister Jack, Jack Morton?"

He said, "Well I call Jack Morton 'Jack Morton' all the time."

So they hit him in the mouth with a blackjack. And this white coach, Mr. Holcomb, he was standin there watchin the whole thing. He was sorta a witness to it all. He said the boy put up a pretty good fight with the cops. They even took him up to the sheriff's, up to jail, and as he was waitin for them to sign him in they were standin over the counter. There was about fifteen policemen and him.

While people were standin around in there Dennison said, "And this boy got enough nerve to call Mister Jack 'Jack Morton.'"

And Willie said, "I'll call Jack Morton anything I want to call him."

They started shakin him. They even beat him after they got him in jail.

We had an assembly in the school about three days later and all of us were sittin in there—the whites were on one side and we were on the other. And what was so funny—Buck Doyle, he's the assistant to the sheriff's department or somethin, his daughter goes to school up there, you know, and man, he was really puttin those policemen down for what they had done. Way back they had passed a list of things that we had to do in school, and one thing, no matter what's goin on in an assembly, no one can walk out, not even the teachers, or else we get three days out. So these girls, Buck Doyle's daughter was the first one to get up and walk out. Boy what'd they do that for? Woooo. I thought there was gonna be a riot. Everybody was hollerin and screamin and Mr. Sommers dropped his glasses and he couldn't see and he was feelin for the microphone and everything. That was really funny. So they said, "OK, we're gonna close the meetin and we're goin back to class."

After we came outa the assembly we were supposed to go to lunch. So we went to lunch, but didn't nobody report to class. Everybody went to lunch, came outa lunch, outa the campus. And those that did go back to class, they ran up and down the halls—"Get your blank-blank outa class, get your god-damned ass outa class."

Well anyway, the teachers got scared, you know. They thought the students'd probably come in the classroom and pull em out or somethin. And they let their students all out. And we got outa school for a day. That's how it happened cause we were supposed to have a test the next day and I didn't have to go back.

After we got back in class we got some of the things settled and they moved policemen off the campus. And I felt real good because, you know. We did it and we succeeded with most everything that we had given our support to. We did it on our own. The students. And the teachers were kinda upset, you know. They figured that if we had any kinda grievances that we'd bring it to them. But we kinda felt, "Why should you lose your job? As long as you've got your job you shouldn't worry, you know. Let me get my thing on my own." Everybody went out and we succeeded.

There was one white boy that was with us all the way. I don't know his name, but he went all the way with everything we did. And there was this other one, he was his best friend, and they played in the band with these Black students. And this boy, they don't like him mainly because he was associatin with Negroes. He had told the kids if they was gonna do somethin, do it together, and he was tryin to get the whites to go along with us because they didn't agree with what the board was layin before us, but they didn't want to help us straighten it out. But it looks like everybody's happy about it now. At least the students have done somethin.

Mosta our teachers are Black now, but we don't have a Black counselor no more. That's one thing they changed. We got a white one now. The Black counselor was really nice. If it wasn't for him durin my junior year I don't know where I'd be. He helped us a lot and gave us some really good counselin. This one, all he ever talk about is college, you know, and never want to discuss the problems that's happenin in school. I mean we want to know somethin about college too, but we want some help and some understandin and communication from him about the situation of the school and everything. But all he wants to talk about is college. College. Every time he goes through with that.

The educational system is poor. That's all there is to it. They just don't know better. The quality is real low. Like when I was in New York in seventh grade I was behind, but I guess I was kinda apt, and I almost caught up. And if I hadn't've come home I would have gotten better. Even the white teachers have poor education. I mean this whole thing is just rotten. When I went to New

York I was in Buffalo for a year at my cousin's. Mosta the teachers said that New York and California have the best educational systems. And when I got up there I felt like I was in first grade and the others were in seventh grade and I didn't know nothin. Not really. But after I got down to it I almost caught up. I was almost a "B" student. I was a "B" student in mosta my subjects.

Our English teacher, he's the senior English teacher, he was tellin us yesterday he was surprised when he came down to teach here. He started us all over with eighth-grade English because he gave us a test. I made a 84—it was about five of us made in the 80s. It didn't go over the 80s. And that's eighth grade, and see, we're supposed to be seniors. And some of the kids—10s, 5s, you know, zero and stuff like that. He's gonna try to help us. He's about the best teacher we got up there. He comes from Texas and he was explainin to us about the low education that the system here—how low it was and everything. Really, this is why I'm worried about goin to college. One time they sent this girl, she was white and she had just graduated, you know, last year, and she was tryin to get some money to go to college. She was tryin to teach us and what she was tryin to teach us we hadn't even—I don't know, we could tell her and she couldn't tell us anything cause she didn't know. If she didn't have the handbook with all the answers in it she couldn't've told us nothin. And they let somethin like that come up and try to teach us.

PART VIII

"WE OUGHTA TAKE ALL THESE SONSOFBITCHES OFF AND KILL EM"

1969–1970

The year following the Hobson incident is spotted with outbreaks of violence. John McFerren was beaten and nearly murdered on December 15, 1969. Within months Shote Wilson was fatally wounded in a gunfight with police and tortured in his dying moments. Then on December 21, 1970, Scott Frank-lin, one of the founders of the league, was discovered shot to death in the smoldering ruins of his store.

John McFerren

Anytime a Negro stands up and be a Negro leader for his people he meets the thugs put up by the power structure to fight you and put up traps for you. Back in 1962 I had a lady claim she was sightseein on my buildin—claimed she fell and turned around and sued me for fifteen thousand dollars. Claimed she got hurt on a scaffold. Later, durin that same time, her daughter and her boyfriend's daughter gave affidavits that it was trumped-up charges to get me in trouble. Anyhow, the day I got beat I went down to the courthouse with Mr. Reed to cover a voter-registration drive, and when I started to approach the courthouse steps five thugs started to closin in on me. One had his knife out and I knocked one down and run and the five of em chased me and caught me about a quarter of a mile away from the courthouse steps. Durin the time I was approachin the courthouse steps—the highway patrol, I stopped him and told him there was five men chasin me and the highway patrol told me that he was on another detail, that he couldn't give me no aid. When they got after me at the courthouse steps, they chased me about a quarter of a mile. They caught me and beat me. They knocked, hit me on the head and legs with a bar. They knocked my teeth out and gave me other bodily harm. When the police came they carried me into the city hall, they carried me into the back, and when John Thomas ran around to see what they had me for, the five thugs jump on him and beat him up.

Viola McFerren

Then there was the beating. This was in 1969, during the boycott that was launched after the Hobson women were beaten. The community was really well together on this boycott. There was very little shopping done—there certainly wasn't enough to keep the stores open. One day John had gone to town with another fella. He walked through the courthouse yard—he was going down into the basement of the courthouse to check on voters registration. Harpman Jameson was down there working with registration. John claims this group of Black young men started walking after him and started talking after him. And he said he refused to talk because he knew they were trying to get something started, and he felt that if he were to have nothing to say that they'd finally leave him alone. Then he said that they just kept coming closer and that there was a large group of them. And he said he walked over to a highway patrolman's car that was parked nearby and he told him that those people were picking after him and asked the patrolman if he would stop them. This highway patrolman told him he had other business to attend to. Anyway, by this time they were really coming on him close. And he claims that there was one of the city police standing not far away, but nobody seemed to care about this happening and yet they were able to see it. And he says as they began to get closer and he saw that they were going to attack him, he started to run. He ran from the courthouse to a block out of the heart of town. And he says it was in the yard of a white lady that they caught him and then they started beating him. He said that all of them—there were about five I believe—he said that all of them beat, stomped him, and walked on him. And he said that there was another one of the group that had this gun—a double-barreled derringer pistol-type gun—that he drew on him while they had him down beating him. And he said that one of the other fellows pushed this gun up—he wouldn't really let him take sight on him. John says the man with the gun had taken sight right on his head when this other fellow pushed the gun away. The beating continued for several minutes until the white lady who was living in this house apparently called the police.

The police came. John couldn't get up, but I believe he told me the police dragged him to the car. They all got in the car and drove back to city hall. John called the store—I was at work at the store. He was seriously beaten and they wanted to have a hearing on it and he wanted me down there before they proceeded with the hearing. I'm surprised he could speak well enough to call anyone. My brother-in-law, Harpman Jameson, who was down there working on voter registration found out that John had been beaten and carried to city hall and he jumped in his truck and drove back to the store to get me. The two of us went back down to the place where they were holding him under arrest. Just as Harpman drove up I was getting off the phone from speaking to John. My niece, Eula Towles, had called me to the telephone and she was almost—she just couldn't take it when he told her John had been beaten up. And I ran to the phone and he told me to hurry down, to come at once, but not to come alone. So I jumped in Harpman's car and went back down there.

When we walked in John was sitting in a chair across from the group that beat him up. And they were laughing and having fun—it was really funny to them. There was one of the city police standing over there by them and he was laughing—it was really funny to him. They were all having a good time laughing at what the men were telling him they had done to John.

As I walked in I saw John squeezing his chest. He was bleeding from his mouth. He had bruises on his face. And his trousers were torn on the back where it seems he'd been scurrying along on the ground. His lips were swollen. It was a very horrible sight to see. Then I asked him what they were going to do with him at the time.

He said, "I'm here under arrest and they're getting ready to have a trial now."

I went into the office and asked the officer, "What is John charged with?"

And he answered in a very angry voice, "For fighting!" Then he said, "The judge is here and he's fixing to have a trial now. If there's anything else you want to know you gotta ask him."

So I went out in the hallway where this judge was coming through. And I asked him when were they setting the trial.

And he said, "Now. We're fixing to have it now."

So John and these other men went into the trial area and John requested that he have time to contact his lawyer.

So this judge said, "Well, I'll set this trial for nine-thirty tomorrow morning. You can find a lawyer anywhere by that time. You can go to the courthouse if you want too."

The next morning we went back and John's lawyer was with him. Meantime, John was driven into Memphis to our family doctor and received medical attention. He didn't go into the hospital because it's pretty hard to get him away from it all. This doctor gave him some medication that he continued on for quite some time. He was banged up pretty bad. He complained of his body aching. In the mornings when it was time to get up, get dressed, he couldn't get out of bed alone. We had to help him get up. The bruises remained for quite a long time before they disappeared—the bruises on his face. After, he wasn't able to do that much for a while. He'd complain of the pain in his body, but he was on the scene most of the time.

Those workers, the close civil rights workers that believe in equality and progress, were very concerned, but there were not, in my opinion, enough people concerned. I was surprised to hear how few people were even calling to say, "We heard about it, we're sorry, and how is he doing?" There were very few people that called and there were very few people that even drove by. This bothered me a lot because I couldn't figure out if they were afraid or if they really didn't care. However, I do know we have lots of people who feel they would be getting along better with white people here if there was not this Original Fayette County Civic and Welfare League.

At the hearing the next day the judge took the men that beat him up first and he asked them how did they plead, guilty or not guilty.

And they all said in concert, "Guilty."

And he then said, "I will fine each of you five dollars."

And there was this Black woman who had been leading this group and had been instrumental in encouraging people to shop in town and been instrumental in getting fights set up to run the picketers out of town. Well she came in the courtroom and one of the police got up and gave her his chair. First time I seen a white man anywhere in Somerville get up for a Black person before. But he got up. He was sitting up near the area where the hearing was being held. He got up and gave her this seat—right up front. And she sat there with just a stack of greenbacks in her hand displaying that she had money to pay these fellows' fines. And as soon as the judge told them that he was fining each one of them five dollars she said, "I have the money right here." But I didn't see her give anybody the money—I don't know if they collected money.

Then they dismissed these fellows and told them they could go. And they left while John was waiting to present his side of it. That's how they handled a case of attempted murder. They wanted to charge John with disorderly conduct even though he had been run down from the courthouse—run down until they caught him. And yet, this is what they wanted to stack on him. And I remember this judge telling John, "We're just tired of this stuff you got going on around here. We're just sick and tired of it." It appeared to me that he was saying this was one way to end it. This was my interpretation of what he meant.

The men who attacked John appeared to be the type of Black people that would do anything for a few pennies. I don't feel that they disliked him, because I have seen all of them, including this Black woman, come around to the bar next door. I have seen one of them that helped beat him up come inside of our store, but John didn't say anything to him rude. He wasn't purchasing anything. He just came in to ask directions. John saw him, but he didn't say anything to him. This Black woman that serves as a—I can't really find a good name for it—she has sent her children over here on errands and still do. They're over here all the time. She has sent other people over here to pick up things for her. I still don't think that this is something that they did because of their dislike for him or us. I think this is something where they had a job to do—someone had given them a job. And the people you saw them with on the street, whispering with the police and having a good time. Drive through town or walk through and you'd just see her walking side by side with the police. I haven't seen them that friendly with other Black people. And they live, all of them—this woman and these men that beat John up all live with white people and they work for white people. So I guess they feel that they are safe because they are surrounded with whites at every hand. And I definitely feel that this is something they were doing for some white people. The rumor got out—well some people came to me and told me that I would be the next one they would get, that they were supposed to catch me, and beat me, and really scar my face up. Up to this time I haven't gotten mine, but I don't put anything past them. I feel that they'll do anything.

Alberta Graham

I'm Alberta Graham. I'm forty-three. Well, I guess it was about nine o'clock, I reckon, and Shote and me just had went to bed. And we heard a car drive up. We was in bed and I come to the door and I went back and told him who it was. So he said, "Well open the door and let em in." And so I went back and opened the door and let em in like he told me. They had rifles. I really think they come there that night to mark him because there was too many of em there. And see, I didn't have a telephone there so they had to have been already outside someplace. They brought that mob there that night.

And so these two mens come in the house and they was askin—his name was Benny Wilson but we all called him Shote—they was askin him about his son. They was policemen—it was Jed Blackwell and I don't know the other one's name. So they went back in the bedroom and asked him somethin about his son. His son had did somethin and what it was I don't know—somethin like breakin in a store. You know how boys are. I don't know what it was. And so they wanted to search the house and he told em he didn't want em to search the house. He said they had to take his word for it. He said the boy wasn't here and so they insisted they was gonna search the house anyway. Without a warrant. They didn't have a warrant. I knew the son wasn't there. He hadn't been there. They wouldn't take his word for it. You see they never did like him anyway because, you know, he would stand up for himself. You know what I mean? He always had stood up for hisself. He would treat em nice, but he just didn't take it. He just had let a lotta white men know that he was a man just like they were.

So he said somethin, but I don't know what it was cause I was in the livin room, but anyway I heard him sayin, "I'm tired of you all sonofabitches fuckin with me!" Now that's what he said. And by that time I heard a shot. I think that he had shot one of em. But I don't know how it was because I was scared and frightened. And then afterwards I heard another shot. By that time I ran down to Mr. Solme's house and told him about it and so we all come on back up there.

When we got back up there he wasn't dead, Shote wasn't dead, but this white man was layin in the hall with all the top of his head blowed out and brains was all over the house. Shote wasn't dead then. They carried him back to this bedroom in there. Some more police come in the house. I don't know who they were. So they carried him in the bedroom and they wouldn't let none of us go in there. What they did to him in there, I don't know. They finished killin him, but there wasn't a shot. He had stabs all around his face. I don't know what they did to him. But anyway, that's the way they finished killin him. After the house got full of em they said, "I'll tell you, we oughta take all these sonsofbitches off and kill em." And so they stayed there about two or three o'clock that night. They kept him there that long in the bedroom.

I knew he was alive after the shots because I heard this other man back there talkin with him and some more come in there and I could hear em talkin with him. They wouldn't let nobody go in there. I could hear his voice but I couldn't understand what he was sayin. I know he was alive. They tortured him. That's what they did. Finally, somebody went out and called the ambulance. And after the ambulance got there they stayed a long time in there. They had him covered when they brought him out. I saw him at the funeral parlor next mornin. He had marks all up on his face. I don't know what instrument coulda did it, but it looked like a knife. He had stabs all in his face. And they mighta tortured him down here somewheres [pointing to the genitals] because it was water all over the floor. They tortured him bad.

Floyd Franklin

Gettin to the problem about my father and his actions in Fayette County. There's a tremendous amount of things that my father's interested in. And he always tried to lead me to believe in organizin ourselves as a race and doin somethin for ourselves. Now this is a firm belief of his. And channelin our money to a stream where we can use it to better our own conditions. Now this is one of his main convictions. He'd challenge anybody to make this not be the real way to success for Blacks. Take your dollars and pile em together. If you had a Black grocery and it wasn't nothin but a shack, spend your dollars in that shack until you can make somethin outa that shack worth comin to. You have to crawl before you can walk. It's best to work your way up. And once you work your way up it'll be pretty doggone hard for you to come down or for anybody to bring you down, because this country is run by the dollar. If you ain't got a dollar—even though you got the vote—you're almost powerless. You got a problem. And that problem can be an outstandin one if you don't think. And this is one of my main, one of my dad's main convictions—that we don't use our dollar wisely. We spend our dollar wisely, we could help each other. We wouldn't have to have you comin round. We could do things. Out here I'm survivin. I'm survivin. And I thank God for it. I'm survivin under pressure. They give me ten years to pay for this property here and I don't feel like they intend for us to get it. And I'll tell you one thing, I'm proud that I bought it when I did because I'm just ahead of the squeeze. Just ahead of the squeeze. Had I not put a small deposit down I never woulda had it.

Now my dad when he got murdered, the first thing the sheriff did is run to the newspaper and said my dad wasn't an activist for some time so we don't believe that this had anything to do with civil rights. Well, so far as the sheriff knowin about my father bein active in civil rights or what may you, my father knew enough about peoples to not jump up and run tell everybody what he believes in and how he intends to get a problem solved. There is such a thing as workin with the Devil, with your hand in his mouth—and once you get it out you can run free. So this is somethin the sheriff might well not understand. So he firstly run and says there wasn't no civil rights or nothin. But anytime a person is supportin a cause of person's rights, I feel like he's involved. Just because he haven't been out—like I did, walkin from John McFerren's downtown every Saturday in the boycott—just because he didn't do that, that does not mean he wasn't involved. His money—any number of peoples, when I was in the city of Memphis workin in the NAACP any number of white peoples said, "Just take this fifty dollars and just don't mention my name. Don't mention my name." There's plenty peoples want things done, but they'd rather to keep the name out. But still they're helpin the cause. For you to go to interpret with your own state of mind and say whether a person is involved in civil rights or not—that's just a thing of opinion. My father's an old man and I don't blame him not gettin out walkin, tryin to walk miles in the boycott march. I'm a younger man and it got me tired.

It was the twenty-first of December of last year which was 1970. In mornin, somewhere in the area of four o'clock it was, I got a phone call and this was my cousin callin. Asked did I know the store was on fire. I started to leave without even puttin on anything. My wife told me to put on some clothes and I got some clothes. Within minutes I was up there. I was the first to get up there. I coulda got electrocuted myself cause I drove my car all up in those electric wires. It's a wonder we didn't get burned up. But somehow or other I backed outa those wires. By that time one or two other cars were drivin up. Well, the structure was down to the ground then. There wasn't any erection standin up at all then. Just a pole or somethin, a two-by-four standin, and that's about all.

When the fire department got there, which was a considerable amount of time after I got there, they sprayed a little water on the fire to extinguish the blaze, get it down, and we looked around and we discovered a skull in the blaze. And we knew that he was in there. That's the onliest way. His car's sittin there. It was burnin on the side. But we knew that he was in there. We felt that he was in there to begin with, but we didn't know it and we looked around and discovered him in there. And when the ambulance come, they picked up what—they got the fire kinda cooled down enough for them to get what they did get, which wasn't much. And they taken it to the coroner.

When you got fire, arson, and murder, it oughta be necessary for you to use every means you have at hand to find out somethin. They don't get the dogs. They found some reason to not get the dogs—somethin about the dogs runnin somewhere or somethin. They didn't take any fingerprints and some of the suspects they picked up, themselves said they didn't fingerprint em. The cash register they picked up, they said somebody erased the fingerprints offa it. So every bit of the information they could've gotten was all destroyed. I feel like more efforts coulda been exhausted to try to get the facts about it. This is a case of arson and murder. All they done is run from house to house. Well who gonna tell anything? Ain't nobody gonna come up and tell you. When somethin like this happen, the first thing somebody thinks, "If they did that to him, they'll do it to me. I'm not gonna get involved." Now you have to have some physical evidence that you can get beside just goin up to somebody talkin outa their mouth. So they didn't do anything so far physical evidence is concerned. They didn't get any.

I'll tell you the same thing I told the sheriff. He says to me, "You all are satisfied this thing was did locally, aren't you?"

I told him, just like I'm sayin now, "I have mixed opinions about what may or may have not happened. It could very well have been a case of somebody knowin about the problems in the community and takin advantage of that problem in the community to get a job done that they had been wantin to get done ever since the early sixties and all the way through—a job that they wanted to get done and could get away with by layin it on the community disturbance." I'm not sure whether it was local or no because somebody might well have had this already planned to the earliest convenience and this might well have been a time when they could use the opportunity and lay it on the people of the community. The sheriff didn't have anything to say. He moved out. I say it could've come from the east, I say it could've come from the south, I say it could've come from the north, I say it could've come from the local area. This is the way I see it. I don't have any facts or nothin definite on what happened, but I know there is a chance for any one of those things to have happened. They have shot pistols and what-may-you over the phone tellin him, "This mean you." Stuff like that. "We're gonna get you," and all that type of stuff.

Another thing I'd like to mention is we're not satisfied with the way things turned out after his death. We're not satisfied. I'm just tellin you—this is just about all I'm sayin. We're not satisfied. We haven't got too much cooperation so far as information is concerned—from peoples that he did a lotta business with in the handlin of his cash money. As a matter of fact, to me there's a feelin now about it. It's to me a feelin. Some of the peoples is refusin to give the type of information that we feel the court administrators deserve to have. This is a thing that leads you to know that things ain't just what they oughta be in Fayette County yet. A man's dead and his business hasn't been altogether revealed to satisfy the administrators that we are gettin justice. Now this is up until today. We're not satisfied that we have been open to all the facts and all the details of his financial standin up until now.

My father always have been what you could call a brilliant man. I believe one fellow in this community now called him, "One of the best well-read niggers in the county." One of the best well-read niggers. This I understand was mentioned in one of the White Citizens Council meetins. Well the old man was always good at pickin up books and readin. And when you read, the more you read the more you learn. He was pretty up on law. He knew law pretty good. And the white superiors couldn't, just couldn't run him around any kinda way. I mean you just couldn't push him around. He almost was just like an attorney when he come up to court. If the judge allowed him an opportunity to defend himself and wouldn't call him for contempt of court, well he'd be just like an attorney in court. But this is a thing that the Negroes, they just didn't do in his day back. They'd be scared, you see. And he taught us the same way. He never did believe about bein overbearin. When you're right, you're just right. And when you're wrong, you're wrong.

And this is the thing—he grew up as what you could call an orphan child and he laid on his stomach and studied books by lamplight, as he often told us. And he believed in havin what it takes and in order to have what it takes you have to go out and make a go outa it. In young life he was a darn good mechanic and he had whites and Blacks comin to him. When I was a baby there was this fire. I'd like to've burnt up myself, but he throwed me out in a quilt. Years later he used to whip me and he'd mention, "Haaaaa, supposed you got burnt up when you was a baby." He used to mention that sometimes. But anyway, he took advantage. I believe he finished school in eighth grade and he done good. And he'd always tell these high school students, "Ain't any one of you got no sense. Ain't none of you got no sense. You can't beat me at figurin and you can't do nothin. You don't know this, that, and the other. You don't know nothin about nothin." He always said that. "You don't know nothin and if you know anything, you prove it."

But anyway he fought in Michigan City against Arlegys—Ransom and Marvin Arlegy who was peoples that controlled the whole area down there. And he won. In many cases he won. And he won this up here. He got the majority of this land suit even though he was in jail. He got the majority outa it.

Well, if you want to know what he was in jail about, he was in about moonshine. He was tryin to make a little buck. He had a big family. Twelve of us. Eleven of us livin. He was tryin to make him a little money. So they slipped up on him and caught him, so he had to go to jail for that. Well, to tell the truth about it, they didn't catch him in that. One of his friends that he was tryin to help lied on him. They made him say that, "Scott Franklin was a partner with me makin moonshine, furnishin me the sugar outa his store to do it with. So we're partners." Now that's what put him in jail. Went to court down in Memphis, Tennessee, down there and had pictures showin how they beat his friend to make him say it. And he would have won that if the guy hadn't've got right up there in front of the judge after they went and taken him and showed all those scars and bruises where they dragged him—they had this Negro so conditioned till he was scared to use what evidence he knowed my dad found. So when he got up there he turned state's witness. They tortured him. Those pictures showed the scars that were there, but when he got up he chickened out. He turned against my dad. That's what put him in jail.

He was a brilliant man and the people knew it. It had been said, the rumor had been out from the whites, "If we can get that nigger outa the county we can handle things like we want to. If we can get him out, we can take care of the resta em.

PART IX

"I DON'T KNOW HOW I CAN STOP"

There is no end to the history of the civil rights movement in Fayette County. The people who have spoken up in this book are still engaged in their struggle. In this concluding section some of these people offer a tentative summary of what they have been through and what they expect. Feelings are varied— from anger and disgust to firm and hopeful commitment—but one thing is abundantly clear—the movement has changed people's lives. A process of conflict and growth was started thirteen years ago and there is no way to reverse a thing that has become so deeply ingrained in so many lives.

Maggie Mae Horton

Law and order. We got the best laws in Tennessee. I don't think they got no better in Washington. But we don't go by em. We don't enforce em. I don't fight the law, I fight the white crackers and the white churchgoin people. We don't only have a problem with our law enforcement, we have a problem with our best citizens—both Black and white. "We won't talk. We won't say anything bout what's happenin. Regardless if they kill me, I don't wanta get involved." Well my goodness, you're already involved—you live here in Fayette County. That's the biggest problem we have here—of gettin involved.

We have a lotta Negroes who feel that "I'm gonna wait on Jesus." But God don't fix it. God give you two plus two and man I'm tellin you, you do what you wanta do yourself. You already made. You ain't gonna come into a damn thing from him. It's hard to get that over. All the peace that's gonna be made is gonna be through you and me and all of us. God ain't gonna come in here and make any peace. Even the ministers, they wanta stay outa this. They say, "We gonna stay here and pray until Shiloh come." Hell, Shiloh here. Anytime a white man can beat you up and do what he want—come to your house, kick you outside—Shiloh hasn't got here? To me, I ain't waitin. Jesus ain't doin nothin for me. He give me my hands and knowledge to do it. All I need is just give me the strength and I'll do the thing myself. That's what we gonna work forward to—tryin to get peoples to quit waitin for God to come do somethin for em. You know, we ain't afraid as we used to be, but we have a custom of what have been taught us all our lives, that God gonna feed you. We don't have enough knowledge to know that it's already picked. All we have to do is get up and get it.

That is what we'll be workin on from now on—to engineer somethin or design somethin that will destroy what our folks' parents have just nailed into us. The most of the sixty- and seventy-year-old peoples, they're goin by what they was taught, and you can't change this. We haven't taught our kids that. We taught em—yes, there's a livin God. I believe there is. But I don't believe he gonna do a damn thing for me. I believe he give me my hand and things to do it with. I'm gonna have to do it and that's what I teach my children—to get up off your stool and do somethin for yourself or ain't anything'll get done. But most of the older ones are waitin for that great day God come in and fix everything. That's why the movement has sagged awhile. And it's a misunderstandin. Yes, I'll go along with what God gonna help me do. But the misunderstandin is that we wait for him to come here and do it for us. And I pointed out what it means to groups of people—God didn't fix it so we could vote; he didn't come down here and go up there and make those white peoples let us vote. We gonna have to do the same thing we did then—to put our bodies up there and speak up and say what we want and what we don't want. There aren't too many religious peoples that think for themselves. And, my God, if I said "damn" around em it'd scare em to death—I'm goin to hell. I'm already in hell. This is it. This is hell here. This is all I expect to go to. Well we've had our portion of it. I'm not gonna wait around I don't think—it's not up to me, but I don't think I'll wait around for all this peace and happiness to come. I'm gonna raise all the hell I can to move some of this away.

I do my hair like I done it now. You know, sometimes you see me and I look like a movie star. When I get ready to raise hell, I get really nappy kinky hair and wash it and stick it up over my head like it is and I go to talk to boss and master. I got a message for him and he gets it. And I just about get what I want when I go. Cause I don't go to come back. It doesn't matter to me since I get what I go for. And I think that's why Negroes, when they got a problem, they come to Maggie Horton. I got a good thing goin with the Welfare Department. If they cut em off today, I bet you I reinstate em tomorrow. Cause all I do is bush my hair up and go in and see what happens. I wish I had the dollars in welfare checks that I've gotten back for peoples cut off for no reason at all.

Most people says Fayette County's in good shape—hell, it's worse than it ever has been. We have worked like hell to come this far, but honey it's all fucked up now. That's a word you hardly use, but I'm tellin you it's in bad shape now.

They ain't done a damn thing with Rossville and don't think we haven't tried. We have done everything that we know possible. Only thing that they've done. We asked for a Negro policeman, they didn't have one. What do you think they done—they went and got one that they could engineer, one that's like—what you call those things—computers? They punch him and use him when they get ready. That's what we got here. One Black Negro. And when we got him in he wasn't Black, he was white. That's the only thing we say we accomplished Rossville and we didn't do it.

Now I'm nonviolent. This is true. I fight the hell outa you, but I don't believe in goin out there burnin up things. This is not my way in the movement. But I'm gonna tell you this and this is a fact—I wouldn't give a damn if they'd go down there and just tear up everything in Rossville. I wouldn't say just one word. No, I wouldn't do it, but I sure wouldn't try to stop it because I believe the police department, the mayor of the town, and all the good churchgoin folks created the problem. So let them cope with it. The only answer to Rossville is that those boys—well, who they call boys—to let em know that they're men. And let em know that they can stand on the street if they want to. On Saturday night now and Friday evenin you can't be on the streets in Rossville. We have one little cafe there that's the only place Negroes have to go. At ten o'clock it must be closed. When they get through takin a bath it's nine-thirty. So you got about thirty minutes to go in get a sandwich and maybe a beer. This has just been goin on for about two weeks. All because the white policeman walked out and looked in somebody's bag and then thought he oughta curse him. He only had a baloney sandwich. He took the bag away from him, looked in it, and then cursed him out. And the Negroes just got to sayin everything. When you get us like that we act real ugly. They hauled three off to jail. Now we can't change Rossville, but we got a right to say who's gonna beat our heads. Especially since there are 70 percent Negroes there.

I just wouldn't want to comment on a man like Nixon. You know, I can't find words to say about him. I don't understand him and I never will. I don't even know what his angle is. Things have really gotten worse since he became president. They really have. Cause he has really showed the whites that all the work that all of the best thinkin peoples have done, all that the civil rights workers have did—he has assured em, "Hell baby, I'm gonna put you back in the driver's seat." And most whites feel that. Things have been much tougher for us. The civil rights agents that are around, you know, even their attitude have changed. Most of em give you the runaround. They don't come out and say what are available or what are law or what you can do. They say they don't know. What the hell is they doin in their job? I talked to quite a few and the only thing they can give you—"I will take your affidavit and I will see what comes of it." He got no information. Why do we need a Civil Rights Commission? You don't need it if they can't answer the questions. They don't know what my rights are. So I guess it's about time people find out the hard way.

To think that we been here all our lives and that could happen to us. Negroes been here eighty or ninety years and they don't even count. They don't even know we here. The civil rights commissioner, he was here and askin me about things in Fayette County.

He said, "How do the Negroes stand?"

I said, "Don't nobody know they're here but you and we Negroes."

He said, "What do you mean?"

"Your white folks don't even know we exist."

And he said, "I can't believe that. I think you should concentrate on what you're sayin cause we want the truth.

I said, "Mister, this is true, the white peoples don't know we exist. If you think they do you go count the jobs what they got. Go in there and see how many Negroes you find. And when you get outa there go in all the stores—all the various places where whites are employed for better than $1.25 an hour. See how many Negroes you find there. And you come back and tell me if we exist in Fayette County."

He said, "Well, if you put it that way, I have to agree with you."

I said, "That's what you should be investigatin. Not lettin me tell you what's happenin. You can see. Go out there and look for yourself. See it's not covered up. We don't have jobs."

I'm madder now than I ever been in my life. All the time that I been in the movement I've had determination that we shall overcome. I did have that. But things have changed. I don't think that we gonna overcome by lettin you do my job; I don't think we gonna overcome by lettin FBI see who is wrong and who is right. In the movement you learns yourself. You out there to see what is to be done and how to do it. And in bein out there you learns how to do it. And bein me for twenty years, I been tryin to get this thing done. Nobody can come here and get my rights for me. I got to get it myself. And that's what I tell my boys. They can bring a whole lotta hell. Much more than I can—they scare me. White folks think I scare em—they should see what my boys can do. And my girls aren't slow.

I'm not filin complaints because I feel they'll do somethin about em. I'm filin em so that when the violence happens I'll say, "I used to file complaints and affidavits. You know, I really believed that somethin goin to be done."

Whenever I called the civil rights commissioner or I'd call into Washington I'd have some hopes that I'd call there and they would come and see about the wrong bein done. I don't feel that way anymore. I don't feel that they gonna do a thing. But I do want em to know that this is so, so that when somethin happens they'll have to say, "We knowed about it; we just didn't do a damn thing about it." That's all they can say. I'll say, "You coulda prevented this cause you seed it comin. I hope you put the blame where it belongs."

Right now I think Negroes are like this. You know you can just peck on somethin and peck on it, long as you don't hurt it too much. But now Negroes are against the wall—a stone wall. We can't go backwards and forwards. We're being detained and we gotta get out. We don't give a damn what it takes to get me outa here. I've been sweatin so much, I've been humiliated so. And how it ends—I don't give a damn. If it's to cut out, knock out, shoot out, break out—anyway I have to get out. I'm comin out. I don't care who I have to fight. I don't care who it is—we gonna fight him. We breakin out.

And since they got Nixon in office, they say that in the cities that Negroes are bein deprived, they think. And how they're bein detained—there's no rules. They're gonna break out. And when they break out all hell's gonna break out. You can get the National Guard, you can get the army, you can get whoever in hell you want, but when Negroes break out it's gonna be worser than the Vietnam war. It's gonna be like a Sunday school to what these Negroes gonna do. And I'm gonna be right there too. It's not gonna be long. We are nonviolent, but that's gonna end. None of us have witnessed what we been witnessin the past two years. I'd rather have George Wallace than have Nixon. At least I know how the man thinks. But here's Nixon sittin in the White House talkin outa both sides of his mouth and there's nothin to it. You don't know what the hell the man means. He'll talk for Negroes at night and go in the country next day and talk against em. He'll make some kinda plan for Negroes this afternoon and take it away from em before nine o'clock tonight. So we don't know what Nixon's doin. We don't even know the man. Wallace, we know he hates the hell outa us. We coulda lived with Wallace. And Goldwater, he just wanted the job anyway. He didn't hate us as bad as they said he was. He was just makin a promise. We'd been somewhere if we'd've had him. But you don't know how to work with no Nixon—hell, he'd have you down in chains and bust your hide open before you know it. Hundreds and hundreds of people on food stamps in Fayette County gonna be off because of this damn thing he signed a few months ago. I don't know anything about him. He's at war within himself. I don't think the man knows one thing from another. I don't think Nixon thinks for himself nohow. I think somebody tells him what to do. I think Nixon holds the chair and somebody else does the plannin and says what's on. It's just like our police in Rossville. He's the police, but the man that hires him is the policeman. He's bein used. That's what I think about our country.

I saw about five guys sittin down talkin. They wasn't talkin to me and I only know one of em. They all out of service now.

One said, "Man, hell, I been here now a year and I ain't got nowhere. I can't get into school. They're all crowded."

The other said, "Well, I been here six months and I ain't got no job."

And the other said he had been on unemployment four years. He said, "Well, it ain't got much more longer. We're gonna have to take what we want."

Now I don't feel that these boys was wrong. That's the only way to survive. If you don't let him work, he'll try to get on welfare and then he won't be on welfare. How in the hell he gonna eat? Somebody gotta do the job. Square and I ain't doin a damn thing but standin and sayin the same thing—"We goin by the law"—and ain't gettin nowhere.

Robert Horton

If the Black folks get together and they need marchin they march, but the main thing what Black folks can do that they ain't doin is to get in your pocketbook. You get in that white man's pocketbook you gonna stop that man. You get in that store where he ain't sellin nothin but chicken and that old fatback meat, molasses, and stuff, and you gonna stop him. But until you do that, you go up there and buy, you keep him fat, you keep him where he can sit there in business and operate. They want to keep you down to a level—he got you down to that level—he want to keep you down to a level where he can absorb everything that you can get. All your finances and money. He wants to keep you where every time you get ready for somethin you got to come to him. If you don't go directly to the one that's doin it you still got to go to the white man somewhere. You got to deal directly with whites. Mosta what you make you don't get. That's what he wants. He don't want you to get on the same level as him. If Black men would sit in Congress of the United States the Black man would be on the same level as the white man and get the same quality education and go out there and get the same jobs and live. Shit. With the old dumb education—I got about two- or three-grade education—with what I done did as a Black man, me, just me, I got a brick house. If I got a college degree or a master's or somethin—well. . . .

The only way you can really learn about Fayette County—go on down here and buy you a home in a Negro neighborhood. You don't have to get no Black skin. Just be in your home over here in the Negro neighborhood. They'll get you some Black skin. You don't have to worry about no Black skin cause they'll give it to you brother, cause they'll burn you right down to cinders.

I'll say this, you take when they killed Chaney and all of em, if them white people wouldn't've been with him doin what they were tryin to do—why do you think they killed him? They said, "If we kill these whites and that Negro that's gonna stop the movement." They say, "If we kill Martin Luther King that's gonna stop the movement." They say, "If we kill Robert Kennedy and John Kennedy that's gonna stop the movement." That's just a damn lie. They ain't gonna stop it. If they kill Maggie Mae, that ain't gonna stop it. That's right. That ain't gonna stop the movement. The movement's gonna keep on goin. Reverend Abernathy. That ain't gonna stop it. The movement is goin brother. It's gonna keep movin cause somebody's ready for Maggie Mae's place, somebody's ready for Ralph Abernathy's place, somebody's ready for Kennedy and all of em, all of em that's fightin for the movement. Only way they's gonna stop it is to kill every Black Negro that lives in the United States. And they gonna have to kill some whites, cause if they kill all the Blacks there's gonna be some whites that'll still be fightin for us. For progress, for equal rights for every citizen of the United States. They gonna be fightin.

Magnolia Horton

My parents been here all this time, and all the stuff that they went through— look like things would've changed and people would have some foresight to see that my skin is dark and yours is light, or somethin like that, but still it's the same—but it just don't work like that. Outa all these years and all the generations past, it's still the same thing. It just makes me mad to see things happen like this. To see Black people all over the world can't get a job—they're fightin for our country, but when he comes back it belongs to the white man. It just really tears me apart to see it happen. My mother keeps hollerin nonviolence, but I don't see how she can take it. I know she been fightin it longer than we have, but I'm about ready to start throwin somethin or shootin or somethin. And she still says nonviolence, and I mean she's taken a lotta stuff.

It kinda scares me. There was this girl that went to school with me and her family was prejudiced. They didn't like her to have nothin to do with anyone Black, but she did. When she was sick she'd write letters to me and everything. In school, if we were in the bathroom we could carry on a conversation, but not when her friends came around. Her friends always hated her because she had a lot to do with Black people. This made me feel real bad to wonder—we got the same thing, I'm a girl, she's a girl, the only thing's different maybe, her skin's light and mine is dark. We're about the same size and everything. And still they say we're different. I don't see why. I don't understand. I guess it's just somethin that they got in their minds from the first generation that come here.

Their ancestors have been passin it along from child to child and it just runs in the family. Most of it lies on the elderly people—what they told their children.

I wish I had a wish. I wish I had three wishes. The first thing I'd try to do is just one year I'd divide up things fifty-fifty. All the Blacks would have 50 percent of everything. I'd put em equally in all the positions—but I'd have a Black president. And I'd just see how things would go. And if that wish shouldn't work out, I'd take another wish and put all Blacks in office, cause all whites had been in office for so long. And if didn't anything happen then, I'd put everyone under my command and then I'd be president.

Everybody say, "God got his Heaven; Devil got his Hell." If the white and Black can't get along here, how they gonna get along in Heaven? So everybody'll go to Hell and we'll still be fightin.

Cleotis Williams

When I was young the attitude I had was, "Everybody that's white is rich." Now that's a fact, that's exactly what I thought. I thought that everybody white was rich. That's the whole idea. We used to be sittin around watchin TV and my mother would be out here in the garden. If a Black person came on the TV then we'd jump sky high. And we'd call her and we'd call everybody else—"Hurry up, there's a colored person on TV! There's a colored person on TV!" And this is just the way it was. It was the whole attitude we had. And nobody had phones. In fact, we used to walk up to my aunt's house to watch TV. It was way over a mile. And phones, man, we'd have to drive down to the highway to get to a telephone. That's a pretty weird life. I don't know, I kinda adjusted to it. We never had anything. We never took any trips. We just made the best of the situation.

The whole civil rights movement kinda slipped up on me, but I think it was about 1960, when the people were startin to register to vote, when they were gettin kicked out just like that, kicked off the land they were rentin, when Tent City went up and all of this, and students started comin down—that's really when I became aware of the whole problem.

One thing I'm proud of is what that white man forced us to do—and I don't think he was aware of what he was doin—when he started puttin all Blacks offa his farm. Now you see Black people buildin their own homes and all this. But the white man didn't realize this at that time. Tent City made a lotta Black people see that what they were doin all these years, sharecroppin, was a waste of time. Valuable time. Precious time. It didn't make any sense at all. I heard people, "You know, I cleared three hundred dollars last year." Oh wow. He'd get up every mornin in the cold for three hundred dollars. It didn't make any sense at all.

The situation is still the same. We're held down by the people in power—the mayor, the county court, and all this type of thing. They don't want any industry in here. Say, for example, you're a poor white man. Now I'm in power, and this Black man is poor too. "Well now if no industry comes in here, no labor unions, we can always keep us up, we can always keep you people down. And if I ever need somebody to come back and work for my farm I can always get it because there's nothin else for him to do." They got him trapped. They don't want any industry here. They got cheap labor.

Old racists like Pulliam have the slave-master complex. They like the old days. They're very considerably opposed to change. You know, they don't like it. Now you take this Somerville Police Department, to show you how racism is. No Black policemen there. And when they did hire a Black policeman, the only place he came was to Black joints. Now cops, they've stopped me lotsa times. The things they don't ask me—"Where you been, boy?" "It's none of your business where I been." "Where you goin? What'd you do?" All this kinda—I don't know. The best thing to do is go on and answer em and split. You know, it hurts you. Whatever he asks—a straight yes-or-no answer. You know, I'm straight. I've been stopped several times, but I never was doin anything. Just stopped. "What're you doin? Where you goin?"

I don't think nonviolence will work. I think it's over. Gone forever. Now eight years ago all the Black people around were hollerin, "Integration, integration." But the whole thing just turned. Heck with white people. Just give it to us. The heck with you people. Get lost. It's a tragedy for us Black peoples now. In many ways some of us is just as sick and racist as white people. They become violent and they don't care anymore. One way or the other. I hear talk about it every day. Every day. The whole attitude has changed. There's hate now. I think real shootin is a long ways off, but so far as conversation's concerned I don't think people will budge anymore. The whole attitude now among most Black people is, "Go for yourself." Their usual attitude is that "white people ain't no good." That's the whole idea. Heck with em. And they got that idea about you and anybody else. Kennedy, anybody. Heck with all white people because white people don't feel nothin about you. That's the whole attitude. This is it. It's not our fault. We tried. See, while the Jews were gettin emselves together, Catholics gettin emselves together, and they put a guy in the White House, we were runnin around tryin to get into the mainstream of society instead of gettin together ourselves and makin our own. Like the Jews. See, we weren't doin it. We were tryin to get in. Just kept tryin to get in. And we're still not next door. Heck with em.

Frankly, I don't consider myself prejudiced. I just consider myself as just bein rational. I just think it ain't gonna work. It ain't gonna be. That's all. So I stick with Black people. See, I'd love to see a world with everybody just bein together. True. But the people aren't never gonna do it.

I took my attitude, this white people attitude, in '68, when Nixon was elected. My idea was that everybody was around sayin, "Man what're we gonna do now?" You know, Nixon just came to em. When Johnson was president he did a lot for Black people. Kennedy was president. He got stopped. But man, you been poor all your life—no matter who's in office that don't make you anything. You gotta do it yourself. So heck with the politicians. Right now I don't care about votin. That's the truth. So it didn't make me any difference who we elect. It just don't bother me. This is just the attitude I have. Maybe I'll change as I mature, but right now this is how I feel. If you don't have any motivation yourself to want to do anything, you can even have a doctorate's degree, but if you're lazy you ain't goin nowhere.

You know, frankly, people here in this county—I don't know what—it's kinda a passive attitude. You know, I've made a lotta friends. I've spent the night in a lotta different homes. A lotta people don't even watch the news. They aren't concerned about social problems. They really aren't aware of what's going on. An act of racists can be faced right up on em and they don't even see it, they don't realize it, cause they aren't concerned. They don't care. Not many of my friends want to stay here. They don't think that at all. You can ask em, "What are you gonna do?" "I'm leavin here." There's no form of interest here. There's nothin, nothin to do. No type of motivation. Nothin.

Edward Gray

My older brother Hugh—he is very very high tempered. If we was sittin in here—he can just not stand whites. I don't know. He would probably fly off the handle with you just goin back over some of the stuff we went through. I'm a little different than him in this respect in that I try to curtail it, to control it a bit. But the situation was the kinda thing—this stuff was naggin at you. Like no way you turned, there was no way out because you was gonna bump into the white man. There was no way out. Everything that you did you was gonna run back into him. You was gonna end back in his arms sayin, "Mr. So-and-so I need this to help me build so-and-so." You had to have money to live on—OK. You had to go down to the bank that he controls. You had to get a new truck, you had to go to the bank and then to the white man that owned the cars. It was things like that. You could see this. The tension.

I'll tell you somethin that used to burn me up. It still do in some respects. I got down to the point where I just don't tolerate it. School made me like this. Remember, we had our own farm and I was still a kid—this is all bout how

built-in hate develops—OK. Used to be white people would come to hunt at
our farm. Now they never would get permission from our father—they'd just
come drive on down over whatever they want like it was theirs. Now when I
got ten or twelve or thirteen years old I just told my father, "This kinda stuff
just don't go with me." Me and him had some discussions about it. It just don't
go with me. It woulda been entirely different if this man had come on by and
said, "I'm gonna park my car down by the road and hunt for a couple of hours."
The thing was if you wanta hunt on his farm you gotta go by his house and
ask at the back door for permission. And the point is he can come to your
house, drive right on down through your fields, and not say nothin about it
to you, see. And sometimes, if he was ridin a horse and goin huntin, he'd cut
your fence just to let his horse through to quail hunt all out through there,
see. That's right. Today, to this very day, I do not allow white people to hunt
on a single inch of land I got. Now when my father's there they can ask him,
but they know me—if they wanta hunt and they see I'm there, they just don't
worry about it cause they know that I just do not tolerate it. That's just one of
those things. If it had've been different, if they had've respected my father as
bein owner, this is one thing I never would've thought of. It never would've
been a built-in thing for me to act like this. It never would've been. Things like
this—little things—I consider em little things—they goes to build up inward
hate. Things like this, they become a part of you and you carry em into school
and on into society. It becomes a hangup.

In school I felt, "How can somebody my same age, how can he know to
hate me? I don't have any hate for him. Why should he throw pennies and
coins at me cause I never did anything to him?" I could say, "If this guy had
been thirty or forty years of age I could kinda see. There's a difference in our
age. He's in one generation and I'm in another." But, really, I'm gonna be very
honest—Fayette's got some of the dumbest-assed white people you got. I don't
see how in the world the Lord put such a dumb bunch of fools together as
he did in Fayette. Not only the older ones, but the young ones. I come to talk
to my mother about this. I told her I'm comin back there to live. She said, "I
don't know. I don't see how you can in some respects. Cause the young white
people feel the same way that the older ones do. Some of em are more-so." In
the picture we had, the class picture, they didn't even want the Black students
picture on there with theirs. They made a suggestion that they put our pictures
on a separate corner of the big picture. I wonder how young people can feel
that way, you know.

This thing prejudice, man, it's not somethin that comes just like that. I feel
that it's an inward thing comes along step by step. There ain't no way in the
world that if a white man came to my door I'd let him hunt. But the point was

I understood it became a parta me over the years—seein the white man drive over my father's property. Not a bit of respect for what I have and go hunt as much as he want, kill as much as he want, and then cut my fence and stuff like that. You see this is not a thing that happened just one time—it's a thing that happened year after year after year. It's not a thing you can just look at and shake your head. It's a built-in thing of hate. I think in Fayette County it grows in the minds of the young as much as the old. I really do.

One thing about the Black people in Fayette County—they're poor people but they're good people. That's one of the reasons I wanta go back there. And I'm determined to go back there. No matter how bad the bad might be, the good is eventually gonna win out if they keep the right goal in mind. It's always been my brother's and my plan also—my brother wants to go to law school and come back in the county and set up his own law firm, his own law practice. And my ambition—not only is it my ambition, but this is my desire—and I'm definitely gonna see this desire fulfilled to the fullest of my extent, so help me God—to be able to finish medical school and go back in Fayette County and work with my people, Black people, not for the sake of money, or not for the sake of glory, but for the sake of helpin people that need to be helped.

Now there's some situations and cases in the county that you really need to see in order to appreciate it. I'll tell you some of the things. When I go down home some of the times I see these old people that I believe could've been helped as far as their medical situation. Another thing that burns me up is you go to one of these clinics where these white physicians are. They take their own time. No matter what's wrong with you. If you're havin a baby and there's a white person in there, you're just gonna have your baby cause he's not gonna take any time for you. Another thing I have to express—I tend sometimes to confuse, to put too much for the Black—I think medicine is a field, it's not a thing that has a color. Now I don't wanta go back to the county with the intent only to help Blacks. I wanta help the people that need help. But my primary aim is to help my people. There will always be that primary aim. Nobody else is gonna do it. It's gonna take bone determination to do it, but I'm determined to do it. No doubt about that.

Mary Sue Rivers

All I can say is what I'm doin for myself. I'm still boycottin Fayette County. I'm stayin with my people. I do most of my buyin up at John's when I go up there to buy gas. I drive miles to keep from buyin in Fayette County.

I don't know why whites hate and don't want their child sittin alongside this little Black child here in school. I just really don't know. They got these Negroes still cookin for em. They out havin a ball, a big time, and comin back home and look for everything to be right there to eat. Why they don't know what their Negro cook done put in there—it could be they're gettin their last meal. But they don't want their child eatin aside of this child in the schoolhouse. I just don't know what's wrong with em.

Fayette County is a county I don't know what they gonna do with it. It's a county just is not gonna do the right thing. Fayette County ain't doin nothin, and nothin ain't good in my opinion. They got a buncha little Ku Klux boys round there—jump on everybody in town, beat em up, and don't even go to the jailhouse. I don't go to Somerville much. I go there for my check and maybe a few more things. I haven't been doin much in Somerville since the Hobson girls was beat up. Of course now my job carries me over there, but otherwise I have no part of Fayette County cause Fayette County has made me sick. I mean the whites in Fayette County just don't have no care for the Negroes at all.

Elvin Jones

My son just got back from Vietnam. From what I gather from him things were pretty good when he was overseas—he didn't have too much of a problem with the race situation. But the thing that bothered him was back in the States—that when he got back to the States it was different. Especially when he got South. He left from California and when he came back here he had some problems because he was Black. He was with the same people he served with, but they sure were different when they got back to the States. The same people. In fact he was involved in a fight with one that he had served thirteen months with overseas. They got back here and got with more peoples in Georgia and started talkin about niggers. That conversation ended up in a fight.

He said his captain was one in particular—would always be tellin him about his country, fighting for your country. My son hadn't been around here for some years—when he was about ten he went to California. When he come back and came South and found out what I had been goin through, it was somethin different than what he had been goin through in California. He said, "I begin to wonder, dad, how could I be fightin for my country and hearin you say what all you go through here in the South? I don't see how it could be our country, yet we gotta fight for it. I don't see how you can say you're fightin for a country and Blacks don't have no controllin power over what go on. Especially here in the South. And yet they're drafted here in the South."

I don't know if these things will work out, but I have a whole lotta dreams and I'm hopin they'll come true. I'm gonna do all I can. As a poor man—I'm poor now and I'm sure I always will be—all the money I get ahold to, mosta it I spend for gasoline, oil, and tires tryin to find and meet people to see what I can do for em to help. And I hope that things will get better, but it may take a turn for the worse. I need a lotta improvement myself and I guess if I spent what money I do get on myself I'd be better off. But I just can't see myself goin off and leavin other peoples not attended to. Sometime they'll try to buy you out or give you a good offer that you might get set up in a nice home with a new car and maybe even get you a job if you just keep your mouth. But I can't see it that way. We have some people, I suppose, what take this kind of thing just to live in luxury emselves, but I can't sleep very well when I know there's other people almost starvin. It ain't goin to have too much unity here until they realize a man is nothin but a man regardless of his color. And not only bein Black—you can be white and when you stand up for what's right you're branded as a Black individual in this county. They don't look at the color when you start that. I'll tell you, I have a lotta plans and I hope they work out. It's a struggle.

Square Mormon

I have to give my wife a whole lotta credit. I mean, I couldn't have done nothin without her no kinda way if I didn't have the right kinda woman. But she was able enough to see what I like to do and able to see how things was. Many times I was gone day and night ridin to and fro and she was here cookin for her big family along with all the white civil rights workers. And all time of night she would get up and make a bed up and they'd be layin on the floor. And she felt about those whites the way she felt about her own children. She would go from the time of mornin till night tryin to find somethin to cook and make it as pleasant as she could. I'll tell you, it seems like all the civil rights people, they appreciated what she did. I think she had just about as hard a job as I did. My trouble was, I was walkin, talkin, and losin rest, and trouble was she was workin, slavin, tryin to feed us. She has helped me be what I tried to be. The children, they was a lotta help too, because they believed that what I was doin was right and they felt how they was human too. So they was willin to take a stand. So that made me feel real good. Once you doin somethin your family think is wrong and not joinin with you, then you have difficulty. Everybody have to have a partner to do a job. This way I felt pretty free all along. This way I'll work really hard, just as long as they let me love.

The way I feel now, let's say this, let's say Fayette County don't be able to reach the top of the mountain, I still won't be goin down in grief about it, because I feel I have did my part. But now if I thought there was somethin that I coulda done that I didn't do, then I'd have a great big grief on me. I have been told by

some of my peoples, "Square, you take too big a step. You gonna get killed."
I had my half-brother come sit down with me and talk hours at a time tellin
me, "You oughta drop this kinda stuff because, man, you got a big family before
you." And I told him, "I think about what Martin Luther King said—'A person
that haven't seen nothin worth dyin for, he's not fit to live anyhow.'" This is what
we really got to realize, because Jesus seen somethin worth dyin for, and King
discovered somethin worth dyin for, and anytime you think about what gonna
happen to you, you ain't gonna do nothin nohow. I also think about this—I told
the people the other night—that a lotta folk is scared of dyin, they're scared
to get in the civil rights movement, they scared to boycott, but still they'll run
down the road at ninety miles an hour. Wheel'll run off and kill em; old tires'll
blow out and kill em. I noticed when we had one holiday I member about 405
people got killed in that one holiday and I told em in the whole civil rights
movement ain't hardly that many people killed. I told em, "You get confused
when you talk about gettin killed." I thinks more about God's will than I do
about dyin because dyin will always take care of itself.

Harpman Jameson

When I was growin up I was always around a good number of whites. All my
neighbors around in the country houses was white. Whites was never a strange
person to me. Mosta my playmates was white. One old playmate is in business
in Fayette County now. When we was growin up every birthday cake he got
my grandmother cooked it. And when she cooked his cake she brought me a
slice of his cake. And when she cooked mine she carried him a slice of mine.
This particular fellow, he don't speak to me today. And I haven't done no more
to him than I have to you—only registered and stood up like a man. We used
to trade birthday cakes. Now he won't even speak. I go in his store maybe, to
buy a part—the dealership he's in, I use that brand on my car. And I go in his
place to buy a part now. He'll say, "Yes, what can I do for you?" And I'll tell him
what I want. He never acts like he ever saw me before or that he know me at
all. And my grandmother cooked these cakes until he went off to college. We
live in the same neighborhood, we vote in the same precinct, but we haven't
spoke since I registered to vote.

I have another neighbor. He's white. We used to hunt together. He was born
on one side of the highway and I was born on the other side. We never did have
no trouble. We used to break horses together. We used to swap goats together.
And, well, back in the years we even had an ox team. He had a pair of oxes and
I had a pair of oxes and we used to get together and have more fun. When he
heard that I had registered to vote, well he haven't spoke no more. And we still

don't stay no more than three blocks apart. And I see him every mornin and I'll be goin to the farm and he'll be on his way to work and, well I have throwed up my hand to wave hello at him but he seem to turn back and look the other way. But anyway, I been knowin him all my days and he been knowin me. As hard as our faces has gotten now, we sure can't forget each other.

We used to have a grapevine on the path between our house and the white people who live across the pasture. We used to swing across the ditch on that vine—you know, like Tarzan do. So we had a lotta fun there. Well one of these boys climbed up in the tree and cut this grapevine and left it hangin. I went to takin a swing on there and I swung across the ditch and I fell in the ditch. I got a scar on my back—it's up there where you can see it. This was a close friend. We hunted together. Years after that they moved out and I went in service and they went in service. We come back and met once. That was in 1946. Then last year, in 1971, we met at a big auction up here in Hickory Valley. I didn't recognize him, but he did recognize me.

So he asked me, he said, "Don't I know you?"

I said, "No, you don't know me."

He said, "Yes, I do."

I said, "No, you don't know me."

He said, "Yeah, I know you. Many times we used to fight and you mean to say you don't know me?"

I said, "Naw, you don't know nothin about me."

He said, "Yes, I know you. Remember the time that I cut the grapevine and you fell in the ditch?"

So I looked over at him then. And so anyway I called his name, he called mine—we run together, we hugged right out at this big auction sale. So we walked around there maybe like a girl and a boy the resta that day. He had his arm on my shoulder. I had my arms around his. Some of my other white neighbors, they looked at us like maybe we was somethin wild walkin around there. But meantime, he wasn't interested in nothin that was goin on in the sale. We just had to talk about the olden times—the good old days that we lived so hard back in the fields. I asked him about all his sisters and brothers; he asked me about all my people. And after we got through with that we began to go through farmin and regular life.

Then we came up to the main point—he said, "Harpman, you know it's a hell of a world now. You see somebody you think you know, you're really scared to go over and speak to him."

I said, "You're damn right."

He said, "Just like we met up."

I said, "That's right. I sure was lookin at you."

And then he went on to speak about how he'd been teachin his boy that a man was a man and how you have to recognize a man to get through the world these days. There have been so many changes.

And I said, "Well I have been tellin my boy the same thing. Mine recognize these points in life. He don't look up and see color and turn you a short answer. He's gonna check with you and see whether you really mean business. And if you is a man, well he's ready to talk with you."

He said, "I got one the same way. Whenever I run up on him here today I'm gonna introduce him to you. He's around here somewhere."

So as the crowd moved around we moved up ahead of the crowd and got us a good seat. We sat there and talked. The crowd'd come by as they auctioned somethin off, but we'd be too busy to see what was goin on. They'd leave us, we'd set there talkin, and then catch up with the crowd again. We spent the whole day like that. In the evenin we run up on his boy and he introduced his boy to me. And the boy seemed to be a real nice young man—he was just finishin high school. We quick got tired of the sale and I walked with him out to his car. He was drivin a Chevrolet and he asked what I was drivin and I told him a Ford truck. Then we had a little argument then about the Ford and Chevrolet. So anyway he wanted to walk down and see my truck. We walked down to see my truck and we got in the truck and drove it back to his car. And that's where we set until the men that was with him got ready to go. We set out there and talked. And he got my address and I got his'n. And we're supposed to visit. We're gonna visit some of the graveyards. He wants to visit the graveyard where my parents are buried. And he wants me to take him to a old graveyard around here where one of his younger sisters was buried at. He done forget just about where the graveyard was. I told him I knowed where the graveyard was and just about where're the graves. And he's supposed to come down some time and we're supposed to take this visit to these graveyards and walk back over the old land where we used to have so much fun at.

I has little faith from our federal government now, under the Nixon administration. Things could be workin better than I have any idea, but I don't have much faith or nothin in the Nixon administration. Some things was done right off. The local government works ahead of the main parta the government. The local part, right here in the county, what we have dealins with—when Nixon was elected to office they went ahead and started doin their thing that day, before Nixon had a chance to do the change. They had so much faith that he was gonna do exactly what they want to—with his law and order and whatnot—they made a particular start the day he was elected to office, makin the change. They knew by the time the Democrats got outa office they would have things shaped like they wanted. And whenever civil rights or anything would try to go directly into the federal government—well, there was nobody there to hear em. So that's what makes the idea of the government so rotten. Cut off from the federal government you have nothin to look forward to—and you just got to wonder. And it's hard to help the people because you don't have nothin really down in mind that you might can get done. Anyway, I hate to tell somebody somethin that I know I can't do. And when the people come to me or some of the others for advice—well, I just have to kinda draw up and kinda talk outa one side of my mouth and wonder. I don't know what it might work out to be, but I don't have no faith in the Nixon administration.

Right now the people need more employment. And along with employment they need a fair shake in the laws—drawin up the laws of the county. You take this school-zonin law and drawin up the laws for these new taxes and stuff like that. Now we got to pay some of these taxes and we need a voice in there. They take two or three judges, maybe the county lawyer, and one or two more big men—they get together and draw up for higher taxes for the poor people to pay. Well that don't only mean Black people—that mean white people too. Some of them's dissatisfied, but they seem to be afraid to attack the big men on that base. Now you take the whole county—they don't believe in payin a top price in wages for nothin. Anytime anybody workin in Fayette County—the wages is higher up most anywhere else on any kinda job. If it's schoolteachin, if it's truck drivin, if it's bricklayin—the wages is higher up. They keeps a lower-payin level in Fayette County than they do anywhere around I know of. You take this little town over in the edge of Mississippi, they got more high-payin production wages than there is in Fayette County. They got a good number of people employed. It look like here they dig up anything they can to get a man outa a job and they don't seem interested in gettin him back unless'n its pullin him back to a two-dollar-a-day job. Well nowadays a ten-dollar-a-day job ain't nothin, but what they want is to turn the clock back to two dollars. Well there ain't no way in the world to turn the clock back to two dollars cause a whole lotta things gotta be turned back. Just go back just a few years ago—I remember buyin mud-grip tires in Sears and Roebuck for twenty-three dollars apiece. Well today that same tire costs you thirty-seven dollars. So there's no way to turn the clock back.

There's a whole lotta things that make me say I will stay. I have spent mosta my life here. I like Fayette County. I have a lotta friends here. Leavin the county—maybe I'm crazy that much. That was the first goal the White Citizens Council set out. I remember when our little local newspaperman said in 1960 they expect to have three thousand Negroes moved by fall. So I'm contrary to their words. That was 1960 and now it's 1971 and I'm still here. I probably will never get rich—least I know I never will get rich—but I'm intendin to stay here as long as I can, to do what I think is right. Like I say, I was shipped out to war when I wasn't nothin but a child—so I come back a soldier and I'm still a soldier out there fightin. If I don't get it—some of the good benefits—I intend to fight till I go down for the younger generation, to make a better livin for em in Fayette County.

I come to find out I went overseas fightin for my country and the war wasn't exactly overseas—it was here. I never had a idea, when I was overseas, that when I come home things would be like they is. And the war's just beginnin here. Now I'm for progress for the Black man and for the white man. And I want to see the children, Black or white, have the best that there is to offer—an education, pleasure, or anything that they want.

John McFerren

The southern white has a slogan: "Keep em niggers happy and keep em singin in the schools." And the biggest mistake of the past is that the Negro has not been teached economics and the value of a dollar. Negroes in West Tennessee still buys big fine cars—the schoolteacher buys big fine cars and especially the preacher—and the average child come up, he sees em with big fine cars and he think that's the thing for him to do. But in the long run they should buy cheap cars and channel their money to what will help em. Back at one time we had a teacher—we used to call him Bilbao because he come from Mississippi—and he pulled up and left the county because he was teachin the Negroes to buy land, and own land, and work it for hisself, and the county Board of Education didn't want that taught in the county. And they told him, "Keep em niggers singin and keep em happy and don't teach em nothin."

When my children started in the integrated schools—they were the first children in the county to start in their school—when they sit side by side with the white child they receive and learn that the white child does not have a superior intelligence because his skin is white. The Negro has the same portion of brains as the white child and he learns how the white people think and he learns exactly what they believe and he learns much more by experience of what the white person thinks and reacts than he do when he's separated. And I'm in favor of any integrated schools because your child, when he comes up in an integrated school, knows exactly what life's all about. When he gets out to facin life, it makes a much stronger child. You take, for instance, my children got the equivalent of education at twelve years old as I had when I was thirty.

Any nation regardless of what nation or nationality cannot live alone in the world by itself. In this county at the present time the white people have put up private schools tryin to keep their children isolated from the public.

China made its mistake a million years ago tryin to keep its people isolated from the world. Anytime you isolate your people from the world then your people become like you cut your arm off—you die. When you mingle and pick up ideas from other nationalities and other people and put em all together in your own brain and make it work for yourself, you make much more progress than from isolation. With the Negroes in West Tennessee, when the white man cut him off and put him to thinkin for hisself, the white man done him a favor. The white man say he can replace the Negro with more machinery, but I want you to know that chemical farmin has already begun to fade because the chemicals are hurtin the earth. There are bare fields where nothin grows. He's gonna bring a starvation on his own self. This country is too poor to afford this big high-priced machinery when the machinery price is gettin higher and the farm produce products is gettin lower. Back in 1960 and '61 the big bankers told the big farmers, "We'll furnish you, get the niggers offa the land." Now he got the land and now he don't know what to do with it. And it's only a period of time that the big bankers will have to build a big parkin lot for the machinery and stuff they got to pay for.

Negroes in this county have made much progress in ten years and also have much progress yet to go. Durin this ten-year period I reached the opinion that the Negroes, while they are fightin for their rights, must enter into businesses of their own and study economics, because you cannot be free when you're beggin the man for bread. But when you've got the dollar in your pocket and then got the vote in your pocket, that's the only way to be free. The Negro race now is just enterin to the money stream. Business and economics is the money stream. And until Negroes can do that—what is votin to civil rights when a man can buy your rights from his pocket? You cannot have civil rights when you beggin for bread. You gotta be independent in economics. It's the only way you can demand your civil rights. And I have been successful and made good progress because I could see the only way I could survive is to stay independent.

Down through the years the Negro in West Tennessee—Fayette County, especially—this county has been controlled and dominated by two sets of families. They been controllin the county since the Civil War. It's been handed down from one generation to the next generation. And through the years the Negro has been the white man's shade tree in the summer and his wood pile in the winter. The Negro has woke up and the white man, more than ever, is drivin tractors for himself. But in the West Tennessee section the land do not produce enough to afford this high-priced equipment. It's only a matter of time when the white man—who's payin six hundred dollars for private schools and collectin food stamps at the same time—it's only a matter of time when all this will come to pass because the economics will automatically force him in line. The Negro is no longer goin back. He's goin forward.

Viola McFerren

Through my role as a community figure—with my anti-poverty work and perhaps with my civic work—I was chosen by the executive director of the National Poverty Program, Sargent Shriver, to serve as a member of the National Community Representative Advisory Council to the Office of Economic Opportunity. This goes back to the mid 1960s. At that time I felt that we were really having a good program. You could communicate with people in Washington, Atlanta, state offices, wherever necessary, and you could get the information you were seeking. And they tried hard to help you get a program for your people. I really enjoyed that. I served one year on the committee and then I was reappointed for a second year. We had some voices of the poor speaking for a while. They wanted to hear what the poor people had to say. Those were good years for the Poverty Program.

Then after that we were changing presidents—Nixon came in—so we never heard anything after that. They abandoned the committee and the programs that were going also. With President Nixon there have been a number of changes. There's not emphasis placed on civil rights, less enforcement of civil rights law, poor legislation. It's to the point now where you can't even protest peacefully without violence occurring from the police side of it. There's not that freedom of speech that we used to know about.

We are starting integration and then we hear our president speak out against this bussing and his voice goes right with the mass of people who're not interested in integration. In my opinion it's not bussing. Bussing's not what's bothering them. It's integration. But seemingly some of them try to cover the word "integration" with the bussing issue—"We don't want bussing. We want neighborhood schools." You hear so many politicians saying "neighborhood schools" because they know this would cut down on desegregation, they know that with housing patterns, especially in white communities, there would be very few Black people, Black pupils, to enroll in schools in their community. It's not bussing. Black children in the South have always been bussed and nothing was said about that by whites. And white children have always been bussed here in Fayette County. I have seen them bussed from one end of the county to the other. As long as they are being bussed past the Black school, then bussing was all right. But if they got bussed to a school where you go across race, then bussing was wrong. So this issue of bussing is nothing more than a way of saying, "We don't want to desegregate the schools."

All of this is bad. There seems to be more unrest among people in these United States now than I have witnessed since I've been living—for forty years. And I think a lot of our politicians have helped sort of to set people on edge from the statements they have made. It has even gotten to the point now where it's very difficult to get a person elected if he believes in fairness, if he believes in equality. He's got to be all the way on the other side, against things that would benefit the oppressed people. A good man's chances are so much less.

Back in the beginning I was totally against the movement because I thought I knew what would happen to people who were for the rights of Black folk, and I was afraid of what would happen to Black people, especially the leadership in the Black community. And, well, I couldn't discourage John. I didn't feel it was wrong. I was just afraid. I couldn't discourage him at all. And he would always say, "It's not worth it, things as they are. Life's not worth living. So what does it matter if a few people have to go to make it better for others?" And then finally, after I could see all of what was happening to people, all this wrongdoing that was being brought upon Black folks, then it just got me into the attitude that I don't care what happens to me as long as I'm trying to do what I feel is right and something that is necessary to be done. And as soon as I could manage to get a little time away from the babies then I started participating in every way possible. I think it just happened. I don't think my becoming involved with John's involvement, I don't believe this is something the individuals decided to do. I think there must be some power beyond us that somehow permitted us to be involved. I think about this work as something that nobody knows how it's gonna end or when it will end. But you see so much that should be done and very few people that really will hold out there and get going with it.

And sometimes I get a little tired physically, and sometimes I get depressed about the reaction of some other people—Black and white—and I wonder, "Why is it this way?" And I feel many of the things one does is not appreciated, but on the other hand I look around and I say, "There is so much that has been done. Things are bad yet, I agree. But there is such a big change from, I'd say, 1950. There is so much of a change, in spite of the changes that we need yet." Until how can you be sorry about your involvement? And again I'll say it has been very difficult. We have suffered tremendously. There have been other people who have suffered just as much as we and some might have suffered more because of this kind of movement, but I feel that this is something that has to be done. I feel that God has the stronger hand in it. I feel that I'm just a tool that is being used and I don't really have full control of myself. I haven't known yet how I could withdraw from it. I know I neglect my children a lot. I spend a lot of time away from them. I think they understand now, though, what I'm doing when I'm away in this kind of work. And they seem to be very concerned about it and they appreciate it now. But sometime I wonder. I look at other people who stay home and take care of their families and just do everything for themselves alone and do nothing for other people and couldn't care less about other people. I look at other people who are enjoying life better, it appears, from a social and economic point of view than we are. But on the other hand I believe I'm one of the happiest people in the world because I want to do something that's going to help somebody. I want to feel that the things I'm doing are things my Eternal Father would like me to do and I'm fully convinced within my own mind that he must be fairly satisfied with the kind of work that we're doing because he's been so good to us to allow us to even be here now. It has been so difficult and any number of things could have happened, and it was not man that prevented it from happening—I know it definitely was not man.

I don't know, I don't know of anything that I have done that I would not redo. For example, spending too much time away from home or from the children or not having very much of a family life when it comes to my husband. I know that we're short on these things. But at the same time I feel that the things that we're doing are worthwhile. I don't regret it. I don't think I can stop yet. I don't know how I can stop. It could be old age that will finally stop me. I hope that will be the thing that will finally stop me. I often think about a statement that Dr. King made a few days before his assassination. He said an awful lot, and I can't get it off my mind at all. He said that he knew all of the dangers of his work, but he also knew the need for this kind of thing. And he said that everyone would like to live to get to be of old age, but he said it's not how long you live, it's how well you live. I think about this and it gives me something to carry with me as I go about my community work. It's not how long you live, but how well you live. And I feel that I have lived real well up to this point. There has been an awful lot that our civic group has done.

I've learned a lot about people through all this. I have learned that our people need progress, but too many of our people are ready to give up the struggle if it means that our Great White Fathers are going to be disturbed. They say, "Then let's forget about it. Let's live as we are." Some people have become set and satisfied in the old way of living. I have learned that all oppressed people are not interested in progress. I have learned that you sometimes get less respect from those that benefit from your struggle. And I have also learned that you can't stop just because people seem not to be concerned—that when you know there's worthwhile work to be done, I feel that you have to keep working towards that. I found that you just got to continue to work on these goals and just forgive a person for his attitudes and hope that someday he will learn. I've seen a lot of people change. There sometimes comes a time when these people get in trouble and they come to you and confide in you. And you've got to be big. You've got to love people to help people. And you've got to help them when they need help if you want to live up to what you're supposed to be—a person interested in human beings.

AFTERWORD TO THE NEW EDITION

When *Our Portion of Hell* was first published, I kept my personal observations to a bare minimum. The book was an oral history, and my part in it was to facilitate the chorus of voices composing the narrative of a tenacious grassroots civil rights movement. But the passage of time invites reflection, and now, some forty-nine years later, I'd like to add a brief account of how the book came about and how it was written, along with a few thoughts on the current state of affairs in Fayette County, the once-embattled corner of Tennessee that is the subject of my book.

My first contact with Fayette County came in March of 1965, when I joined a group of University of Chicago students who went there during spring break to help the Original Fayette County Civic and Welfare League build a community center. For most of my fellow students it was a one-time experience, but for me that short visit set in motion a life-altering involvement that continues to this day. In the years immediately following my first visit, I returned to Fayette County several times—occasions that anchored deep and abiding friendships with the Jameson and McFerren families. Then, in 1970, I learned that John McFerren had been assaulted right outside the county courthouse, barely escaping with his life. I was beside myself. I wanted to rush to support him, I wanted to do something, anything, that might relieve my sense of watching helplessly from 1,100 miles away. But what? Rashly, I suggested that I write a book about the Fayette County civil rights movement, though, really, it wasn't a proposal at all, but rather an impulsive wish that such a book should exist. Months passed without any word from Tennessee, so I assumed that my friends had taken my idea solely as an expression of solidarity. Then Minnie Jameson telephoned me out of the blue to tell me that the community wanted me to do the book and that they were prepared to work with me.

Minnie's call set everything in motion. I'd said there ought to be a book about Fayette County, and now I had to make it happen. But what kind of book should it be? A history of the movement, of course, but what kind of history? My friends expected me to write their story, and on the surface that made sense. I was the one who'd suggested that a book might do some good, and I was the one who knew about books: I read them, I taught them in college, and presumably I had the skills to write one. But the more I thought about our book, the more inappropriate it seemed that I—a white, middle-class guy from the North—should be writing it. After all, one of the essential achievements of Fayette County's indigenous movement was that ordinary people, whose voices had been muzzled by a political and social system constructed to silence them, had summoned the courage to speak for themselves and, as the expression goes, to walk their talk. It wasn't for me to write their story. If there was to be an account of their lives, it would have to come from the people who lived it. But how to do this? Few members of the Black community had more than an eighth-grade education; the world of books was far removed from their everyday lives. Still, I was convinced that the history of the movement had to emerge from the experiences and voices of the people who made it. The book I promised to bring into existence had to be an oral history. Without further reflection, I bought a cassette tape recorder and drove to Tennessee to get to work.

I still marvel that the book happened at all. I was a freshly minted PhD in English literature, a very junior faculty member at the City College of New York—producing an oral history of a Black community in the rural South was something for which I had no practical training. To say I was flying blind would be an understatement. Today oral history is a recognized academic discipline. Books and scholarly papers are written about methodology, purposes, and perspectives—but back in 1971, I had no viable models for my work. Studs Terkel's oral histories, *Division Street America* and *Hard Times*, had appeared in recent years and were hugely successful with a popular audience. But Terkel, I'd been told, used only a fraction of each interview, heavily editing them, then using these brief individual sketches to illustrate the large themes of his books. Also, the first volumes of Robert Coles's valuable Children of Crisis series had been published—a vast and admirable undertaking to represent the voices of American youth across diverse ethnic, geographic, and economic lines: children who'd experienced the first wave of public school integration, but also children of immigrants, sharecroppers, Eskimos, Chicanos, and Indians, even children of the rich. Yet the experiences and reflections of Coles's hundreds of subjects come to us not in their own voices but in Coles's sympathetic and expressive rendering of them. Coles regarded tape recorders as a distraction intervening between him and the people with whom he spoke. Instead, he listened carefully to his subjects and channeled their words into his own version of their stories. Coles's decision served his mission well, but to follow his lead in my project would, in my view, have been to insert myself into the narratives I gathered, implying that my Black friends needed a white "translator" to put their stories across effectively. In fact, when I sought a publisher for *Our Portion of Hell*, several editors suggested that I do just that. They strongly supported the civil rights movement, yet the marketable book they wanted was one written from my perspective, a book *about* Fayette County rather than a firsthand testament by the very people who made that history. But I would have none of it. I was driven by this overriding conviction: that like the movement itself, *Our Portion of Hell* had to be a community undertaking.

With that in mind, I set to work. Each morning, Harpman and Minnie Jameson, whose home became my own, served me a hearty country breakfast before I set forth in my secondhand Volkswagen Beetle. I stopped first at John McFerren's grocery, where Viola McFerren filled me in on the people she thought I should interview. But arranging meetings was difficult. Many homes did not have telephones, which meant I had to drop in unannounced—and people were wary of strangers, especially a white guy pulling up to their home with a tape recorder and a funny foreign car. It was my great good fortune that Viola paired me with William Henry "Gyp" Walker, a free-spirited man in his mid-sixties, who accompanied me as my guide and who vouched for me and explained my mission to the people I sought out. Gyp gained his nickname by hoboing and riding the rails during the Depression—a gypsy life where he earned meals and a floor to sleep on by pounding out barrelhouse blues on juke-joint pianos and by drawing what he called "French pictures" for bar patrons. Was he ever gainfully employed? I never found out. But he was beloved by Black people throughout the county. Every morning, he'd slide into my car, turn on WDIA, the Memphis soul station, and off we'd go with him growling and baying to the music. Day after day, we'd turn off the highway onto unmarked dirt roads, one road after another, until we pulled up to the sharecropping bungalow I sought. People were delighted when Gyp emerged from my car. "Why, Gyp," a typical greeting went, "where you been keepin yourself? Come on in!" Gyp would gesture at me and explain, "This feller here is writin a book about civil rights, and Mrs. McFerren told him he should speak with you." That was enough to get things started. Once I explained my purpose and eased into my interview, Gyp drifted outside to play with children or just poke around in the yard. He lived very much within himself. I never got to know him as well as many people I encountered, yet I was fascinated by him and deeply grateful for his generous assistance. When I think of Gyp now, Thoreau's celebrated line from *Walden* comes to mind: "If a man does not keep pace with his companions, perhaps it is because he hears a different drummer. Let him step to the music which he hears, however measured or far away." That was Gyp, for sure—a free spirit in every way.

I remember a hot, dusty day in early September when we were barreling south on Highway 76 to an interview in Rossville. Suddenly, with no explanation, Gyp told me to take a sharp left turn and park at a nearby elementary school. I followed him inside, past clusters of startled children, and into the auditorium, where he sat down at the piano and began banging out his raunchy blues. Within minutes teachers were hustling students into the room for an impromptu assembly, and soon the principal arrived to greet him warmly. For students and teachers alike, it was a brief recess, as well as an unexpected opportunity to experience Fayette County's cultural treasure: a blues tradition that counts Tina Turner, Isaac Hayes, B. B. King, and Mississippi Fred McDowell among its celebrated local artists. I'd like to believe that those astonished and delighted schoolchildren sensed that this unkempt man who shook the auditorium with churning, soulful music, this man their teachers seemed to adore, had a life lesson to impart to them: no matter what obstacles one faces, a resolute person need never submit to the expectations of others.

As for my interviewing method, I kept things simple. A typical interview began with me telling people the obvious: that no one was a greater expert on their lives than they themselves. A self-evident truth, but it was the basis of all that followed. I invited people to talk about their childhood, about the material circumstances of their early lives, about their parents and their schooling, about their earliest views of white people and their first encounters with segregation. Only after we'd settled into a comfortable rhythm would I ask them about events directly pertaining to the civil rights movement. In most cases, folks were quite forthcoming—as if they'd been waiting for this opportunity to have their say—but in a few instances people's emotions remained so raw that they could barely speak about what they'd faced. In those situations, I often felt predatory and uncomfortable. What right did I have to distress people by dredging up agonizing memories? It was incredibly difficult for them and for me. Only a shared determination to set the historical record right got us through. Those months in which I gathered my interviews were uncommonly intense—so enriching and deeply transforming that when I returned to New York, I sometimes felt unable to fully express to friends and family what I'd experienced. In a sense, I felt most understood, most at home, in Fayette County, my adopted community.

After I'd completed my interviews, I spent the better part of a year transcribing them and then arranging them into a community-told history: *Our Portion of Hell*. My editing process required numerous judgment calls. For example,

I resolved never to correct the grammar of people's spoken words, but the question of how to render dialect speech was open to many considerations. Here's what I mean. Back in the 1930s, the Federal Writers' Project sent teams of researchers into the rural South to collect life stories from sharecroppers, factory workers, and people in low-paying service occupations—a remarkable undertaking that led to *These Are Our Lives*, a classic forebear of oral history. The interviewers' scrupulous efforts to render the language they heard led to passages like this: "The feller that was drivin' the truck wa'n't wuth nothin'; so we couldn't get no damages out'n him." This is true to the ear, but I worried that if I adapted this level of meticulous phonetic transcription, it would impede my readers' access to what was actually being said. And the primary purpose of *Our Portion of Hell* was to document a rare occurrence of grassroots activism through the voices of the people who lived it, rather than to capture their precise speech patterns. I wanted to convey the flavor of local dialect without slowing down the flow of language with improvised spellings and showers of apostrophes. I did nothing to "improve" people's language to a standard English norm, but I avoided laboriously imitating colloquial speech. For example, here is a transcribed sample from Elvin Jones, a man whose life was transformed by the movement: "I was seein I wasn't getting anyplace drinkin, so then I started readin the Bible, studyin the Bible. . ." As far as I was concerned, Mr. Jones and all the other speakers I encountered expressed themselves thoughtfully, feelingly, and often eloquently, notwithstanding their dropped *g*'s. To my way of thinking, inserting apostrophes to indicate missing *g*'s would have been a form of condescension suggesting that the speaker's words needed tidying up. Nevertheless, one editor I encountered argued that the absence of apostrophes invited confusion. What about "goin," he asked? Wouldn't this mislead readers to hear it in their minds as if it rhymed with "coin" and "join"? I stood my ground, though I'm sure that in his eyes I was a headstrong, young writer who defied constructive criticism. I make no apologies. I was driven by my determination to be worthy of the trust my friends had placed in me—to render their words and their history truthfully.

Our Portion of Hell was published in 1973 and was praised by Robert Coles, Julian Bond, and Dr. Kenneth Clark, the renowned psychologist whose "doll test" provided electrifying evidence for the plaintiff in the hallmark *Brown v. Board of Education* decision. In later years, prominent scholars such as Howard Zinn, Leslie Fiedler, and Stanley Kutler expressed admiration for the book, as well as Janet Reno, the former US attorney general, and William Ferris, former chairman of the National Endowment for the Humanities and founder of the Center for the Study of Southern Culture. It is gratifying to know that these people whose voices figured so prominently in America's fraught encounter with racism understood that *Our Portion of Hell* offered living testimony to the great historical epoch we call the civil rights movement. But what pleased me the most was that I'd delivered on my promise: the Black community of Fayette County had their book in hand—*their* history, presented in their own words.

◆ ◆ ◆

Much has changed in the sixty years since the trial of Burton Dodson, the event that galvanized the Black community of Fayette County to stand up for themselves and thus led to the making of this book. Some of the greatest changes took place in the mid and late 1960s when President Lyndon Johnson's administration put forward the bold and transformative initiatives known as the Great Society program. The most visible change is in housing. When I conducted my interviews in 1971–72, the homes I visited were nearly identical: timeworn, uninsulated bungalows with no indoor plumbing. It was not uncommon to see walls patched with cardboard. But with the advent of the Great Society, federal programs compelled banks to provide affordable mortgages to poor people throughout the South, allowing them to build new homes with running water, decent bathrooms, modern kitchens, and air-conditioning. Today, it's nearly impossible to find one of the old bungalows. In 2002, I returned to Fayette County to produce a short documentary film, and I wanted to interview Harpman Jameson in front of the wood cabin where I'd lived with him and his family on my first visit to Fayette County. But there was nothing there. Not a trace remained of the home that had been in his family for three generations. It had melted into the earth.

The end of segregated public schools is another area of striking change. In 1973, when *Our Portion of Hell* was published, Fayette County's schools had only recently been integrated and, simply put, things were a mess. Many schools were decrepit and poorly maintained; teachers were often unqualified; and white students and faculty were hostile to Black students. Also, it is hardly coincidental that school integration sparked the establishing of private schools. In 1965, Fayette Academy opened: "A [private] school that would provide excellence in education and a focus on family and Christian values." Its official policy states that it admits students of any race, color, or nationality and that it follows appropriate nondiscriminatory policies, but in reality it became a haven for white flight from the integrated public schools. More Christian-based private schools followed, draining off more white students. As a result, in a county that is currently 68 percent white, the public schools have just 38 percent white students. Yes, public schools are integrated; Black and white students study side by side—but this is integration with an asterisk. While it's true that handsome new public schools have been constructed and that teachers are far better trained than in the 1960s, statewide statistics reveal that Fayette County public schools are underperforming, with white students scoring significantly higher than their Black counterparts. Still, since the 1970s, Black students have graduated high school and gone on to attend college in increasing numbers. Many have received advanced degrees, moving on to outstanding careers in education, government, the armed forces, and business and earning salaries that would have been unthinkable before the civil rights movement. Their accomplishments rest on the dogged efforts of their parents, the everyday heroes of Fayette County's struggle. It is a story that reaches well beyond the time frame of *Our Portion of Hell*, but it is very much a continuation of that history, embodying as it does the aspirations that brought Fayette County's grassroots movement into being.

This change has been extraordinary. But, inevitably, the surge in education and opportunity has led a generation of young Black people to settle far from home, totally upending the county's demographics. Back in 1959, 70 percent of Fayette County's nearly 25,000 citizens were Black and just 30 percent were white. Since then, the population has grown to close to 40,000, but the Black population has diminished considerably. Today 68 percent of the county is white and about 28 percent is Black. Simply put, Fayette County is transforming into a mostly white Memphis suburb. Big new homes have sprung up everywhere, with rail fences, broad lawns, and Jacuzzis. There are three country clubs in Fayette County now—cotton fields have been replaced by golf courses. The days of sharecropping are long gone, and the days of independent farmers, Black or white, working forty or so acres are quickly passing as well.

Here is something else I could not have envisaged when I wrote *Our Portion of Hell*. In 2019, the Benjamin L. Hooks Institute for Social Change at the University of Memphis collaborated with Fayette County Public Schools to host a traveling exhibit that presented the story of Tent City and invited visitors to share their personal stories about voting. When vehicles transporting the exhibit crossed from Shelby County (Memphis) to Fayette County, they were met by a convoy of police cars that escorted them along Highway 64—an honor guard that rolled past the very courthouse where, sixty years before, Black citizens eager to register to vote had been harassed and turned away, and where John McFerren had been beaten, almost murdered. That motorcade was a stirring event—a welcome sign that there are good and decent white people in Fayette County, among them public administrators and law enforcement officers who respect Black people and genuinely seek to support racial harmony. I could not have written these words in 1973.

Still, it is one thing to say that things have improved for Black people in Fayette County but quite another to say that the underlying issues of their struggle are behind them. They are not. The best that can be said is that the situation for the Black community in Fayette County today is no worse than for Black people in the rest of America. Income inequality remains; 40 percent of America's prison population is Black; white nationalism is on the rise; and according to the Brennan Center for Justice, at least nineteen states have passed thirty-four laws restricting access to voting, and more than 440 bills with provisions that restrict voting access have been introduced in forty-nine states—an all-out effort by fearful white Republicans to suppress the Black vote. This current crisis is part and parcel with the unfinished story of struggle that *Our Portion of Hell* tells. Cruel and ruthless forces of oppression exist at every point in history, and powerless people will always be faced with the choice of submitting passively or standing up for themselves—of going it alone or banding together with others who share their views and their determination to seek justice. For this reason, the grassroots movement depicted in *Our Portion of Hell* stands as a forbear to ongoing events. Black Lives Matter, especially when people of all races march together insisting that the time is now—long past, in fact—for our institutions and our leaders to take note of America's embedded racism. If you acknowledge the value of grassroots political activism, then you'll see why the personal testaments that make up *Our Portion of Hell* remain vital even though so much has changed. The trailblazers who spoke up for this book left an inspiring legacy to their children and grandchildren. Because I was fortunate enough to have been drawn to Fayette County, their experiences are ingrained in my sense of the best and the worst in human nature. And if you open your mind and your heart to this community-told history of ordinary people who rose up in the face of oppression to accomplish extraordinary things, their unwavering mission will become a vibrant presence in your life too.

ACKNOWLEDGMENTS

In the years following the publication of *Our Portion of Hell*, I received occasional letters and phone calls—often from Fayette Countians who'd loaned their copy to friends and never managed to recover it—asking me if I had spare copies they could buy. I was sorry to disappoint them, but the book was out of print. With the advent of the internet and online access to used-book sellers, a few copies turned up—but at prohibitive prices running into the hundreds of dollars. Over the years, I tried intermittently to find a publisher to bring *Our Portion of Hell* back into print, but to no avail. In all likelihood, this book would not have found its way to the University Press of Mississippi without the active support of Daphene McFerren, executive director of the Benjamin L. Hooks Institute for Social Change at the University of Memphis. Daphene is one of the many "children of the movement" who built on their parents' sacrifices to forge successful careers that at the time of Tent City would have seemed like pipe dreams. During her years at the Hooks Institute, Daphene has carried her parents' mission forward, assembling the core of a rich collection of Fayette County materials at the University of Memphis library and coproducing with me *Freedom's Front Line*, a documentary about the Fayette County movement that has aired frequently throughout southwest Tennessee on WKNO, the local PBS TV affiliate. Her search for an appropriate publisher to reissue *Our Portion of Hell* brought us to the University Press of Mississippi—and so, some forty-nine years after it first appeared, *Our Portion of Hell* is available once again. Thank you, Daphene. This book owes its new life to you. In this vein, I'd be remiss if I didn't express my deep gratitude to Kathrin Seitz, Verne Moberg, Elaine Markson, and Danny Moses, whose belief in my project made the original edition possible way back when.

Fifty years ago, when I was seeking a publisher for *Our Portion of Hell*, I doubt that any university press in the South would have shown interest in taking it on, yet today those same universities are in the vanguard of addressing Black history and the civil rights movement. The University Press of Mississippi has played an important part in this turn toward reexamining our nation's egregious record of slavery and racism, and I am honored to be one of their authors. I would like to thank Emily Bandy and all those involved at the press for making *Our Portion of Hell* available to a new generation of readers.

Thanks, too, to the photographers whose powerful images do so much to support the spoken words of the text: Michael Abramson, Ernest Withers, Nick Lawrence, Art Shay, Barnet Sellers, Jim Shearin, and Archie Allen. In this regard, I'm deeply grateful to two archivists who responded to my every request with diligence, dispatch, and patience. Without the support of Gerald Chaudron, head of Special Collections at the University of Memphis, and Connor Scanlon, research and licensing specialist at Withers Digital Archive, several of the images in this book would not have seen print.

For those of you who want to know more about the Fayette County civil rights struggle, here are a few recommendations. Before the writing of *Our Portion of Hell*, one book about the Fayette County movement already existed. *Step by Step* (New York: W. W. Norton, 1965) was created by members of the Cornell Fayette County Project and provides a valuable account of the efforts of forty-five student volunteers to bring fair elections to the beleaguered community. Since the appearance of *Our Portion of Hell* in 1973, various articles and doctoral dissertations have contributed to a fuller understanding of the events recounted in my oral history. Readers interested in looking deeper will find no better starting point than Katherine Ballantyne's excellent essay, "We Might 'Overcome Someday': West Tennessee's Rural Freedom Movement" (*Journal of Contemporary History* 56, no. 1 (2021): 117–41). Not only does it provide a compelling overview of events, but its citations offer a path to most of the scholarship devoted to Fayette County. I would be remiss if I didn't direct readers to the University of Memphis website Tent City: Stories of Civil Rights in Fayette County, Tennessee. It offers a wealth of information that includes a timeline of events, video clips, and stirring images. For those readers in the Memphis area, I urge you visit the university library's Special Collections to explore the fascinating materials gathered by Daphene McFerren and others. With advance notice the library can arrange for you to listen to the taped interviews from which I prepared *Our Portion of Hell*, and they can arrange a viewing of *Freedom's Front Line*, the documentary mentioned earlier.

LIST OF ILLUSTRATIONS

ABOUT THE AUTHOR

Photo by Ilene Raye Sunshine

Robert Hamburger is the author of six books ranging over oral history, personal journalism, biography, travel memoir, and fiction. He produced and conducted interviews for *Freedom's Front Line: Fayette County, Tennessee*, a thirty-minute film about the civil rights movement that was broadcast on WKNO, the western Tennessee PBS station. He is the recipient of two NEH research awards, three Fulbright teaching fellowships (France, New Delhi, Kolkata), three residencies at the MacDowell Colony, and a New York Foundation for the Arts award in creative nonfiction.

Printed in the United States
by Baker & Taylor Publisher Services